MW01517906

HP ASE Cloud Architect
OFFICIAL EXAM CERTIFICATION GUIDE
(Exam HP0-D14)

First Edition

Ken Radford
HP ASE – Cloud Architect

HP Press
660 4th Street, #802
San Francisco, CA 94107

HP ASE CLOUD ARCHITECT OFFICIAL EXAM CERTIFICATION GUIDE (EXAM HP0-D14)
Ken Radford

Published by:

HP Press
660 4th Street, #802
San Francisco, CA 94107

ISBN-978-1-937826-16-1

Printed in Mexico

WARNING AND DISCLAIMER

This book is designed to provide information about the topics covered on the Architecting HP Cloudsystem Solutions (HP0-D14) certification exam. Every effort has been made to make this book as complete and as accurate as possible, but no warranty or fitness is implied.

The information is provided on an "as is" basis. The author, HP Press, and Hewlett-Packard Development Company, L.P., shall have neither liability nor responsibility to any person or entity with respect to any loss or damages arising from the information contained in this book or from the use of the discs or programs that may accompany it.

The opinions expressed in this book belong to the author and are not necessarily those of Hewlett-Packard Development Company, L.P.

TRADEMARK ACKNOWLEDGEMENTS
All terms mentioned in this book that are known to be trademarks or service marks have been appropriately capitalized. HP Press or Hewlett Packard Inc. cannot attest to the accuracy of this information. Use of a term in this book should not be regarded as affecting the validity of any trademark or service mark.

GOVERNMENT AND EDUCATION SALES
This publisher offers discounts on this book when ordered in quantity for bulk purchases, which may include electronic versions. For more information; please contact U.S. Government and Education Sales 1-855-4HPBOOK (1-855-447-2665) or email sales@hppressbooks.com.

Feedback Information

At HP Press, our goal is to create in-depth technical books of the best quality and value. Each book is crafted with care and precision, undergoing rigorous development that involves the expertise of members from the professional technical community.

Readers' feedback is a continuation of the process. If you have any comments regarding how we could improve the quality of this book, or otherwise alter it to better suit your needs, you can contact us through email at feedback@hppressbooks.com. Please make sure to include the book title and ISBN in your message.

We appreciate your feedback.

Publisher: HP Press

HP Contributors: Colin I'Anson, Richard Hykel, Henrik Elmgren, James Drover and John Cosgrave

HP Press Program Manager: Michael Bishop

HP Headquarters

Hewlett-Packard Company
3000 Hanover Street
Palo Alto, CA
94304-1185
USA

Phone: (+1) 650-857-1501
Fax: (+1) 650-857-5518

HP, COMPAQ and any other product or service name or slogan or logo contained in the HP Press publications or web site are trademarks of HP and its suppliers or licensors and may not be copied, imitated, or used, in whole or in part, without the prior written permission of HP or the applicable trademark holder. Ownership of all such trademarks and the goodwill associated therewith remains with HP or the applicable trademark holder.

Without limiting the generality of the foregoing:

    a.   Microsoft, Windows and Windows Vista are either US registered trademarks or trademarks of Microsoft Corporation in the United States and/or other countries; and

    b.   Celeron, Celeron Inside, Centrino, Centrino Inside, Core Inside, Intel, Intel Logo, Intel Atom, Intel Atom Inside, Intel Core, Intel Core Inside, Intel Inside Logo, Intel Viiv, Intel vPro, Itanium, Itanium Inside, Pentium, Pentium Inside, ViiV Inside, vPro Inside, Xeon, and Xeon Inside are trademarks of Intel Corporation in the U.S. and other countries.

About the Author

Ken Radford is certified in HP ASE – Cloud Architect, HP Accredited Presales Professional, HP Accredited Presales Consultant, HP Accredited Sales Professional, HP Accredited Sales Consultant, HP Certified Systems Administrator, and HP Certified Instructor. He was a courseware developer for the *Architecting HP CloudSystem Solutions, Rev. 11.41* course.

About the Technical Reviewers

John Cosgrave; Senior Consultant, Enterprise Architecture & Cloud Computing. MCSE, MCSD, MCDBA, ASE, ITIL V3 Expert.

James Drover; Chief Technologist CI. Master ASE: SAN Architect, MCSE, MCDBA, VTSP.

Henrik Elmgren; Enterprise Architect and Senior Strategist at HP. MSc, ASE Cloud.

Dr. Colin I'Anson FIET; HP Distinguished Technologist, Cloud Computing Architect.

Introduction

This book helps you study for the Architecting HP CloudSystem Solutions (HP0-D14) exam. You can benefit from this guide when you are attempting to achieve the HP ASE – Cloud Architect certification.

To pass the exam, you will need to demonstrate your ability to correctly explain Cloud computing; describe and position the HP CloudSystem solutions, their purpose, benefits, and components; explain the HP Cloud Functional Reference Architecture; analyze customer requirements and recommend the correct HP CloudSystem solution; and demonstrate key features and benefits of HP CloudSystem.

HP ExpertONE Certification

HP ExpertONE is the first end-to-end learning and expertise program that combines comprehensive knowledge and hands-on real- world experience to help you attain the critical skills needed to architect, design, and integrate multi-vendor and multi-service converged infrastructure and cloud solutions. HP, the largest IT company in the world and the market leader in IT training, is committed to help you stay relevant and keep pace with the demands of a dynamic, fast-moving industry.

The ExpertONE program takes into account your current certifications and experience providing the relevant courses and study materials you need to pass the certification exams. As an ExpertONE certified professional, your skills, knowledge, and real-world experience are recognized and valued in the marketplace. To continue your professional and career growth, you have access to a large ExpertONE community of IT professionals and decision makers, including the world's largest community of cloud experts. Share ideas, best practices, business insights, and challenges as you gain professional connections globally.

To learn more about HP ExpertONE certifications, including storage, servers, networking, converged infrastructure, cloud, and more, please visit: www.hp.com/go/ExpertONE.Audience

Anyone who deploys complex solutions based on HP technologies including: HP Reseller and Service Authorized Partners, Customer IT Staff, HP Field Presales and Competency Center Solution Architects, HP Services Field and Call Center Support Engineers.

Minimum Qualifications

You should have a thorough understanding of HP Converged Infrastructure and its components, including HP servers, storage, networking, power and cooling, software, security, and services.

To achieve the HP ASE – Cloud Architect v1 certification, you must first achieve the prerequisite certification, APC – HP Converged Infrastructure Solutions [2010], or one that supersedes this certification. Then, you must pass the Architecting HP CloudSystem Solutions (HP0-D14) exam.

Audience

Although anyone can take the exam, most successful candidates have two years of real-world experience architecting HP Converged Infrastructure solutions. Exams are based on an assumed level of industry-standard knowledge that may be gained from training, hands-on experience, or other pre-requisites.

Relevant Certifications

After passing this exam, your achievement may be applied toward more than one certification. To determine which certifications will be credited with this achievement, log into The Learning Center and view the certifications listed on the exam's More Details tab. You may be on your way to achieving additional HP certifications.

Exam Details

- Number of items: 62
- Item types: multiple choice (single response), multiple choice (multiple response), drag-and-drop, scenario
- Exam time: 105 minutes
- Passing score: 68%
- Reference material: No on-line or hard copy reference material will be allowed at the testing site.

Exam Topics

- Identify fundamental architectures, products, and solutions for HP CloudSystems
- Identify HP CloudSystem offerings
- Plan and design an HP CloudSystem solution
- Describe HP CloudSystem implementations

Preparing for the Exam HP0-D14

This self-study guide does not guarantee you will have all the knowledge you need to pass the exam. It is expected that you will also draw on real-world experience and would benefit from completing the hands-on lab activities provided in the instructor-led training. The exam tests knowledge and skills necessary for an individual to be certified as an HP ASE. The exam contains questions that are complex and demanding, reflecting the challenging nature of the tasks that the ASE often faces in complex, real-world cloud implementations.

Recommended HP Training

Although not a requirement to qualify for the certification exam, it is highly recommended that you complete the following training course and its associated prerequisites.

Architecting HP CloudSystem Solutions (course ID 00405026)

Delivery format: Instructor Led Training (ILT), typical duration: 2 days.

To learn more about training options and prerequisites for the exam, visit www.hp.com/go/certification.

Obtain hands-on experience

You are not required to take the recommended, supported courses; and completion of training does not guarantee that you will pass the exam. HP strongly recommends a combination of training, thorough review of courseware and additional study references, and sufficient on-the-job experience prior to taking the exam.

Exam Registration

To register for this exam, please go to http://www.hp.com/certification/learn_more_about_exams.html

CONTENTS

1 Cloud Fundamentals

EXAM OBJECTIVES

✓ Describe cloud computing and its benefits to enterprise datacenters.

✓ Describe the different types of cloud implementations.

✓ Explain key cloud processes and terminology.

ASSUMED KNOWLEDGE

You should be in possession of the HP APC - Converged Infrastructure Solutions (2010) certification.

INTRODUCTION

Many people have said many things about cloud computing, and there appear to be almost as many definitions of cloud as there are people commenting on the subject. In this chapter, rather than attempting to provide a precise definition, we will list several key attributes of cloud computing that should help with our understanding of the subject. Once we have gained an appreciation of the fundamentals of cloud computing and of the terminology that we can expect to encounter when working in the cloud arena, we will be much better able to understand and articulate the business value that HP CloudSystem solutions bring to customers. We will begin by answering the question *what is wrong with the way compute infrastructure is managed today?*

The Problem with Today's Infrastructure

Traditional datacenters have become siloed, with stranded islands of server, storage, and networking resources creating an environment that is overly complex, costly to maintain, needing lots of managing, and human resources. The processes to get things done are cumbersome and time consuming and, in short, unsustainable. For example, to support a new business initiative, the organization has determined that it needs to run a new application and new servers, storage, and networking equipment will need to be purchased, provisioned and deployed. This process, from the initial decision to deploy new applications to the time when the applications go live on the new infrastructure, can take weeks or even months.

Figure 1-1 illustrates how complicated it can be to deliver an application infrastructure. It requires many processes and teams coordinating to order the system; locate equipment; secure approvals; set up servers, storage, and networking; load and patch the operating system (OS); set up virtualization and application software; and bring it all online.

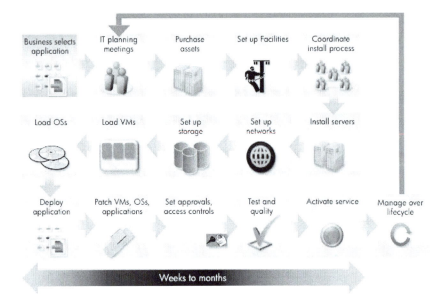

Figure 1-1. The problem with today's infrastructure

HP recognized this problem years ago, and set out to solve it by automating the steps, accelerating service delivery, and improving service quality, while reducing the total cost of ownership.

Business is Outpacing IT

The time-consuming process we just described can be very frustrating for business users, and many of the users will be aware of the advantages of using cloud-based solutions. Indeed, in some cases, users are bypassing the IT department and registering for services such as those from Amazon and Microsoft.

Many businesses are concerned about adopting cloud solutions, because they may have heard about challenges with security, management, and efficiency. Many are worried and a little confused about how they can integrate their traditional IT environment and workloads with private and public clouds. They are concerned with security, the potential for vendor lock-in, performance, availability, and also with how internal and external services will be integrated. They view the cloud as a complex puzzle with many pieces and can feel as if they are attempting to complete the puzzle without having seen the big picture. CIOs are necessarily concerned with security and maintaining service level agreements (SLAs), yet they are always under pressure to accelerate service delivery, reduce costs, and improve availability. These CIOs may have the feeling that cloud solutions could be the answer, but they just need to understand how their concerns can be addressed. The HP CloudSystem solutions address these concerns and are set to make a major difference in the way CIOs view the cloud.

Before we talk about the HP CloudSystem solutions, we need to address the question *what is cloud computing?*

Cloud Computing Defined

According to HP, cloud computing is a model for enabling on-demand access, via a network, to a shared pool of configurable resources (for example, networks, servers, storage, applications, and services) that can be easily and rapidly provisioned and de-provisioned.

The key attributes of cloud computing are:

- **Service based and available on-demand on a self-service basis**—Users can provision computing resources, such as server, storage, networking, and/or applications, automatically, when they need them, without needing to concern themselves with the hardware and software that the service requires. They simply select the service they require from a portal and begin to use the service.

- **Scalable and elastic**—Resources can be assigned and unassigned dynamically, enabling logical servers and their associated storage and networking to be *flexed up* (also referred to as *dialed up* or *scaled up*—in other words increased) and *flexed down* (also referred to as *dialed down* or *scaled down*—in other words decreased) according to the needs of the users' application workload(s). As a result of this dynamic and rapid *flexing* of resources, the consumers could be forgiven for believing that they have access to unlimited resources. This is, of course, not the case, and the manager of the underlying infrastructure must see to it that there are enough resources to meet the needs of the users.

- **Shared access to pooled resources**—The cloud provider's computing resources are pooled, and these pooled resources are made available to users on a shared basis; potentially with many users sharing the same resources. The resources are dynamically assigned and reassigned to users according to their needs, and the users do not know, and really should not care, precisely where the resources are located. Examples of resources that can be pooled include CPU, storage, memory, and network bandwidth.

- **Metered by use**—Cloud systems provide a metering capability that will keep track of how much resource has been consumed by each user. The usage data can then be used for reporting purposes and/or for producing a bill. This is similar to the way in which consumers are charged for their use of electricity and gas; a meter records each unit of electricity or gas that has been consumed, and the utility provider uses the data to prepare a bill at the end of billing period. It is for this reason that the term, *utility computing*, is often used to refer to this type of service.

- **Delivered via a network/the Internet**—Resources are available over a network and are accessed through client systems (for example, smart phones, laptops, and PCs).

To connect this definition to a real-life example, consider the Gmail service from Google. It is:

- **Service based and available on-demand on a self-service basis:** When we want to send or receive email, we do not have to think about the infrastructure that underlies the Gmail system.

Also, we do not need to install an email client onto our computer system, and we do not need to concern ourselves with having to set the service up, we simply log in to our Gmail account, click **Compose message**, type the message, and click **Send**.

- **Scalable and elastic:** The service can grow to accommodate new users, and the storage space per user can be expanded virtually endlessly. The user does not need to know what is happening behind the scenes; all they care about is that the service works.

- **Shared access to pooled resources:** The Gmail servers and storage systems are securely shared between multiple different users. This is also referred to as *multi-tenancy*.

- **Metered by use:** The Gmail service is actually free (paid for by advertising), but if you were to run out of storage space, you could buy an additional 20 gigabytes of storage for as little as $5 a year.

- **Delivered via a network/the Internet:** The Gmail service is hosted on servers that are owned by Google and delivered via the Internet.

Why Cloud?

To thrive in today's business environment, it is vital for companies to be able to very quickly deploy new applications to support new business initiatives, products, and services.

The cloud is one approach organizations are taking to address the need to become Instant-On Enterprises. In a world where everything and everyone is connected and everyone expects immediate gratification and instant results, cloud computing plays a key role. HP believes that enterprises will provide services using a hybrid delivery approach—delivering some services through traditional channels, others through internal private clouds, and others sourced from external public cloud service providers.

They will use a combination of all of these models to realize the benefits of the cloud, such as faster growth, increased agility, and lower cost, while protecting their existing investments (see Figure 1-2).

Faster Revenue Growth
Business and IT aligned

Increased Agility
**Respond to opportunity
immediately**

Investment Protection
**Integrate traditional IT and
new cloud services**

Lower Cost
Reduce CAPEX and OPEX

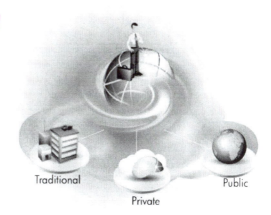

Traditional

Private

Public

Figure 1-2. Why cloud?

There are many advantages of the cloud computing model. These include the fact that business and IT are aligned, meaning that when the business has a need for a new service or solution, IT responds immediately (and even automatically) to deliver the necessary infrastructure. This is often referred to as *increased agility*.

Service functionality and business outcomes are key to influencing the choices made; individual technical components are less relevant. HP solutions provide access to a broad and flexible service portfolio—from infrastructure, platforms, software and applications, to business processes. In addition, services can be accessed on-demand—often with variable availability and capacity levels—from outside the office, across the Internet.

Cloud service consumers are charged only for services used, resulting in a reduction in capital and operational expenditure. In addition to saving money, organizations see the benefits in terms of increased agility for business and IT operations, shorter time to market, and more opportunities for innovation.

There are also some potential disadvantages that will need to be considered. One key concern relates to **security and risk**. The service provider could be hosting sensitive business data in a multi-tenant environment. Assurances will need to be made regarding the security of the data. Certain service models (PaaS and SaaS) provide the service provider with the opportunity to lock the consumer into their service, with a potentially expensive exit route. In addition to this, what happens in the event of a service outage or in the event that a service does not scale to the required extent? SLAs will help, but they won't provide much comfort if the service provider has just gone out of business.

Another important area for consideration is regulatory issues. What would happen in the event that a service provider goes through a technology refresh and upgrades their storage devices? The disks may contain highly sensitive customer data, and this data should of course be removed without trace before the discs leave the data center (and maybe end up on an online auction and shopping website). If the service provider fails to sanitize the disks, the resulting potential for non-compliance could be extremely hazardous to the health of the organization.

There may also be some organizational challenges. Moving services into the cloud could involve outsourcing an entire solution, and outsourcing normally brings with it personnel implications. What will happen to the people who were supporting the service that has just been outsourced?

Enterprise-Class Attributes for Successful Cloud Solutions

To take full advantage of the benefits of cloud solutions, and to mitigate the risk of the potential disadvantages, HP believes that a cloud solution must be:

- **Secure**—delivering agreed-upon security levels (for example, threat protection, privacy, compliance) and data and intellectual property protection

- **Open**—comprising modular infrastructure and services that support heterogeneous environments and do not lock customers in to proprietary architecture

- **Automated**—incorporating policy-based automation and management that integrates cloud with legacy assets and services to provide integrated service catalogs and end-to-end service quality

- **Resilient**—providing consistent delivery of agreed-upon availability, quality, and performance service levels

- **Seamless**—combining public and private cloud services with traditionally deployed services and outsourced services to deliver a seamless experience

Some of the many potential benefits of cloud computing are presented in Table 1-1, along with their associated attributes and features.

Table 1-1. Attributes, features, and benefits of cloud computing

Attribute	Feature	Benefit
Service based and available on-demand on a self-service basis	Users can rapidly gain access to required services without having to concern themselves with the under-lying infrastructure.	Rapid time to productivity and reduced cost of ownership
Scalable and elastic/rapid elasticity	Logical (typically virtual-ized) servers, storage and networking can flex-up and down as required.	Flex-up—Servers can be configured with *just the right amount* of resources, resulting in high utilization ratios and reduced costs. Flex-down—When resources are no longer needed, they are returned to a *free pool* and can be reused by other services. This results in elimi-nating stranded islands of resources and lower costs.
Shared access to pooled resources	Infrastructure is shared between multiple users, organizations, or compa-nies. The cloud provider's CPU, memory, storage and networking resources are pooled, and these pooled resources are dynamically assigned and reassigned to users according to their needs.	Utilization of physical resources is maximized and costs are reduced. Eliminates *stranded* islands of resources, resulting in greater flexibility, increased agility, and lower costs.
Metered by use	Users only pay for what they consume.	Reduced up-front capital expenditure and predictable operational expenditure.
Delivered via a network/the Internet	Services can be accessed from any network-connect-ed client.	Workers can access their data from anywhere, leading to enhanced productivity.

Cloud Service and Deployment Models

There are two dimensions of the cloud model that will be considered: service models and deploy-ment models (see Figure 1-3).

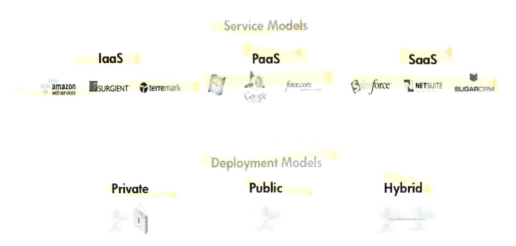

Figure 1-3. Cloud service and deployment models

Service Models

The first dimension, service models, determines the level of resources that are provided to the consumer. Is it, for example, a virtual server with an operating system (IaaS), does it also include software development tools (PaaS), or does it include full applications as well (SaaS)?

Infrastructure as a Service

Cloud infrastructure services, or *Infrastructure as a Service (IaaS)*, is probably the easiest model to understand. IaaS delivers computer infrastructure, typically a virtualized environment, as a service. Rather than purchasing servers, software, datacenter space, power and cooling, or networking equipment, clients instead buy those resources as a service. The service is typically billed on a utility computing basis (see Measured Service, above) and the cost will be calculated based on the level of activity. This effectively gives users the opportunity to buy services by the hour, day, week or month.

Amazon Elastic Compute Cloud (EC2) is one example of infrastructure as a service; it delivers a computing environment with an operating system on which users install and run their own applications. EC2 is a central part of the Amazon.com cloud computing platform, Amazon Web Services (AWS).

Let us take a closer look at how to go about provisioning an Amazon EC2 logical server. We will create a virtual machine (Amazon Machine Image, or AMI, in Amazon-speak) and allocate a specific amount of CPU and RAM to it. It will automatically be allocated some disk storage onto which the Amazon Linux operating system will be installed. This example will highlight the main features of IaaS, namely, the ability to create and deploy a virtual server running Linux (or Windows).

Note

The instructions that follow are not intended to be an exhaustive guide to using the Amazon EC2 service. Full instructions can be found at http://docs.amazonwebservices.com/AW-SEC2/latest/GettingStartedGuide.

After creating an account at http://aws.amazon.com and signing in to the AWS Management Console (https://console.aws.amazon.com/s3/home), press the **Launch Instance** button to start the **Request Instances Wizard** (see Figure 1-4), and this wizard will lead you through the process of creating an Amazon Machine Image (AMI).

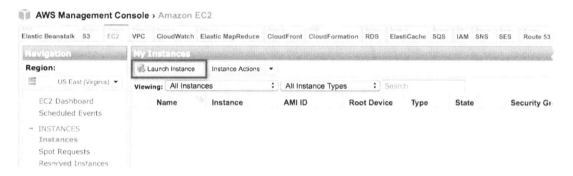

Figure 1-4. Amazon AWS Management Console

The Request Instances Wizard first needs to know which software will be running in the new Amazon Machine Image (see Figure 1-5). The software on offer includes 32- and 64-bit Amazon Linux; 32- and 64-bit SUSE Linux Enterprise Server with Apache Web Server, MySQL database, PHP and Ruby programming environments; 32- and 64-bit Red Hat Enterprise Linux; and 32- and 64-bit Microsoft Windows Server 2008 with SQL Server, IIS web server, and ASP-NET programming environments.

So, an AMI can contain all of the software needed to act as a web server (for example, Linux, Apache, and your web site), or all of the software to act as a Windows database server (for example, Windows and SQL Server).

Note

Strictly speaking, IaaS is about choice of operating system. As soon as we begin to include programming environments, such as PHP, or software, such as SQL, we begin to move in to the PaaS model.

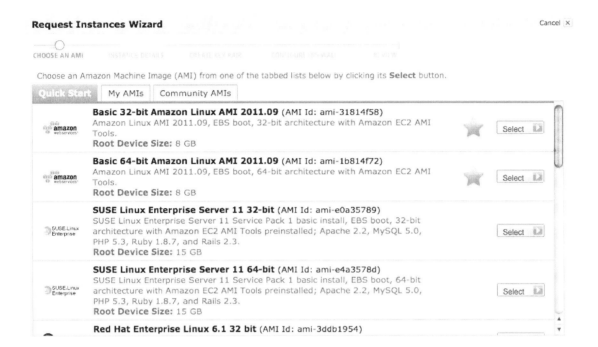

Figure 1-5. Request Instances Wizard—Choose an AMI

After selecting the software — **Basic 64-bit Amazon Linux AMI** in our example — the wizard now needs to know the amount of CPU and RAM to configure (see Figure 1-6). The smallest configuration is the "Micro" AMI with 1 CPU core and 613 MB RAM, and the largest is the High-Memory Quadruple Extra Large with 8 CPU cores and 68.4 GB RAM. The CPU units are measured in ECU (EC2 Compute Units). These units will be discussed in a later chapter.

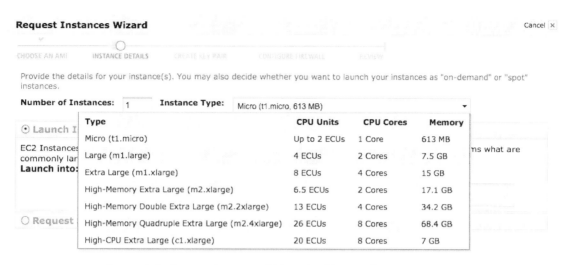

Figure 1-6. Request Instances Wizard—Choose the instance type

The final screen of the wizard reviews the AMI configuration (see Figure 1-7). Pressing the **Launch** button will create the AMI and boot the operating system.

Request Instances Wizard   Cancel ×

CHOOSE AN AMI   INSTANCE DETAILS   CREATE KEY PAIR   CONFIGURE FIREWALL   REVIEW

Please review the information below, then click **Launch**.

AMI: Amazon Linux AMI ID ami-1b814f72 (x86_64)

Name: Basic 64-bit Amazon Linux AMI 2011.09

Description: Amazon Linux AMI 2011.09, EBS boot, 64-bit architecture with Amazon EC2 AMI Tools.   Edit AMI

Number of Instances: 1
Availability Zone: No Preference
Instance Type: Micro (t1.micro)
Instance Class: On Demand   Edit Instance Details

Monitoring: Disabled   **Termination Protection:** Enabled

Tenancy: Default
Kernel ID: Use Default   **Shutdown Behavior:** Stop
RAM Disk ID: Use Default
User Data: This is a test inst...   Edit Advanced Details

Key Pair Name: testkey   Edit Key Pair

Security Group(s): sg-857073ec   Edit Firewall

‹ Back   Launch

Figure 1-7. Request Instances Wizard—Review details

The **My Instances** window shows that the new AMI, **TestInstance**, is running (see Figure 1-8). Selecting the AMI displays its configuration information. Take note of the **Public DNS**, as this will be used to connect to the AMI in the next step.

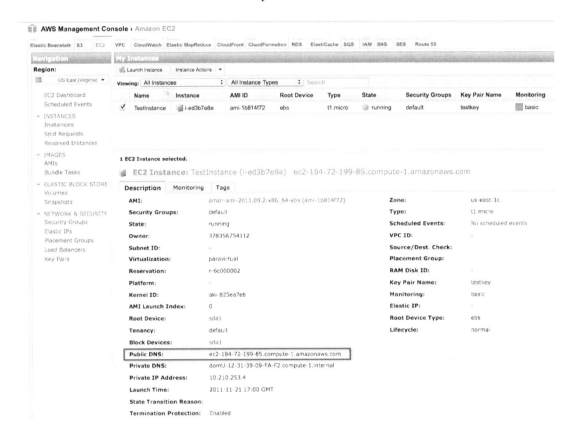

Figure 1-8. Request Instances Wizard—My Instances

Now that the new AMI is running, we can use a terminal emulator, such as PuTTY, to connect to it. Copy the **Public DNS** address from the **My Instances** window and paste it into the **Host Name (or IP address)** field of the **PuTTY Configuration** window (see Figure 1-9).

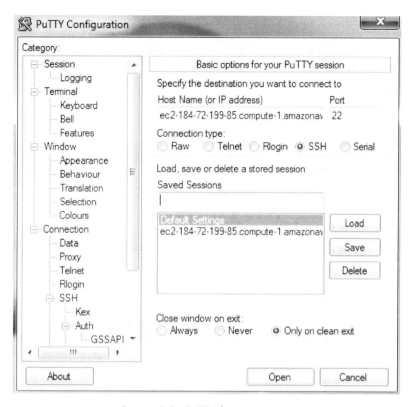

Figure 1-9. PuTTY basic options

Log into the AMI using the username **ec2-user**, and you now have access to the operating system console (see Figure 1-10).

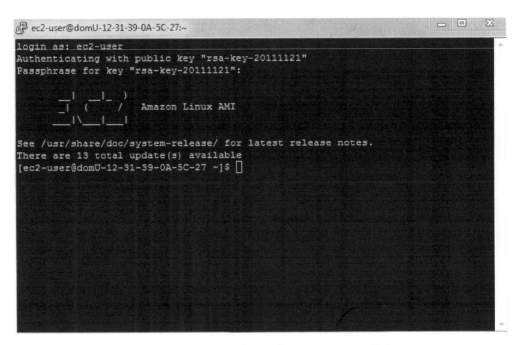

Figure 1-10. Logged in to the AMI using PuTTY

This particular AMI does not have any additional software, such as Apache, MySQL or PHP, so if additional packages are required, they will need to be installed from one of the Amazon package repositories using the **yum** tool. Amazon maintains package repositories that include hundreds of common open source applications.

In summary, we have just used Amazon EC2 to create a virtual machine (AMI, in Amazon-speak). The AMI was configured with a specific amount of CPU and RAM, and was automatically allocated some disk storage onto which the Amazon Linux operating system was installed. This example highlights the main features of IaaS, namely, the ability to create and deploy a virtual server running Linux or Windows. Additional software, such as MySQL, PHP, and Apache, can subsequently be installed if required and, as previously noted, will take us into the PaaS model.

 Note

The Amazon EC2 service is provided free of charge to new users for a period of 12 months. After this time, or in the event that the user exceeds the limits of the free usage tiers, a standard pay-as-you-go service rate is payable. Pricing details can be found at http://aws.amazon.com/ec2/#pricing.

Platform as a Service

Cloud platform services, or *Platform as a Service (PaaS)*, deliver a computing platform and/or solution stack as a service. PaaS enables deployment of user-created or acquired applications, created using programming languages and tools supported by the provider, without the cost and complexity of buying and managing the underlying hardware and software layers. The consumer does not have control over the underlying infrastructure (networking, servers, operating systems, or storage), but does have control over the applications that are deployed. Installing Linux, Apache, MySQL and PHP/Perl/Python (commonly known as the *LAMP stack*) on a virtual machine is one example of PaaS.

Google App Engine is another example of PaaS. It offers a full development stack for people who want to develop and host applications on Google's infrastructure. Google App Engine supports apps written in several programming languages. These programming environments are:

- **Java runtime environment:** Applications can be built using standard Java technologies, including the JVM, Java servlets, and the Java programming language, or any other language that uses a JVM-based interpreter or compiler, such as JavaScript or Ruby.

- **Python runtime environment:** This environment includes a Python interpreter and the Python standard library.

- **Go runtime environment:** This runs natively compiled Go code.

The programming environments are determined by the PaaS provider, so if the programming environment that you are using is not supported by a particular provider, you'll need to look elsewhere.

Let us take a look at how to go about developing an application using Google App Engine. We will use the Google App Engine SDK and the Python programming language to create and test an application on our local system. Following the development and testing of the application, the application will be deployed into the Google infrastructure using the App Engine Launcher. Once deployed, it will be accessible from the Internet using a web browser.

 Note

The instructions that follow are a subset of the full instructions that can be found at http://code.google.com/appengine/docs/python/overview.html.

The first step is to sign up for an account at http://code.google.com/appengine. After creating the account, sign in and download the App Engine SDK (Software Development Kit) by selecting the **Download the App Engine SDK** link on the home page. The Java, Python and Go SDKs are available for Mac OS, Linux and Windows. Select the desired package, and save it to your local system.

Next, download and install the desired programming language.

The following example will use the Python SDK and the Python programming language (available from http://www.python.org/download) on a Windows platform.

Once the SDK and programming language have been installed, it will be necessary to write your application. For the purposes of demonstration, we will write an application that prints a simple message to the screen. The application code has been created using WordPad and has been saved into a directory named **helloworld** with the filename **helloworld.py** (see Figure 1-11).

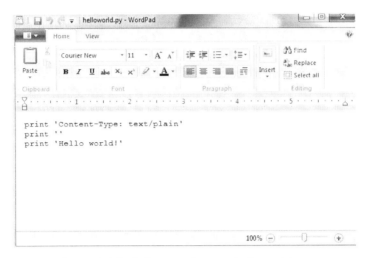

Figure 1-11. Python application helloworld.py

App Engine applications use a configuration file named app.yaml, which describes several important application parameters including the name of the application—helloworld1957 in our example—and the filename of the code itself—helloworld.py in our example (see Figure 1-12). The app.yaml file can be created using WordPad and should be saved into the same directory—helloworld in our example—as the application code itself.

```
application: helloworld1957
version: 1
runtime: python
api_version: 1
handlers:
- url: /.*
  script: helloworld.py
```

Figure 1-12. app.yaml configuration file in WordPad

Next, run the Google App Engine Launcher at:

- c:\Program Files\Google\google_appengine\launcher\GoogleAppEngineLauncher.exe

From the **File** menu, select **Add existing application**. Browse to the location where you saved your application, and click **Add**. The application will appear in the **Launcher** window (see Figure 1-13).

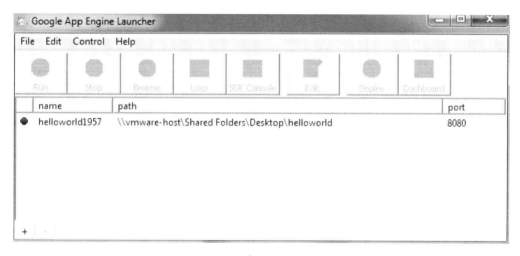

Figure 1-13. Google App Engine Launcher

Now, let us test the application on our local system before we deploy it into the cloud. When helloworld1957 is selected and the **Run** button is pressed, the application will start to execute on our local system. To see the output of the application, enter **localhost:8080** into the address bar of your browser, and the application output will be displayed (see Figure 1-14).

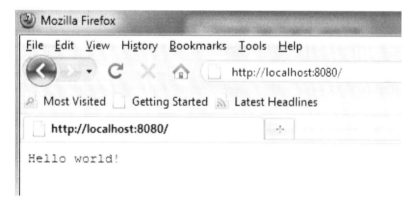

Figure 1-14. Local application output in a web browser

The application can be further developed, tuned, and tested locally before we deploy it into the cloud. When we are happy that the application is performing to our satisfaction, it can be deployed onto a Google server by pressing the **Deploy** button in the App Engine Launcher. An information dialog will open, and after several seconds, the following message should be displayed:

```
Completed update of app: helloworld1957, version: 1

2011-11-22 15:49:39 (Process exited with code 0)

You can close this window now.
```

This means that the application has been successfully deployed onto the Google infrastructure. To see the output of the application, we can browse to the default application URL, which in our example is http://helloworld1957.appspot.com (see Figure 1-15). Rather than choosing the default URL, we could have registered our own domain name and accessed our application using that URL instead of the default one.

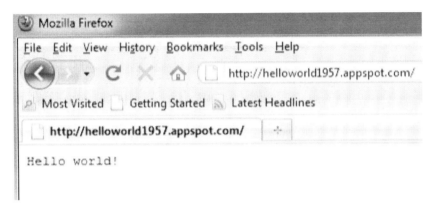

Figure 1-15. Remote application output in a web browser

In summary, we have just used the Google App Engine SDK and the Python programming language to create and test an application on our local system. Following the development and testing of the application, the application was deployed into the Google infrastructure using the App Engine Launcher, where it could be accessed using an appspot.com URL.

The main difference between the IaaS example discussed earlier and this PaaS example is that, with the IaaS example, no application development tools were used. We simply created a virtual server with some CPU, RAM, and disk storage onto which an operating system was installed and booted. In the PaaS example, we used the Google App Engine tools to create, test, and deploy our application into the cloud.

 Note
Google App Engine applications are configured with enough CPU, bandwidth, and storage to serve around five million page views per month for free. Additional resources can be purchased on a pay-as-you-go basis when required. See http://code.google.com/appengine/docs/billing.html for details.

Software as a Service

Cloud application services, or *Software as a Service (SaaS)*, provide access to software applications over the Internet. This means that the users of the software service do not need to develop the application, or even to install and run the application on their own computers, which further means that the users do not need to concern themselves with the management of the underlying cloud infrastructure—or indeed the cost of providing the infrastructure in the first place.

There are two variants of SaaS:

■ **Applications as a Service (AaaS):** One example of AaaS is the Microsoft Office 365 service. Rather than locally installing and running applications, such as Microsoft Word, Excel and PowerPoint, the Office 365 service enables the features of these applications to be accessed via any web browser. By accessing the Office 365 web portal, users can gain access to Outlook email, contacts, calendar, instant messaging and shared documents (via the SharePoint Online service).

■ **Cloud services as a service:** Service providers, such as Salesforce.com, provide access to enterprise Customer Relationship Management (CRM) applications via the Internet. Their services include the Sales Cloud and the Service Cloud. The Sales Cloud is an application that allows sales managers to see in real-time the activities of their teams and enables sales reps to manage customer information easily. The Service Cloud allows companies to meet customers wherever they are—including social networks like Facebook and Twitter, and enables service agents to provide fast, responsive service to customers.

The main difference between SaaS and PaaS is that with SaaS, we are not developing the applications ourselves; instead, we are simply accessing applications that have been developed by someone else. With PaaS however, we are developing and deploying our own applications using SDKs and programming languages.

Deployment Models

The second dimension, deployment models, deals with who manages the resources that deliver the service.

Private Cloud

In a *private cloud*, services are provided to specific users, such as members of departments within a company. Services are delivered via the network, but remain private in the sense that the data remain behind the company firewall rather than being transmitted over the Internet. The underlying resources are shared (also known as *multi-tenancy*, but only between the departments within the company. While private cloud requires an investment in infrastructure and incurs ongoing maintenance costs, it can be made to be highly available and flexible. The fact that the data remain behind corporate firewalls can help to address concerns regarding security, governance, availability, and control.

HP recently introduced a service known as *HP Enterprise Cloud Services – Compute* that is hosted on HP infrastructure. This type of remotely-hosted service is known as *virtual private cloud* and provides server, storage, network and security bundles that are provisioned and configured using a self-service web portal, consumed as a service, and paid for on a pay-as-you-go basis. We will take a closer look at *HP Enterprise Cloud Services – Compute* in a later chapter.

Public Cloud

With a *public cloud* (also known as an *external cloud*), the cloud assets are owned and operated by the provider (with the exception of the Internet, obviously) and are shared by all users (also known as *multi-tenancy*). The services are typically ordered via a self-service portal and are accessed over the Internet, and are provided to users on a utility computing (pay-per-use) basis, which means that the users do not have to invest in the acquisition and maintenance of the computer infrastructure. The users could be employees of different companies, located in different countries, legal jurisdictions, time zones, etc. Unlike the private cloud scenario, where the data reside securely behind the company firewall, the public cloud sees users' data being transmitted over the public Internet and being stored, well, who knows where? This clearly raises concerns regarding security, governance, availability, and control. Sensitive business data may be stored in a different country, with a different legal system, with potentially many barriers to remediation in the event of an outage and/or loss of data.

The examples of IaaS, PaaS and SaaS that we saw earlier in this chapter all fall into the pubic cloud category. The entire infrastructure was owned by Amazon (IaaS example), Google (PaaS example) and Microsoft/Salesforce.com (SaaS example), and the services were delivered over the Internet and were charged for on a pay-per-use basis.

Hybrid Cloud

Figure 1-16. Hybrid cloud

We mentioned earlier that cloud users sometimes fall into the trap of believing that they have an unlimited amount of resources at their disposal, and with the public cloud, this belief may not be far from the truth as providers, such as Amazon and Google, make a massive amount of resources available. In the private cloud however, the resources may be limited to, for example, a single CloudSystem Matrix system. While the CloudSystem Matrix, when correctly sized and configured, can provide a large amount of resources, it will not be able to match the resources of the HP, Amazon or Google datacenters! To overcome this potential resource limitation, a hybrid cloud environment makes use of services sourced from internal and external providers and seamlessly manages services delivery from public, private, and traditional IT sources (see Figure 1-16). This is achieved using bursting and bridging.

Bursting

Bursting is a way to temporarily increase resources to handle peak loads or an unanticipated spike in activity. For example, the HP CloudSystem solutions use internal resources under normal conditions, and when increased demand is experienced, the systems will automatically begin to use resources sourced from either external providers, such as Amazon (EC2) and Savvis (Symphony Virtual Private Data Center), or from other internal infrastructure resources.

Bursting can also be more of a long-term solution and could involve electing to run an entire layer of a multi-tier application on the infrastructure of an external service provider. An example could be where a mission-critical database is hosted on private resources, securely locked away in the data-center, but the client access layer is provided by a low-cost service provider.

Bridging

Bridging is when the IT department provides a service that is sourced from multiple providers. For example, IT may provide a database offering that includes Disaster Recovery (DR) capability. Rather than providing the DR capability themselves, the IT department may commission a third-party company to provide the DR functionality. The user is not normally aware that part of the service is provided by a third-party, and should not really care. As previously stated, the third-party company may be in a different location and legal jurisdiction, so great care must be taken in selecting companies that will take part in these *bridged* solutions.

HP believes that a hybrid cloud will be typical for most enterprises in the future.

Community Cloud

A fourth type of deployment model is the *community cloud*. This is where the cloud infrastructure is shared by several organizations and supports a specific community that has shared concerns, including mission, security requirements, policy, and compliance considerations. It may be managed by the organizations themselves or by a third party and may exist on or off the premises. Because of the special attributes, the community cloud provider aims to become the special-purpose cloud service provider to their industry.

Cloud Terminology

There are several terms that will appear throughout the book and will need to be understood when discussing cloud computing. These include:

- **Provisioning:** The process of creating a service from a service template. The provisioning software searches its inventory before allocating the infrastructure resources to all logical resource definitions in the template.

- **De-provisioning:** When a service is no longer required, its resources are returned to the pool of available resources and its storage resources are scrubbed to remove all trace of sensitive data. If cross-charging or billing is performed, a final invoice can be generated.

- **Service template:** A design blueprint that specifies the requirements for an infrastructure service in terms of server groups, networks, and storage, and contains customization points that use workflows during the execution of a request. A template may also include the application associated with the service.

- **Workflow:** A set of actions that execute customer-specific IT tasks. Workflows can define integration with IT processes, including approvals, manual OS deployment, manual storage provisioning, and sending notifications. Making use of the workflow automation engine embedded in the HP CloudSystem solutions (powered by HP Operations Orchestration software), architects can associate workflows with service templates, to be executed before and/or after provisioning based on the associated templates.

- **Monitoring:** The process of collecting server, storage, network, and application availability and performance data across physical and virtual infrastructure.

- **Application lifecycle management:** The process of planning, provisioning, customizing and configuring applications and their associated resources, ongoing patch management, and ultimate retirement of resources and returning them to the pool of free resources.

- **Orchestration:** The execution of a pre-defined workflow used in the process of provisioning and managing infrastructure.

- **Service catalog:** A repository of service templates. System architects create service templates and then save them to the catalog for access by specified, approved users.

- **Hosting:** The process of making services available via a network.

- **Brokering:** Providing access to services from resource pools (such as traditional IT, private, and public cloud). In the event that a resource pool becomes unavailable, the resources from a different pool can be used, thereby minimizing service downtime.

- **Bursting:** A way to increase resources to handle peak loads by using either additional local resources (local bursting) or by using both local resources *and* public cloud services, such as Amazon EC2 (dual bursting). The additional local resources could be another HP CloudSystem.

- **Bridging:** This is where IT provides a service that is sourced from multiple providers. For example, your IT department may provide a database offering that includes a disaster recovery (DR) capability, where the DR piece is supplied by a third-party provider.

- **Cloud Maps:** An HP template for use in creating service catalogs. HP Cloud Maps contain engineering components, such as best practice reference architectures, workflows, sizers, and deployment scripts, as well as white papers to assist with customization. Cloud maps will be covered in more detail in a later chapter.

- **Tenant array:** Servers that host users' application workloads, as opposed to servers that run management software.

Test Preparation Questions and Answers

The following questions will help you measure your understanding of the material presented in this chapter. Read all the choices carefully, as there may be more than one correct answer. Choose all correct answers for each question.

Questions

1. What are the essential characteristics of cloud computing? (Select three.)

    a. Guaranteed dedicated resources

    b. Scalable and elastic

    c. Delivered via network/Internet technologies

    d. No single point of failure

    e. Measured service

    f. Access to unlimited resources

2. What is the meaning of the term *rapid elasticity*?

    a. Users can provision resources themselves.

    b. Resources are paid for on a pay-per-use basis.

    c. Users can request more resources when required.

    d. Resources can be assigned and de-assigned dynamically.

3. What are the benefits of cloud computing? (Select two.)

    a. Resources are available on a self-service basis, resulting in high-availability.

    b. Virtual servers can scale up and down as required, leading to high-availability.

    c. Stranded islands of resources are eliminated, resulting in reduced costs.

    d. Services are delivered via the Internet, resulting in high utilization and reduced costs.

    e. Infrastructure is shared, leading to high utilization and reduced costs.

4. Which statement best describes PaaS?

    a. Computer infrastructure and/or a solution stack are delivered as a service.

    b. Computer infrastructure, typically virtualized, is delivered as a service.

    c. Commercially available software applications are delivered as a service.

    d. Cloud assets are owned and operated by the provider.

5. A customer is concerned with making sure that they always have enough resources to meet the needs of their business applications. Which technology would you focus on in your discussions with them?

   a. Resource pooling

   b. Bursting

   c. Bridging

   d. Private cloud

6. Which statement best describes a community cloud?

   a. Services are sourced from multiple providers.

   b. Cloud assets are owned and operated by the provider.

   c. Services are provided to specific users, such as members of departments within a company.

   d. Cloud infrastructure is shared by several organizations.

7. What is a service template?

   a. A set of actions that execute customer-specific IT tasks

   b. A design blueprint that specifies the requirements for an infrastructure service

   c. A method for providing access to multiple resource pools

   d. An HP tool for creating service catalogs

8. What is the main feature of orchestration?

   a. It plays a part in the process of provisioning and managing infrastructure and is the execution of a pre-defined workflow.

   b. Server, storage, network and application availability, and performance data are collected across physical and virtual infrastructures.

   c. Resources are returned to the pool of available resources when no longer required.

   d. Resources are sourced from internal and external providers.

9. What does a Cloud Map provide? (Select three.)

   a. Workflows

   b. Operating system images

   c. Deployment scripts

   d. Sizers

   e. Pricing tools

   f. Troubleshooting guides

Answers

1. ☑ **B, C, and E.** The essential characteristics of cloud computing include scalable and elastic, delivered via network/Internet technologies, and measured service.
   ☒ **A** is incorrect, because rather than providing guaranteed dedicated resources, cloud computing uses shared resources. **D** is incorrect, because whereas it is highly desirable to have no single point of failure, this is not inherent in the cloud model. **F** is incorrect, because, whereas it may seem like the resources are unlimited, there is always a limit, albeit a very large one.

2. ☑ **D.** Rapid elasticity means that resources can be assigned and de-assigned dynamically.
   ☒ **A** is not the best answer, because it describes *on-demand self service*. **B** is incorrect, because it describes *measured service*. **C** is incorrect, because it only refers to adding resources, rather than adding and removing resources.

3. ☑ **C and E.** The benefits of cloud computing include elimination of stranded islands of resources, resulting in reduced costs, and infrastructure is shared, leading to high utilization and reduced costs.
   ☒ **A** is incorrect, because *resources are available on a self-service basis* is an attribute, not a benefit, and self-service does not necessarily result in high-availability. **B** is incorrect, because *virtual servers can scale up and down as required* is a feature, not a benefit, and it does not necessarily result in high-availability. **D** is incorrect, because *services are delivered via the Internet* is an attribute, not a benefit, and it does not necessarily result in high utilization and reduced costs.

4. ☑ **A.** PaaS is where computer infrastructure and/or a solution stack are delivered as a service.
   ☒ **B** is incorrect, because it describes IaaS. **C** is incorrect, because it describes SaaS. **D** is not the best answer, because it describes the public cloud.

5. ☑ **B.** Bursting is a way to temporarily increase resources to handle peak loads or an unanticipated spike in activity. This can help customers to make sure they have the resources they need.
   ☒ **A** is incorrect, because whereas pooled resources will increase flexibility and utilization ratios, the pooled resources still have a finite, limited capacity. **C** is incorrect, because bridging describes a service that is sourced from multiple providers. **D** is incorrect, because private cloud will provide access to a finite, limited set of resources.

6. ☑ **D.** A community cloud is a cloud infrastructure that is shared by several organizations.
   ☒ **A** is incorrect, because it describes bridging. **B** is incorrect, because it describes the public cloud. **C** is incorrect, because it describes the private cloud.

7. ☑ **B.** A service template is a design blueprint that specifies the requirements for an infrastructure service.
   ☒ **A** is incorrect, because it describes a workflow. **C** is incorrect, because it describes brokering. **D** is incorrect, because it describes cloud maps.

8. ☑ **A.** Orchestration plays a part in the process of provisioning and managing infrastructure, and is the execution of a pre-defined workflow.
   ☒ **B** is incorrect, because it describes monitoring. **C** is incorrect, because it describes de-provisioning. **D** is incorrect, because it describes hybrid delivery.

9. ☑ **A, C and D.** Cloud Maps provide workflows, deployment scripts, and sizers.
   ☒ **B, E and F** are incorrect. Cloud Maps do not include operating system images, pricing tools, or troubleshooting guides.

2 The Instant-On Enterprise

EXAM OBJECTIVES

✓ Relate HP CloudSystem to the HP Converged Infrastructure and to the Instant-On Enterprise.

✓ Explain the capabilities of the HP Converged Systems offerings.

ASSUMED KNOWLEDGE

You should be in possession of the HP APC - Converged Infrastructure Solutions (2010) certification.

INTRODUCTION

In the past, the main role of IT was as a provider of infrastructure and applications, normally operating as a cost center. Today, increasing demands are being placed on business as a result of several trends that are presenting new challenges and opportunities. HP believes that the IT department should adopt the role of service broker; sourcing the right service, at the right time, at the right cost, to make sure that the goals of the business are met. In this way, IT can be much more aligned with the business, and rather than being a cost of doing business, it can be a source of innovation and competitive advantage. In doing so, it can transition from being just a cost center to becoming a business partner that enables the business to perform better.

Mega Trends Shaping Businesses

Three mega trends are shaping the next generation of successful businesses:

1. **Business models**: Driven by technology and extreme markets, customers are demanding very low price points and expecting suppliers to be easy to access and do business with. In times of recession, technology often drives new buying behavior. For example, *as-a-service* models are becoming more and more popular as a way to purchase services.

2. **Fundamental shifts in technology**: Smartphones, tablets, and PDAs are becoming more and more prevalent and are accelerating the number of devices being connected to the Internet. It is expected that the coming decade could see several trillion devices being connected. This exploding Internet-connectedness will provide IT with new challenges and opportunities for new ways to deliver services to enterprises and their customers. On-premise, proprietary computing resources are gradually being complemented and even replaced by the agile and open computing resources of the cloud.

3. **Changing workforce**: Social media, consumerization of IT, and changing demographics are transforming the way that work gets done in enterprises. The growing use of tools such as Facebook, Jabber, Twitter and Office Communicator is providing instant communication between employees, and also between a business and its customers. Major corporations monitor social media communications to find out what their customers are saying about them and their products. This gives the business direct and immediate feedback in a way that has not been possible until recently.

   We are starting to see social media come into play in larger non-traditional enterprises where IT has to deal with not only consumers but also administrators' and managers' expectations regarding social media.

In response to these trends, HP is driving the evolution of what they call the Instant-On Enterprise. An Instant-On Enterprise is one that uses advanced technology and business processes to better meet the needs of customers, employees, and partners.

The Instant-On Enterprise

HP's expectation for the enterprise of the future is that:

- Everything and everyone is connected.

- Everyone expects instant gratification and results.

- Business and IT are one and the same.

- The business can respond to continuous opportunity and competition.

- Business can be conducted anywhere, at any time, in any way.

HP believes that tomorrow's industry leaders will be those organizations that capitalize on technology to increase their business agility and to respond rapidly to the ever-changing needs of customers.

These organizations will explore better ways to run their businesses and will design new processes and methods to meet changing customer demands. They will build dynamic, flexible systems that meet ever-changing business requirements and enable them to interact with customers, employees, and partners more quickly and with greater personalization. They will govern their organizations and partners to ensure that legal and ethical goals are met, and will conduct transactions efficiently, effectively, and securely.

The characteristics of the Instant-On Enterprise include:

- It serves customers, employees, and partners in whatever way they want and need, instantly, at any point in time and through any channel

- It uses technology to integrate and automate the value chain

- It adapts easily and supports rapid innovation

- It manages risk and environmental responsibilities

- It streamlines everything that is required to deliver a service

To achieve an Instant-On Enterprise, IT must deliver on five critical success factors:

1. **Flexibility:** Applications and services must be available 24x7 and must be able to adapt when presented with new opportunities.

2. **Automation**: Technology resources must dynamically scale up and down to optimize utilization levels and eliminate over- or under-provisioning.

3. **Security**: Assets, resources, and data must be protected against unauthorized access, malicious damage, and failure of any kind.

4. **Insight**: Executives must be able to access information that will help them make better business decisions. Information must be delivered and protected in such a way as to meet the needs of the business.

5. **Speed**: The best delivery model for each solution must be selected and delivered in the right timeframe, and at the right price.

Journey to the Instant-On Enterprise

Businesses will face many obstacles along their journey to the Instant-On Enterprise. Many enterprises are dealing with rigid infrastructure made up of stranded islands of server, storage, and networking resources coupled with the management headache of physical and virtual sprawl. They are experiencing applications and information complexity, driven by an explosion of data and aging assets. On top of that, ubiquitous network access leaves them open to attack from the outside world. Finally, their infrastructures are often built on an old model that required organizations to custom build and manage everything themselves.

Obstacles	Key Initiatives	HP Solution
Aging Applications Brittle and change resistant	Modernize Architect solution for change	**Application Transformation**
Rigid, Sprawling Infrastructure Physical and Virtual Sprawl	Transform Break silos	**Converged Infrastructure**
Unknown Threats Connectedness is an open doorway	Secure Protect assets without constricting flow	**Enterprise Security**
Information Explosion Magnitude of growth driving up cost, effort and risk	Optimize Control and exploit information	**Information Optimization**
Custom built Dedicated stacks of hardware & software	Deliver Right method, right time, right cost	**Hybrid Delivery**
Uncertainty Security, regulatory compliance, integration and interoperability	Build, Transform, Manage & Secure, Consume End-to-end solutions	**Cloud Computing**

Figure 2-1. Obstacles, key initiatives and HP horizontal solutions

There are several key initiatives that will aid the transition to the Instant-On Enterprise (see Figure 2-1):

- **Modernize**: To create an Instant-On Enterprise, business applications will need to be modernized to enable them to better meet the needs of the business. This modernization ensures that new functionality can be added quickly and easily. It also ensures that today's innovation does not become tomorrow's legacy problem. This approach also reduces the ongoing operational cost of the new solution as compared to its predecessor, owing to the fact that legacy applications can be difficult to update when new functionality is required and can be very costly to maintain. The HP solution is application transformation.

- **Transform**: Stranded islands of resources, also known as IT silos, limit business agility and should be eliminated. The Instant-On Enterprise runs on a converged infrastructure that drives out cost and provides the foundation for agile service delivery. The HP solution is Converged Infrastructure.

- **Secure**: To create an Instant-On Enterprise, assets need to be protected without introducing a barrier to innovation. The goal should be to ensure that the right people have the right access to the right resources at the right time. Customers, employees, partners, and consumers should be provided with instant access to the right enterprise assets without compromising risk. The HP solution is enterprise security.

- **Optimize**: Today, millions of terabytes of digital information are created, captured, and replicated, and it is complex, time-consuming, and very costly to manage and utilize information at this massive scale. This is further impacted by the increasing complexity of unstructured data. The Instant-On Enterprise aims to capture, protect, archive, search, and retrieve the data needed to power the enterprise. Once tamed, this data can be exploited and used for the benefit of the business. The HP solution is information optimization.

- **Deliver**: The best method of service delivery should be selected to enable the business to perform the tasks that need to be performed in the appropriate timescale, and at the appropriate cost. The HP solution is hybrid delivery.

- **Build, consume, manage and secure, transform:** HP can *build* a solution that is purchased by a customer and installed into the customer's data center. Alternatively, HP can host the solution and enable the customer to *consume* services on a pay-as-you-go basis. *Management* of services across traditional infrastructure, and the private, and public cloud is brought together into a single *security* policy framework. HP can deliver a range of consulting services to help customers *transform* their operations and move them to the cloud. The HP solution is cloud computing.

Let us now take a closer look at each of these solutions.

Application Transformation

Without applications, IT infrastructure is an expensive way of generating hot air. Many legacy applications were custom-built and may have been revised and patched many times throughout their existence. Add to this the fact that many of the changes may have gone undocumented, and it is not difficult to see how the applications grow in size and complexity over time. This complexity has a negative impact on flexibility and also increases the cost of ownership. With a limited IT budget, every dollar spent on maintaining legacy applications cannot be invested in innovation. The goal of application transformation is to move away from monolithic applications that need to be supported by massive development teams, to service-based architectures where the applications are assembled using trusted, pre-built services, and made available via a public or private cloud. HP has a wide portfolio of solutions for transforming and modernizing business applications, and any transformation project should begin with a clear understanding of the business needs and goals.

The HP Application Transformation Experience Workshop represents an excellent starting point for any transformation project, and helps customers to understand their current situation and to develop a clear understanding of business drivers, challenges, and on-going initiatives related to transformation. It also provides an insight into critical success factors and best practices by leveraging information gained from successful customer projects. The final stage of the workshop involves building a road map for the implementation of one or more of the HP application modernization strategies.

These strategies are:

- **Retire**: Applications and associated data that no longer provide business value are simply retired (in accordance with appropriate data retention policies).

- **Re-architect**: Applications are modernized using contemporary software technologies and techniques.

- **Replace**: Custom, hand-written applications are replaced with off-the-shelf software.

- **Re-host**: Applications are migrated to new infrastructure that delivers more business value. This can be achieved either with or without emulation tools.

Converged Infrastructure

This solution matches the supply of IT resources with the demand for business services in an optimal way, and provides the foundation for agile service delivery. It integrates server, storage, networking, power and cooling, and management resources to deliver the data center of the future. HP Converged Infrastructure has five fundamental requirements (notice that the initial letters spell *vroom*–the dictionary definition being *the loud, roaring noise of an engine operating at high speed!*):

1. **Virtualized**: Server, I/O, storage, and networking are virtualized to separate the applications, data, and networking connections from the underlying hardware. This makes it easy to rapidly reallocate resources when required. It also helps to eliminate stranded islands of resources and, in so doing, drives up utilization ratios.

2. **Resilient**: Fault-tolerant, mission-critical technologies and high-availability policies are utilized to provide the appropriate level of availability for each business application.

3. **Open**: HP Converged Infrastructure is built on standard, common architectures and integrates with the most commonly used hypervisors, operating systems, and applications.

4. **Orchestrated**: The infrastructure to support new business applications is provisioned using automated workflows, creating an application-aligned infrastructure that can be flexed up or down according to the needs of each application.

5. **Modular**: This approach enables the use, and re-use, of common components throughout the data center—from x86 to NonStop systems—and provides the ability to combine existing and new technologies and to scale capacity over time.

The HP Converged Infrastructure is built upon four pillars:

1. **HP Virtual Resource Pools**: This provides a common, modular infrastructure of virtualized server, I/O, and storage resources that can be assembled and reassembled to meet the needs of the business applications.

2. **HP Matrix Operating Environment**: This provides a common platform for the automation and management of resources, including infrastructure and applications. Rather than having many individual, disparate management tools, the HP approach is to provide a *single pane of glass* integrated management solution that combines all the tools into one command center.

3. **HP FlexFabric**: Rather than managing LAN and SAN as separate entities, they are consolidated onto a single virtualized fabric. This approach helps with the building of high-performance, low-latency networks and can dramatically reduce network complexity and cost.

4. **HP Data Center Smart Grid**: This provides intelligent energy management throughout the data center and helps to reduce energy costs. Extensive power and cooling measurements are taken in real time across IT systems and facilities, and these measurements can be used to reclaim stranded capacity and to reduce environmental impact.

HP Virtual Desktop Infrastructure

Traditionally, desktops have been device-centric, with the user's profile, applications, and data tied to a specific PC or laptop. This may have been okay in days gone by, but with today's increasingly mobile workforce and the plethora of devices that they use to perform their work, this approach can be a barrier to productivity. In addition, storing sensitive business information on mobile devices can represent a major security challenge—the unencrypted data on the laptop inadvertently left on the back seat of the taxi could result in serious consequences for the owner of the device and for their company.

The HP Virtual Desktop Infrastructure (VDI) is based on the HP Converged Infrastructure, and rather than the main compute and storage resources residing on the user's desktop, they are securely located in the data center. Secure network connectivity gives end users access to their profiles, applications, and data and provides them with an experience that meets their needs for mobility and can also meet business goals for lower costs, simpler management, and a more flexible infrastructure.

With VDI, a desktop is created in a virtual machine. Applications and user personality are injected into the core desktop virtual machine and a brokering mechanism manages connecting end users to the VM. More than simply a virtual machine, the runtime VDI instance is the real time compilation of the end-user's data, personal settings and application settings with the core operating system instance and shared generic profile. The applications are either installed locally as a fully installed or packaged instance or streamed from outside the VM.

Enterprise Security

As previously stated, security is a major concern of CIOs, and they need to be reassured that adopting cloud technology will not expose them and their businesses to an unacceptable level of risk. Security is not just about firewalls, malware, and antivirus protection. Threats are becoming more sophisticated and unpredictable than ever before, partly owing to the trends in IT consumerization, mobility, social media, cloud computing, and cybercrime. Let us take a closer look at these trends and their impact on risk.

Consumerization

The boundary between work and leisure has become blurred, with many employees taking personal devices to work and taking work devices home. This makes controlling network access, identity management and application permissions more of a challenge.

Mobility

The rise in the use of smartphones, tablets, and PDAs means that it has become easier to work at home, on an airplane, in the back of a taxi, or just about anywhere. These devices, and the sensitive data they contain, must be protected against loss and/or theft.

Cloud Computing

There are many risks associated with cloud computing. Compliance, privacy, and data security must be maintained across the entire services supply chain. This is such an important area, and one of such great concern to CIOs, that we will discuss it further in the Secure Cloud Design section below.

Cybercrime

Protecting critical business resources and sensitive data has always been a challenge, and now that some of these resources can be located outside of the data center and company firewalls, the responsibility for protecting them needs to be clearly defined.

Social Media

Sharing data using Twitter, Facebook, LinkedIn, and other tools makes it easier than ever to accidentally expose sensitive information and compromise security.

HP addresses these risks by using the HP Enterprise Security Solutions framework to link information security management and governance with the operations and technology required to achieve end-to-end security. This framework has three major elements:

1. **Information security management**: This addresses the people, processes, and technologies that are required to protect mission-critical data and information in accordance with internal security policies and compliance requirements.

2. **Security operations**: This addresses risk assessment and mitigation, identity and access management, monitoring and alerting, incident management, and security change control.

3. **Discrete security capabilities for data center, network, applications, and endpoint security**: Data center security includes data and content security, and business recovery/continuity services. Network security involves intrusion protection and securing data in motion. Application security deals with securing data in use and application delivery. Endpoint security is concerned with securing data at rest and security of mobile devices.

Secure Cloud Design

In the traditional data center, with its silos of server, storage, and networking—where one business unit or customer was guaranteed exclusive access to their resources—maintaining privacy was relatively simple. In a cloud environment, with its inherent multi-tenant nature, it is no longer possible to guarantee separation between the resources used by different business units and/or customers.

There are several requirements—over and above those that apply to a traditional data center—that should be considered when designing secure cloud solutions.

Sensitive business information must be protected against accidental or intentional access by non-authorized parties. Data leakage between tenants must be protected against. In addition, protection against the potential for one tenant (customer) to accidentally or intentionally cause a system overload and create a denial of service situation must be provided.

Meeting the legal requirements associated with storing customer data in specific territories and providing associated support for litigation in those territories needs to be considered, as does meeting the compliance requirements in the country where the service is sold.

It is also important to provide identity assurance by establishing trust between individuals, systems, services, and partners while maintaining secure access. All access to resources—either by an employee of the provider or by a tenant user—should be role-based and subject to a centralized single sign-on (SSO) mechanism. All resources (servers, storage, networks, and software) should be protected against intrusion by legitimate users. The resources should also be protected against human error.

All third parties (users, customers, and their subcontractors) should have clearly defined rights and be subject to policy control to manage their ability to modify the infrastructure. In addition, the privacy of any data held by third parties must be assured.

Security mechanisms should be extended across both physical and virtual infrastructure (hypervisors, storage, and networks) and should be centrally controlled. The security architecture should integrate with automation processes and APIs; the cloud makes extensive use of automation, and the security policy will need to permit these automated processes to perform their legitimate functions.

There are a number of mechanisms that can be used to secure the cloud infrastructure. These include:

- **Single sign-on (SSO)**: This allows users to authenticate once using a single authentication authority and to access all of the resources to which they have been granted access without having to re-authenticate. Use of SSO is critical in a multi-tenant environment.

- **Identity management**: This provides a set of tools that allow administrators to quickly and easily manage systems, applications, and users. The identity management policies will be driven by risk factors, regulatory compliance, and business policies.

- **Perimeter security**: This represents the first layer of security and is intended to prevent accidental or deliberate access to resources. In a multi-tenant environment, it is not possible to physically separate one customer from another, so this method of securing resources will need to be complemented by other security mechanisms.

- **Intrusion detection and prevention systems**: An Intrusion Detection System (IDS) monitors networks and systems for malicious activities and policy violations and reports them to a central management system. An Intrusion Prevention System (IPS) detects these activities and takes immediate action to terminate them. Rather than just providing protection of hardware resources, IDS and IPS should also extend protection to the hypervisor level.

- **Trusted infrastructure access**: It is no longer sufficient to simply close the door to unauthorized users and to open the door to authorized users. Authorized users should of course be provided with easy access to their resources, but they, along with unauthorized users, should be prevented from accessing resources to which they are not authorized.

- **Compartments**: These provide the ability to separate (compartmentalize) different kinds of users (tenants), information, authorizations, and activities to ensure that no one user has all the keys, and that activities are broken into individual tasks, each with its own associated privilege.

- **Host security**: This deals with the security hardening/lockdown of the operating system itself, and provides the ability to configure daemons, system settings, and firewalls to be more secure than their default state.

- **Encryption, digital signatures, and key management**: These are fundamental technologies used for securing distributed systems. Encryption and digital signatures rely on the secure distribution of keys, and can be used to protect data on disk drives, and to prevent unauthorized access to systems.

- **Firewalls**: These can be implemented in hardware and/or software and are used to protect against the unauthorized flow of incoming and outgoing network traffic.

- **Network compartmentalization**: Assets can be protected by configuring networks at the physical and logical levels using mechanisms such as demilitarized zones (DMZ) and VLANs.

- **Malware protection**: Operating systems need to be protected against threats such as viruses and worms. This is especially important in a shared infrastructure.

- **Storage protection**: Rather than having one discrete storage device for each computer system, virtualized storage systems are used to provide storage resources to many systems. In this shared environment it is critical to protect data belonging to each system against unauthorized access, modification, or deletion by any of the other systems. In addition, the storage subsystems must be protected against unauthorized configuration changes.

Information Optimization

HP helps businesses rethink how information is gathered, stored, and used—harnessing its power, ensuring its integrity/protection, and making it available to the right people at the right time.

The HP approach to information optimization includes three main areas:

1. **Information infrastructure**: HP offers products and services to store and catalog data for easy retrieval. Paper documents can be digitized and controlled using the HP imaging and printing products and services. Digital information can be stored, protected, and archived using HP's portfolio of servers and storage solutions. Information can be managed, allowing employees and partners to quickly gain access to the right information, with HP content management services.

2. **Information governance**: HP information governance solutions enable businesses to manage, protect, retain, and find information, making it easier to comply with regulatory obligations.

3. **Business insight**: HP's Enterprise Data Warehouse solution is used not only by many enterprise customers, but within HP itself. In addition, HP has a global consulting organization with more than 2,400 consultants who can assist with the implementation of business intelligence solutions.

Hybrid Delivery

HP knows that not every workload is created equal and that enterprises will have a variety of service delivery models in use for a very long time. HP helps with the selection of the best method of service delivery; whether that is using traditional, private cloud, or public cloud architectures. HP can also manage, outsource, and finance cloud implementations.

HP is of the view that the *hybrid delivery* model is the future of cloud computing; spanning all market segments, from enterprises, to small to mid-sized businesses (SMBs), to consumers (see Figure 2-2). Enterprise customers need cloud computing to help them speed innovation and growth, to improve business agility, and to reduce costs and time to revenue. SMBs and consumers are beginning to realize the low cost, pay per use benefits of the cloud, providing easy access to scalable resources. For developers, their focus is to develop, test, and deploy new applications quickly and efficiently, and to be able to develop cloud-based applications once and then have them consumed by users anywhere.

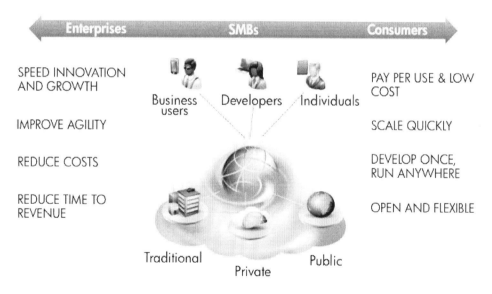

Figure 2-2. Hybrid delivery is the future

With its hybrid delivery model, HP can help businesses deliver the right services at the right time and at the right cost across all these customer segments. HP solutions comprise a complete set of offerings to help enterprises move to the cloud, and can meet the needs and requirements of enterprise businesses by offering private cloud, virtual private cloud and public cloud solutions.

Several service delivery models are available and, depending on their needs and requirements, customers can select one or more of the models.

Figure 2-3 shows the hybrid delivery model, combining the traditional IT and outsourced IT models.

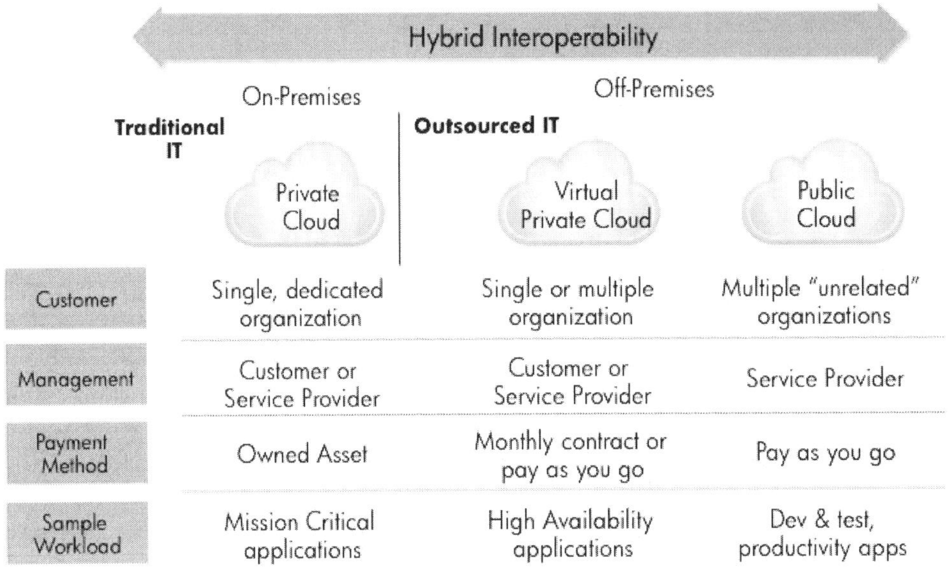

	On-Premises	Off-Premises	
	Traditional IT	**Outsourced IT**	
	Private Cloud	Virtual Private Cloud	Public Cloud
Customer	Single, dedicated organization	Single or multiple organization	Multiple "unrelated" organizations
Management	Customer or Service Provider	Customer or Service Provider	Service Provider
Payment Method	Owned Asset	Monthly contract or pay as you go	Pay as you go
Sample Workload	Mission Critical applications	High Availability applications	Dev & test, productivity apps

Figure 2-3. Service delivery models

Each delivery model has its own unique characteristics and its own pros and cons. In order to select the most appropriate delivery model, several important questions need to be answered:

- Will resources be dedicated to just your organization (single tenant) or shared among multiple organizations or customers (multi-tenant)? If single tenant, either private or virtual private may be the solution. If multiple, unrelated organizations will be using the resources, public cloud may be the answer (subject to other considerations including security, governance, etc.)

- Will the cloud environment be managed by internal resources or by an external service provider? If the environment will be managed by internal resources, public cloud will probably not be the best solution.

- Are the resources owned outright by the organization or will they be consumed on a pay-as-you-go basis? Pay-as-you-go solutions are typically associated with virtual private and public clouds.

- What type of applications or workloads are you considering to put into the cloud environment? Are they business-critical applications requiring 24x7 availability and subject to stringent regulatory requirements? If so, public cloud might be considered far too risky.

These considerations, among others, will influence the selection of service delivery models.

Cloud Computing

The role of IT is changing as it becomes responsible for both building and brokering services. These responsibilities include **building** internal private/hybrid cloud solutions, **consuming** services from the public cloud, **managing and securing** service delivery, and **transforming** infrastructure and applications to take advantage of cloud computing (see Figure 2-4).

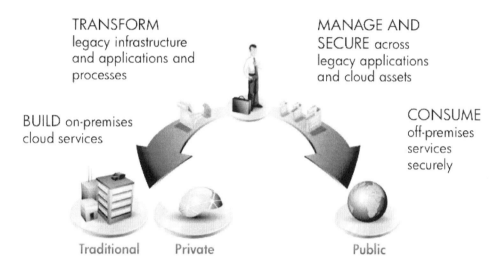

TRANSFORM legacy infrastructure and applications and processes

MANAGE AND SECURE across legacy applications and cloud assets

BUILD on-premises cloud services

CONSUME off-premises services securely

Traditional   Private   Public

Figure 2-4. Delivering complete solutions for hybrid delivery

The HP solutions that will be covered in subsequent chapters of this book cover the four key areas previously mentioned:

- A *build* solution that helps enterprises build a turnkey private cloud. This solution is built around the HP CloudSystem offerings and provides a private cloud solution that is typically located in the customer's datacenter and behind the company firewall, thereby mitigating some of the risks we spoke about earlier (security, governance, etc.). If required, this private cloud solution can make use of external resources using *bursting* technology, which means that the available resources can be scaled almost infinitely.

- A complete portfolio of cloud consulting services to help enterprises to *transform* operations and move them to the cloud. HP has gained considerable expertise with helping customers adopt cloud computing and are ideally placed to partner with enterprises to help them plan their cloud journey and to implement solutions that deliver the desired business outcomes.

- *Management and security* solutions that enables management of services across traditional, private, and public cloud environments, bringing them together into one security policy framework, and making all of those services available in one centralized portal. This is built on the HP Cloud Service Automation software and integrates with the HP Secure Virtualization Framework providing a fully automated and highly secure cloud environment that mitigates the risk of downtime caused by human error, misconfiguration of resources, and attack from inside or outside of the organization.

- Enterprise-class services that enterprises can *consume*. These include HP Enterprise Cloud Service for Compute (ECS-C) and HP Cloud Services that enable mission-critical applications to be run as a service in a cloud computing environment. HP ECS-C is an example of the Virtual Private Cloud that we saw earlier, and can benefit customers who wish to minimize capital expenditure without tying themselves into a long-term contract.

Cloud Starts with a Converged Infrastructure

To achieve the alignment of IT and business and meet the ever-changing needs of the business—while also meeting cost, agility, and responsiveness goals—CIOs are turning to infrastructure convergence.

HP believes that technology has evolved to the point where true convergence has become a reality and that it can accelerate the transition to an Instant-On Enterprise. That technology is known as HP Converged Infrastructure (see Figure 2-5).

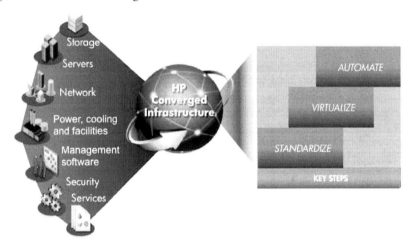

Figure 2-5. Cloud starts with a Converged Infrastructure

What is a Converged Infrastructure? For the last 15 or 20 years all the major infrastructure technologies have been building their own silos. Data centers are even managed in this way, with a separate network stack, server stack, storage stack, and management stack—all built up in isolation and without adequate communication channels to the other stacks.

The HP Converged Infrastructure brings everything back together as one.

Built on industry standards, it does not lock customers in to a proprietary, inflexible system. This standards-based approach is a very important part of the HP architecture.

A Converged Infrastructure enables organizations to transform technology into a business advantage that makes IT one of the most important partners in the organization.

HP Converged Systems

HP Converged Systems simplify and extend the HP Converged Infrastructure by integrating hardware, software, and services into turnkey systems to help businesses harness the full potential of virtualization, cloud, and next generation applications. The HP Converged System portfolio includes the *HP VirtualSystem*, *HP CloudSystem*, and *HP AppSystems* optimized for application delivery in virtualized, cloud, and dedicated environments (see Figure 2-6). Each of these systems is a complete solution that is tested, integrated, optimized, and scalable. Each system is built on a common platform of HP Converged Infrastructure.

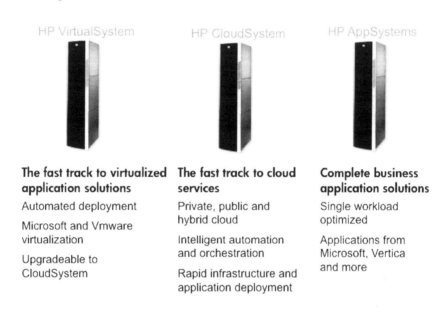

HP VirtualSystem HP CloudSystem HP AppSystems

The fast track to virtualized application solutions

Automated deployment

Microsoft and Vmware virtualization

Upgradeable to CloudSystem

The fast track to cloud services

Private, public and hybrid cloud

Intelligent automation and orchestration

Rapid infrastructure and application deployment

Complete business application solutions

Single workload optimized

Applications from Microsoft, Vertica and more

Figure 2-6. HP Converged Systems

With all HP Converged Systems, there is a choice of three flexible delivery models:

- Turnkey solutions—for fastest time to value

- Built-to-order solutions—for maximum customization

- Hosted solutions—hosted by HP for a balance of optimization and time to value

HP VirtualSystem

Virtualization can introduce a great deal of complexity into an IT environment—not to mention the ever-present potential for virtual sprawl—that results in a proliferation of management tools and security challenges that may be overlooked, and altogether make for a complicated life for IT administrators and the businesses they serve. The HP VirtualSystem represents a range of converged systems that have been tuned for virtualized application environments and provide simplified deployment, management, and security of physical and virtual resources.

HP VirtualSystem simplifies and extends the HP Converged Infrastructure into optimized solutions for server and client virtualization (see Figure 2-7). It delivers a complete, high-performance virtualized environment with pre-tuned server, storage, networking, management, and hypervisor resources. These systems offer leading virtualization technologies, such as HP P4000 and 3PAR Converged Storage, HP FlexFabric networking, and HP BladeSystem with Virtual Connect. All are based on a common architecture, using common management and a common security model.

HP Infrastructure	Deep Management	Virtualization Infrastructure	Services
Optimized rack and blade server configurations Converged, scale-out storage, optimized for virtualization High performance, secure LAN and SAN connections	Intelligent rack and power infrastructure management Integrated system and storage management	vSphere and Hyper-V are the industry-leading virtualization platforms for building cloud infrastructures	Factory integration Installation and support Consulting Holistic delivery

Demonstrating the real benefits of
Converged Infrastructure

Figure 2-7. HP VirtualSystem

HP offers three scalable deployment systems for small, midsize, and large enterprises; each is based on leading virtualization software from Microsoft and VMware and offers support for a maximum of 6000 virtual machines in a single system.

The three configurations are:

1. **HP VirtualSystem VS1**, offering up to 8 HP ProLiant servers, P4500 storage, and support for up to 750 virtual machines

2. **HP VirtualSystem VS2**, offering up to 26 ProLiant servers, P4800 SAN Solution, and support for up to 2500 virtual machines

3. **HP VirtualSystem VS3**, offering up to 64 ProLiant servers, HP 3PAR Utility Storage, and support for up to 6000 virtual machines

 Note
The HP VirtualSystem does not include HP Cloud Service Automation software.

The HP VirtualSystem is built on the same hardware architecture as the HP CloudSystem, so when the business is ready to move to a CloudSystem, a simple upgrade is all that is required.

Availability, performance, capacity allocation, and real-time recovery of HP VirtualSystem solutions can be extended by adding HP SiteScope, HP Data Protector, HP Insight Control, and HP Storage Essentials software extensions.

HP CloudSystem

HP CloudSystem is a complete, integrated, open platform for private, public, and hybrid clouds. The platform is based on proven, market-leading HP Converged Infrastructure. It is built on the modular HP BladeSystem architecture and the highly automated Matrix Operating Environment and HP Cloud Service Automation (CSA) products (see Figure 2-8).

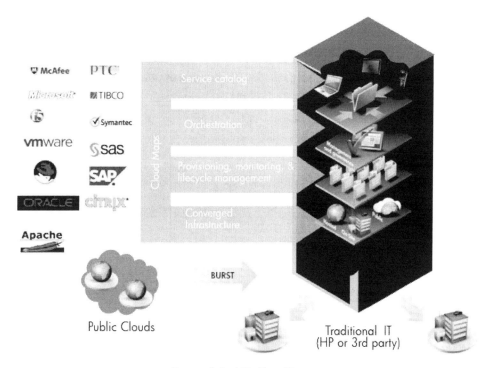

Figure 2-8. HP CloudSystem

CloudSystem is built on the concept of shared pools of servers, storage, and network connectivity that can be provisioned and de-provisioned as needed. An IT architect or designer uses a graphical design editor in CloudSystem to build application infrastructure templates representing physical and virtual servers, storage, and the connections between them. IT architects finalize and then publish these templates into a catalog, which is then available to users to select and request as needed. This process provides standardization and efficient control of provisioning within a shared infrastructure model. After an infrastructure template has been published, an actual instance of it can be created or provisioned rapidly within CloudSystem, using a self-service portal.

HP CloudSystem combines three core elements:

1. **HP Converged Infrastructure:** HP Converged Infrastructure provides pools of compute, storage, and network resources coupled with the Matrix Operating Environment for rapid provisioning of complex infrastructure services.

2. **HP Cloud Service Automation:** HP CSA provides advanced application provisioning, advanced workload optimization and metering, and service assurance through application lifecycle management, service governance and compliance.

3. **HP Cloud Services:** HP Services for CloudSystem helps customers get started and reduces time-to-productivity. We will be discussing HP cloud services in a later chapter, but here are some highlights.

In the decision-making stage, customers can be helped by HP to quickly develop a cloud roadmap for their business with the **HP Cloud Discovery Workshop**. Once the customer has decided to implement an HP CloudSystem solution, the **HP CloudStart** service manages the installation and configuration of a fully operational HP CloudSystem Matrix in just 30 days. The **HP Cloud Computing Curriculum** and courses offered by HP Education Services helps staff to become productive quickly, and **HP Solution Support for CloudSystem,** with a single point of contact for hardware and software, provides assistance for any operational issues.

In addition to these three core elements, HP provides Cloud Maps to help with the creation of service catalogs. Cloud Maps include best practice templates, workflows, sizers, scripts, and reference whitepapers.

The HP CloudSystem will be discussed in much more detail throughout the rest of this book.

HP AppSystems

HP AppSystems are complete, pre-integrated solutions that are tuned and optimized to deliver maximum performance for a single application or a suite of applications for business analytics, data management, and collaboration.

HP AppSystems are built on a Converged Infrastructure foundation and based on a common architecture that is designed to integrate seamlessly with an existing environment. These systems bring together applications with high-performance server, storage, networking, and software (for example, Microsoft operating system or Microsoft Hyper-V). They also include common management and security platforms.

The AppSystem family includes solutions that incorporate top-tier applications from Microsoft, SAP, Vertica, and more (see Figure 2-9). These are all open, configurable systems designed to integrate with current business architecture and applications.

HP AppSystems are appliances that have been tuned and tested by HP to provide optimized performance for particular workloads and offer a choice of best-of-breed applications. AppSystems also provide simplified, integrated management—not building new islands of incompatible IT, but managing these new systems as part of the overall IT ecosystem. AppSystems can leverage HP Cloud Maps to automatically provision infrastructure and applications. Rather than having to deal with multiple different companies for support issues, HP provides a single point of contact for support of AppSystems

Figure 2-9. HP AppSystems

The HP AppSystems portfolio currently includes solutions for:

- **Business insight and analytics**: HP AppSystems for business analytics and reporting include:

  - HP Vertica Analytics System. This solution combines the Vertica Analytics Platform with HP Converged Infrastructure into an appliance that enables real-time analysis of large amounts of complex data, helping customers to gain business insight and to make better decisions. It uses a Massively Parallel Processing (MPP) architecture that enables it to scale out linearly using low-cost industry-standard servers.

  - HP Business Decision Appliance for Microsoft SQL Server. Jointly engineered by HP and Microsoft, this appliance includes Windows Server, Microsoft SQL Server, and Microsoft SharePoint. It is easy to set up and operate and enables end-users to gain access to information and can accelerate analysis and decision making from months to minutes.

- **Data management**: HP AppSystems for data management include:

  - HP Business Data Warehouse Appliance Optimized for SQL Server. Jointly engineered by HP and Microsoft, and based on Microsoft SQL Server Enterprise edition, this appliance provides high-performance and scalability to 5 TB.

  - HP Enterprise Data Warehouse Appliance Optimized for SQL Server. Jointly engineered by HP and Microsoft, and based on Microsoft SQL Server Parallel Data Warehouse, this appliance provides massive scalability—from 38 to more than 500 TB—and shorter query times than traditional SQL Server databases.

  - HP Database Consolidation Solution Optimized for SQL Server. This appliance enables customers to consolidate and reduce database sprawl and to reduce the complexity of managing thousands of SQL instances.

- **Collaboration**: HP AppSystems for collaboration includes:

  - HP E5000 Messaging System. This appliance simplifies the delivery of Microsoft Exchange Server deployments and has built-in high-availability, large mailboxes, centralized archiving and can scale quickly, providing optimized storage for business critical messaging. Preconfigured solutions start at 500 mailboxes and scale up to 3000 mailboxes, while providing mailbox sizes of between 1 and 2.5 GB. Scalability can be achieved by adding more storage capacity and more appliances, enabling support for up to 15,000 mailboxes.

Test Preparation Questions and Answers

The following questions will help you measure your understanding of the material presented in this chapter. Read all the choices carefully, as there may be more than one correct answer. Choose all correct answers for each question.

Questions

1. What are advantages of the cloud computing model? (Select two.)

   a. Responsive IT, by aligning IT with the business

   b. The ability to recycle legacy hardware

   c. The need to only pay for services used

   d. Investment in leading edge technology

   e. Minimising investment in technical training

2. Which attributes should a successful cloud solution possess? (Select two.)

   a. Be able to integrate legacy assets with the cloud

   b. Use highly trained staff to maximize efficiency

   c. Be able to utilize the latest technology at minimal cost

   d. Provide consistent delivery and quality of service

   e. Utilize proprietary architecture for maximum return on investment

3. What is true of the HP VirtualSystem?

   a. It includes HP Cloud Service Automation.

   b. It is based on the HP Superdome.

   c. It offers leading virtualization technology.

   d. It is an open source product.

4. What factors influence the selection of the correct service delivery model?

   a. The ability to integrate legacy hardware

   b. Legal requirements for data protection

   c. Who manages the cloud environment

   d. The implementation of cutting edge technology

5. Which of these key areas is covered by the HP cloud solutions?

    a. Management of the corporate IT network

    b. Enterprise class services for consumption by the enterprise

    c. Administration of application upgrades

    d. A proprietary IT infrastructure

6. Which solution is included in the HP AppSystems portfolio?

    a. Computer aided design and management

    b. Business insight and analytics

    c. Program development and analysis

    d. Information lifecycle management

Answers

1. ☑ **A and C.** The advantages of the cloud computing model are that IT is responsive and aligned with the business, and only those services that are used need to be paid for.
   ☒ **B** is incorrect, because the cloud model is not concerned with recycling legacy systems. **D** is incorrect, because the cloud model is not tied to technology advances. **E** is incorrect, because training investment is not a core concept of the cloud model.

2. ☑ **A and D.** A successful cloud solution should integrate legacy assets with the cloud, and provide consistent delivery and quality of service
   ☒ **B** is incorrect, because the cloud model obviates the need for the user to employ highly trained maintenance staff. **C** is incorrect, because the cloud model is not concerned with utilization of leading edge technology per se. **E** is incorrect, because the cloud concept is based on open standards.

3. ☑ **C.** HP VirtualSystem offers leading virtualization technology.
   ☒ **A** is incorrect, because HP Cloud Service Automation is not included in the basic offering. **B** is incorrect because the cloud model is not tied to the HP Superdome. **E** is incorrect, because the VirtualSystem is not an open source product.

4. ☑ **C.** Factors that influence the selection of the correct service delivery model include who is responsible for managing the cloud environment.
   ☒ **A** is incorrect, because the service delivery model is not concerned with integrating legacy hardware. **B** is incorrect, because legal requirements for data protection do not influence the service delivery model. **D** is incorrect, because technology types are not a major factor for deciding upon the service delivery model.

5. ☑ **B.** HP cloud solutions provide enterprise class services for consumption by the enterprise.
   ☒ **A** is incorrect, because the cloud model is not concerned with management of the corporate network. **C** is incorrect, because HP cloud services are not specifically designed to manage application upgrades. **D** is incorrect, because HP cloud solutions are designed around open standards.

6. ☑ **B.** The HP AppSystems portfolio includes business insight and analytics.
   ☒ **A** is incorrect, because the AppSystems portfolio does not currently include CADCAM applications. **C** is incorrect, because HP AppSystems do not include program development applications. **D** is incorrect, because information lifecycle management is not an area covered by AppSystems.

3 HP Cloud Functional Reference Architecture

EXAM OBJECTIVES

✓ Identify the lifecycle of cloud services.

✓ Describe the HP Cloud Functional Reference Architecture.

ASSUMED KNOWLEDGE

You should be in possession of the HP APC - Converged Infrastructure Solutions (2010) certification.

INTRODUCTION

Cloud environments are dynamic by nature and new applications and services must be able to be provisioned quickly and easily. These services must also be managed to ensure that availability and performance expectations are met.

It is to this cloud services lifecycle that we now focus our attention.

Cloud Services Lifecycle

The HP lifecycle approach to cloud management consists of the following steps (see Figure 3-1):

1. Design service templates that define all of the instructions for building the elements of a cloud service. These templates define server, storage, networking, operating systems, and applications requirements for each service. A service can be simple, comprising a small number of *service elements* such as a single virtual machine with storage and networking, or it can be very complex, and require the provisioning of multiple service elements that combine to form the service. An example of a more complex service could be a multi-tier application with several physical servers, virtual machines, networks, middleware packages, and databases; some of these elements could be hosted on privately-owned infrastructure and some in the public cloud (using bursting).

    In the case of HP CloudSystem Matrix, to assist with the building of service templates, HP provides what they call Cloud Maps. Cloud Maps for many leading business applications are freely available from the HP website at http://www.hp.com/go/cloudmaps. In addition to the HP-provided Cloud Maps, users can create their own with the Insight Orchestration Designer tool.

Cloud Maps will be discussed in more detail later in this book.

2. Publish the service templates into a service catalog, which appears on a self-service portal and allows users to select the service they require from a list. The service may be delivered using public cloud, private cloud, traditional IT environments, or a combination of these. Users don't need to know or care where the services are sourced from.

3. Automate the provisioning and monitoring of infrastructure and applications. HP uses intelligent resource management technology that automates the optimal allocation of resources to ensure that cost, performance, and compliance goals can be met, based on each client's pre-defined business policies. This automation can reduce provisioning time from months to minutes.

4. Manage service lifecycle, including patching of operating systems and applications, compliance verification, reporting, and rescaling systems, and concluding with the de-provisioning of resources and returning them to the pool of available resources at such time as the service is no longer required.

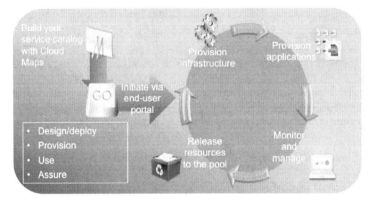

Figure 3-1. Cloud services lifecycle

Many cloud discussions focus only on the provisioning of the services, that is, the activities that take place in the time between when a user chooses the service and when it is made available for use. This is only a small part of the activities that have to happen in the cloud environment. The cloud services lifecycle defines four phases, and these phases encompass everything that needs to happen in order to ensure successful delivery of cloud services. The phases are:

■ **Design/Deploy**: This phase is concerned with the process of making products/services available, with the flex-up and flex-down of the services, and with the final retirement/decommission of the product/service when it is no longer required.

Note
Service providers tend to use the term *products* while enterprises more often use the term *services*.

- **Provision**: This phase takes care of the provisioning of the service and also the de-provisioning of the service when it is no longer needed. Provisioning begins when a user chooses a service and ends when that service is made available for use.

- **Use**: This phase takes care of the things that need to happen while the service is being used. This may include the creation and maintenance of usage records that can be used for billing purposes.

- **Assure**: This phase is concerned with monitoring the service to make sure that it is delivered to an appropriate level of quality, taking into account any service level agreements.

HP has designed the Cloud Functional Reference Architecture, which describes the mechanisms necessary for the design/deploy, provision, use, and assure phases of the cloud services lifecycle.

HP Cloud Functional Reference Architecture

In cloud computing, scalable and elastic IT-enabled capabilities are delivered as a service to customers using the Internet or an intranet. The most important capabilities are a pool of shared resources, a self-service portal, automated provisioning, scale-up and scale-down of resources, a facility to meter and charge for usage, and the eventual release of the resources when the service is no longer required.

In order to ensure a consistent approach throughout all phases of the cloud services lifecycle, HP has designed the HP Cloud Functional Reference Architecture. The reference architecture shows the many functions required to manage a cloud and how these functions work together.

When we look at the CloudSystem solutions in later chapters, we will see that the tasks performed by each functional block of the reference architecture are realized by a particular feature of an HP product. For example, the supply layer *Resource Health* functional block tasks are performed by Insight Control and System Insight Manager. Another way to look at this is that, given a certain set of customer functional requirements, the related functional blocks of the HP Cloud Functional Reference Architecture can be identified. Given that each functional block of the reference architecture is delivered by a particular software product, when we know which functional blocks are required, we are able to identify the software that will need to be included with the solution.

The reference architecture leverages best practices from several sources:

- **The IT Infrastructure Library (ITIL):** ITIL provides a set of best practices for the design and operation of IT infrastructure, and is drawn from the public and private sectors internationally. Some industry pundits have said that 'ITIL is dead' but HP firmly believes there is still great validity in the methods when it comes to cloud.

- **Enhanced Telecom Operations Map (eTOM):** This guidebook defines widely used and accepted standards for business processes in the telecommunications industry. The eTOM model describes service provider business processes and the interactions between these processes.

- **The Open Group Architectural Framework (TOGAF):** This provides a detailed method and a set of supporting tools for developing enterprise architecture.

The HP Cloud Functional Reference Architecture is central to the design of the HP CloudSystem solutions. The architecture uses the three-layer model shown in Figure 3-2.

Note
The HP Cloud Functional Reference Architecture describes an environment—often referred to as the *cloud platform*—to offer and aggregate any cloud services (IaaS, PaaS. SaaS), not the architecture of the workload running within the environment.

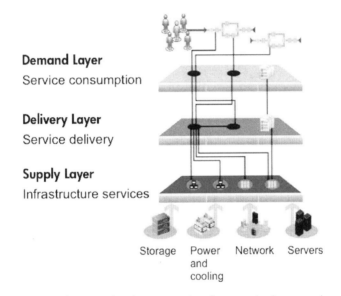

Demand Layer
Service consumption

Delivery Layer
Service delivery

Supply Layer
Infrastructure services

Storage   Power and cooling   Network   Servers

Figure 3-2. The HP Cloud Functional Reference Architecture layers

The *demand layer* contains the self-service portals and is where services are ordered and monitored by end users or subscribers.[1]

The *delivery layer* provides deployment and configuration of the service instance. For example, Cloud Service Automation software enables and manages the delivery of the requested cloud service. In CloudSystem Matrix there are user interfaces that allow infrastructure design, for specifying what assets will be made available and where a service designer can make additions to and manage service catalogs.

The *supply layer* manages all of the infrastructure services for CloudSystem; this is where the physical and virtual assets reside.

---

[1] When we look at the CloudSystem solutions in later chapters, we will see that when HP CloudSystem Matrix is used standalone, the end-user portal is provided by the Matrix OE. In the HP CloudSystem Enterprise, the user portal (line-of-business focused) is provided by Cloud Service Automation (CSA) software. In the HP CloudSystem Service Provider, the user portal (customer-focused) is provided by Aggregation Platform for SaaS (AP4SaaS) software.

The supply layer provides for service delivery of infrastructure elements such as compute, network, storage, and other resources, both physical and virtual. These infrastructure elements may be HP hardware and virtualization, or they may be provided by a customer's existing infrastructure or by third parties, including public clouds.

The infrastructure services of HP CloudSystem are based around HP BladeSystem technology with Virtual Connect and Matrix Operating Environment. In addition, the CloudSystem solutions include a vCenter provider that can deploy/remove from deployment, and start/stop/suspend/restart VMs managed by VMware vCenter.

Note

Matrix OE was formerly known as Insight Dynamics.

Let us now look a little closer at the HP Cloud Functional Reference Architecture. In addition to the demand, delivery, and supply layers previously described, the architecture defines mechanisms by which users gain access to services. These mechanisms are known as *portal and service access* (see Figure 3-3).

Notice that Figure 3-3 introduces key concepts using a *governance and management plane* and a *cloud operations plane*. The governance and management plane contains overall enterprise functionality that is used in the management and operation of both cloud and traditional environments, while the cloud operations plane contains functionality considered specific for cloud environments and includes the demand layer, the delivery layer, and the supply layer.

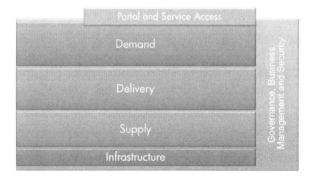

Figure 3-3. The HP Cloud Functional Reference Architecture with portal and planes

Portal and Service Access

The portal provides permission-based access mechanisms and interfaces (GUIs) to access functions delivered through the cloud environment. It supports role-based access needs of the different types of users. The portal also provides access to all relevant functions concerning the cloud services, regardless of whether they are delivered through the cloud operations or governance and management plane. Services can also be accessed using application programming interfaces (APIs).

There are four role-based portal classes found in the HP CloudSystem offerings:

1. **Service designer portal**: This is where the service architect designs the services and their associated infrastructure elements.

2. **User self-service portal**: This provides authorized users with access to predefined service definitions contained in the service catalog and enables them to submit requests for provisioning and utilization of these services.

3. **Service manager portal**: This is used for monitoring the services, events, and processes.

4. **IT administrator portal**: This is used by IT staff to manage resources such as servers, storage, and networks.

Note
Why not have a single portal shared by all roles? This might seem like a good idea at first glance, but doing so would expose certain users, notably the end-users, to excessive complexity and would create a potential security risk. The user self-service portal only shows the end users the functions that are relevant for them, and hides all other designer/ management functions.

Governance and Management Plane

The governance and management plane contains overall enterprise functionality that is used in the management and operation of both cloud and traditional environments. This functionality has been present in datacenters for many years, and has been expanded to support cloud environments. Functions in the governance and management plane include:

■   **Governance,** including risk management, compliance, policies, standards, and architecture

■   **Business,** including strategy, demand, financials, invoicing, procurement, and client relationships

■   **Management,** including service design, service transition, service operation, and continuous improvement

■   **Security,** including identity management (application, information, infrastructure security, and monitoring)

Cloud Operations Plane

The cloud operations plane contains functionality considered specific for cloud environments and includes the demand layer, the delivery layer, and the supply layer.

Demand Layer

This layer focuses on the interaction with the user—either programmatic (via APIs) or physical (via the portal). This layer is also responsible for:

- Authenticating end users to determine their capabilities in creating or modifying services

- Maintaining a catalog describing the services that are available to end users

- Exposing the ability and initiating requests to create and modify services

- Combining one or more customer-facing services/products into an end-to-end customer service

- Presenting both internal services (provided by the delivery layer) and external (aggregated) services

- Providing service billing and settlement information

- Visualizing customer Quality of Experience (QoE) and compliance with Service Level Agreements (SLAs)

- Maintaining mapping of customer to service

Delivery Layer

This layer addresses the service that is being requested and is responsible for:

- Combining all of the elements for the customer-facing service

- Orchestrating and automating the combination of multiple service elements (from one or more supply layers) into a single service

- Selecting the appropriate supply layer, based on policy, demand layer request, and supply layer availability (including bursting functionality)

- Monitoring and calculating service usage by consumer/customer

- Maintaining information mapping service to service elements (supply layer resource pools)

Supply Layer

This layer provides access to the infrastructure and is responsible for:

- Isolating the delivery layer from the resources by providing simple service abstractions, potentially combining multiple heterogeneous resources into a single abstraction

- Providing the necessary governance and orchestration to ensure that the resources deliver the desired customer-facing service

- Optimizing the utilization of the resources within the pool

- Monitoring utilization of the resources, generating usage data records for events that may be potentially billable

- Assuring the health of the resources

- Maintaining a resource pool catalog describing the physical and logical resource repository

Infrastructure

The supply layer directly drives the infrastructure, which includes servers, storage, networking, power and cooling, management software, information, and applications.

The HP Cloud Functional Reference Architecture Functionality

Drilling a little deeper into the Cloud Functional Reference Architecture, we see functional blocks (see Figure 3-4) that describe the functionality that exists in each of the three cloud-specific layers of the architecture.

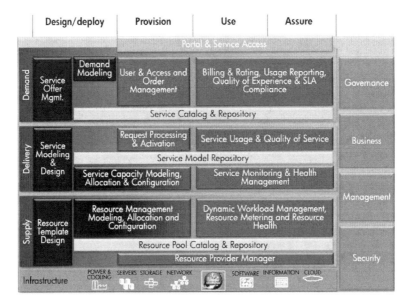

Figure 3-4. HP Cloud Functional Reference Architecture functionality

The HP Cloud Functional Reference Architecture includes a great deal of complexity. To assist with our understanding, we will use an example of provisioning a service to illustrate the operation of the functional blocks and the way the layers interact.

Example: Service Provisioning

This example of provisioning a service will step through seven major activities (see Figure 3-5). It will highlight the tasks performed by the functional blocks and the interaction between the three layers. The example will also illustrate the four phases of the cloud services lifecycle (design/deploy, provision, use, assure).

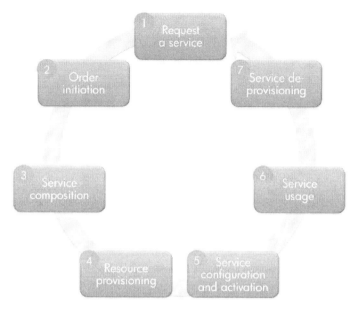

Figure 3-5. Service provisioning example

 Note

Before the service can be requested in step one, the service must have already been de-signed (by a service designer) and deployed (made available to the user). These activities constitute the first phase of the cloud services lifecycle—*design/deploy*.

Step 1 – Request a Service

This step is part of the *provision* phase of the cloud services lifecycle and starts when a user logs onto the system in search of a particular service. The portal will display the services in the service catalog that this user is eligible for. The user makes a choice and requests the provisioning of a specific service.

The individual actions are listed in Table 3-1 and correspond with the numbers in the circles in Figure 3-6.

Note

The actions may not be executed in precisely the order listed. Indeed, some steps may be executed in parallel.

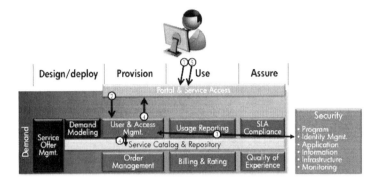

Figure 3-6. Request a service

Table 3-1. Request a service

Number	Action	Functional block
1	User logs on to the portal using identification mechanism (password, smart card, active key, etc.).	Portal & Service Access
2	Portal transfers request to User & Access Management for confirmation of request.	Portal & Service Access and User & Access Management
3	User & Access Management checks with Identity Management to see whether the user is eligible to use the service, and what their role is.	User & Access Management and Identity Management (governance and management plane)
4	Based on identity and rights for the role, User & Access Management identifies the services that this user may choose from in the service catalog; their descriptions are loaded and are presented through the portal.	Service Catalog & Repository and Portal & Service Access
5	User goes through the description of the services in the portal, identifies which service they want to provision, and launches the request for the service(s) they want.	Portal & Service Access

At the end of step one, we know who the user is, and what service they have ordered.

Step 2 – Order Initiation

We are still in the provision phase of the cloud services lifecycle. Once the user has made their request, a final check will take place to ensure the user is eligible to consume the service at that moment in time.

If appropriate, there is a check to identify whether the service is provided by the internal cloud environment or by an external service provider. If the service is to be delivered internally, the request is passed to the delivery layer (signified by the thick black arrow pointing downwards in the middle of Figure 3-7). If the service is to be provided by an external provider, the request is passed to the external provider (signified by the thick black arrow at the top left side of the Figure 3-7).

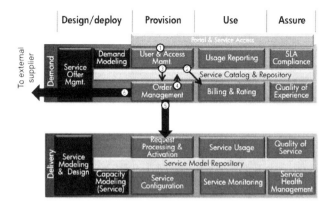

Figure 3-7. Order initiation

The individual actions are listed in Table 3-2 and correspond with the numbers in the circles in Figure 3-7.

Table 3-2. Order initiation

Number	Action	Functional block
1	Optionally, using information associated with the user, an approval process is initiated and approval is gained. If approval is not granted, the user is warned, either via the portal or via email.	User & Access Management
2	User & Access Management checks with Billing & Rating to see whether the user is allowed to consume the service (budget available, pre-payment OK, or service provider invoices paid, etc.). If not allowed, user is warned.	User & Access Management and Billing & Rating
3	User & Access Management creates an order and forwards it to Order Management.	User & Access Management
4	Order Management checks the Service Catalog to see whether the service is delivered by this cloud or by an external cloud.	Order Management and Service Catalog
5	If the service is to be delivered internally by this cloud, Order Management initiates the provisioning of the service by contacting Request Processing & Activation (in the Delivery layer). The request will include parameters including username, ID of the requested service, and parameters for the service.	Order Management and Request Processing & Activation
6	If the service is to be delivered by an external cloud, Order Management initiates the provisioning process with the external cloud, using a set of APIs. When the service has been provisioned, information relating to the service is returned to Order Management and Order Management stores this information in the Service Repository.	Order Management and Service Repository

Step 3 – Service Composition

We are still in the provision phase of the cloud services lifecycle. Once the request to provision, configure, and activate the service has been received, the *service elements* composing the service will be identified. For each element, the associated resources will be defined and the supply layer will check whether appropriate resources are available for reservation. Resources may include servers, storage, networking, software, databases, software license keys, IP addresses, and vLans. We need to make sure that all necessary resources are available before the provisioning process begins, as a missing resource could seriously disrupt the provisioning process. If all resources are available, they will be reserved.

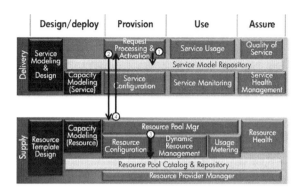

Figure 3-8. Service composition

The individual actions are listed in Table 3-3 and correspond with the numbers in the circles in Figure 3-8.

Table 3-3. Service composition

Number	Action	Functional block
1	Request Processing & Activation gets the description of the service and the list of the service components (elements) from the Service Model Repository.	Request Processing & Activation and Service Model Repository
2	Request Processing & Activation identifies the resources and all of the service components required to deliver the service and sends a request to the Resource Pool Manager to check resource availability.	Request Processing & Activation and Resource Pool Manager
3	Resource Pool Manager checks availability of resources within Resource Pool Catalog & Repository. If all required resources are available, they are reserved.	Resource Pool Manager and Resource Pool Catalog & Repository
4	Resource Pool Manager provides status on resource availability and reservation to Request Processing & Activation.	Resource Pool Manager and Request Processing & Activation

Step 4 – Resource Provisioning

We are still in the provision phase of the cloud services lifecycle. If not all of the resources are available, they may have to be provisioned on an external cloud to host either this service, or to host other workloads that would free up space to run this service on the (local) environment. The resources for each service element are provisioned using the configuration information available in the Service Model Repository.

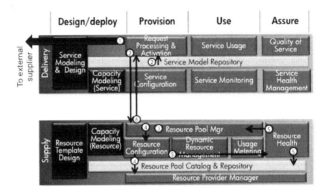

Figure 3-9. Resource provisioning

The individual actions are listed in Table 3-4 and correspond with the numbers in the circles in Figure 3-9.

Table 3-4. Resource provisioning

Number	Action	Functional block
1	If some resources are not available, review whether bursting is an option. If yes, identify workloads that can be moved and initiate bursting using APIs.	Request Processing & Activation
2	If all resources are available, Request Processing & Activation gets the configuration from the Service Model Repository and initiates the provisioning of the resources (using parameters passed through with the request) by communicating with the Resource Pool Manager.	Request Processing & Activation, Resource Pool Manager, and Service Model Repository
3	The Resource Pool Manager identifies the physical resources that have been reserved.	Resource Pool Manager
4	Using configuration parameters received, Resource Pool Manager provisions and configures all resources (physical and virtual servers, storage, OS, middleware, database, software license keys, IP addresses, vLANs, etc). It does so by communicating with Resource Configuration and Resource Provider Manager.	Resource Pool Manager, Resource Configuration, and Resource Provider Manager
5	Resource Configuration instructs Resource Health to check that the resources are correctly provisioned by communicating with Resource Pool Manager and Resource Configuration, updating the resource state in the Resource Pool Catalog & Repository, and reporting successful provisioning.	Resource Health, Resource Pool Manager, Resource Configuration, and Resource Pool Catalog & Repository
6	Resource Pool Manager returns resource provisioning status to the Request Processing & Activation (in the demand layer) together with the actual resource identifiers.	Resource Pool Manager and Request Processing & Activation

Step 5 – Service Configuration and Activation

We are still in the provision phase of the cloud services lifecycle. Now that the resources have been provisioned, software needs to be configured within the virtual machines (or physical servers). Once that is done, metering, billing, and monitoring needs to be initiated.

Finally, feedback is provided to the user that the provisioning has been performed and that the service is available.

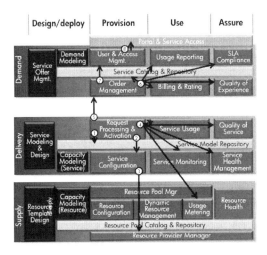

Figure 3-10. Service configuration and activation

The individual actions are listed in Table 3-5 and correspond with the numbers in the circles in Figure 3-10.

Table 3-5. Service configuration and activation

Number	Action	Functional block
1	Request Processing & Activation stores the resource information specific to the service in the Service Model Repository. The user is now associated with the set of resources that will deliver the service.	Request Processing & Activation and Service Model Repository
2	Request Processing & Activation gets the software configuration information for the service from the Service Model Repository and instructs Service Configuration to initiate the configuration of the software stacks in the logical servers.	Request Processing & Activation, Service Model Repository, and Service Configuration
3	Service Configuration specifies the service attributes not under the control of the supply layer and instructs the Resource Provider Manager to configure the software in the logical servers.	Service Configuration and Resource Provider Manager
4	Request Processing & Activation initiates service usage, quality of service, service monitoring, service health management, and usage metering for the service. Note: Quality of service relates to technical SLA parameters such as response time delay, number of fails per second, etc.	Request Processing & Activation, Service Usage, Quality of Service, Service Monitoring, Service Health Management, and Usage Metering
5	Request Processing & Activation notifies Order Management that the service is ready.	Request Processing & Activation and Order Management
6	Order Management initiates billing, usage reporting, quality of experience, and SLA compliance monitoring. Information linking the user with the instance of the service is stored in the Service Catalog & Repository. Note: Quality of experience relates to the user experience, and is presented in a *traffic light* (good, warning, bad) manner. For example, if the service as a whole is running slowly, the user will be notified in a simple, easy-to-understand way, rather than being presented with lots of metric data.	Order Management, billing & Rating, Usage Reporting, Quality of Experience, and SLA Compliance, Service Catalog & Repository
7	Order Management feeds back service activation status to User & Access Management.	Order Management and User & Access Management
8	User & Access Management uses the portal, APIs, or email to advise the user that the service is available for use, and transfers the information required for using the service. This information will include the IP address and credentials for the service.	User & Access Management and Portal & Service Access

Step 6 – Use the Service

Now we move into the *use* and *assure* phases of the cloud services lifecycle. The user can now use the service and execute the appropriate tasks. Using the information provided at the end of the Service configuration and activation step, the user will connect to the service and begin to use it. Monitoring, metering, billing, and service assurance will run and, in the event that a billing limit is reached, the user will be warned and the service may be temporarily suspended. In the event that the service experiences a problem, an ALERT will be generated. Service health information will be forwarded to an external Service Management solution (for example, HP Service Manager), if available.

We will now look at normal operation and ALERT generation. We will assume that the user has connected to the logical server using a terminal emulator and has logged in.

Step 6a – Normal Operation

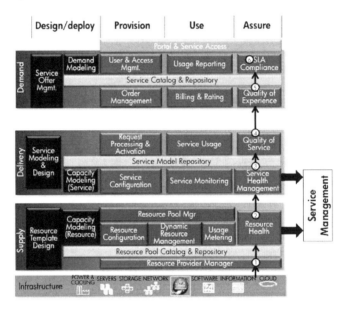

Figure 3-11. Use the service—normal operation

The individual actions are listed in Table 3-6 and correspond with the numbers in the circles in Figure 3-11.

Table 3-6. Use the service—normal operation

Number	Action	Functional block
1	Resource Provider Manager collects the operational parameters such as utilization and temperatures from the infrastructure.	Resource Provider Manager
2	Resource Health monitors a set of parameters over time to ensure each *infrastructure resource* is working in the acceptable range.	Resource Health
3	Service Health Management combines the resource monitors to create a view of the health of the *cloud service* instance. This information will be passed to an external Service Management solution if one is available.	Service Health Management
4	Quality of Service compares the health of the service with technical QoS.	Quality of Service
5	Quality of Experience verifies that QoS meets user service levels as seen by the customer.	Quality of Experience
6	SLA Compliance assesses contractual compliance to SLA as seen by customer.	SLA Compliance

Step 6b – ALERT Generation

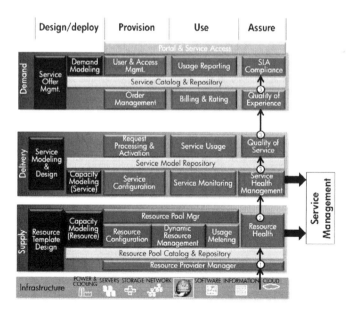

Figure 3-12. ALERT generation

The individual actions are listed in Table 3-7 and correspond with the numbers in the circles in Figure 3-12.

Table 3-7. Use the service—ALERT generation

Number	Action	Functional block
1	Resource Provider Manager collects the operational parameters, such as utilization and temperatures and detects one or more parameters that are outside of the acceptable range. An ALERT is raised.	Resource Provider Manager
2	Resource Health observes a set of parameters over time to ensure each infrastructure resource is working in the acceptable range. In the event that a resource is operating outside of the acceptable range, an ALERT is detected and forwarded to external Service Management system if one is available. As an example, a resource alert would apply to a failed VM.	Resource Health
3	Service Health Management combines the resource monitors to create a view of the ALERTS coming from the cloud service instances and informs Service Health Management and relays data on failed/failing QoS to Quality of Service, Quality of Experience, and SLA Compliance. If an external Service Management system is being used, ALERT data will be transferred to it. Here, the alert applies to the cloud service (logical servers + storage + networking + software), rather than just a single resource (the VM).	Service Health Management, Quality of Service, Quality of Experience, and SLA Compliance. Optionally, external Service Management system

Step 7 – De-provision the Service

Now we move back to the *provision* phase of the cloud services lifecycle. Once the user no longer needs the service, they can initiate the de-provisioning of this service. This returns the resources to the pool of available resources. If cross-charging or billing is performed, a final invoice is sent to the user or to the user's department.

An overview of the individual actions is listed in Table 3-8 and corresponds with the numbers in the circles in Figure 3-13. We will assume that the user has already successfully logged on through the portal.

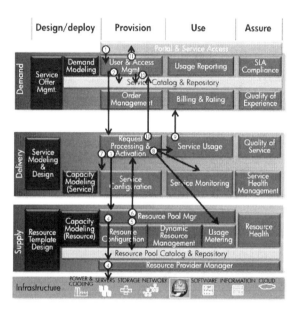

Figure 3-13. De-provision the service

Table 3-8. De-provision the service

Number	Action	Functional block
1	User requests termination of a service.	Portal & Service Access and User & Access Management
2	User & Access Management checks in the Service Catalog & Repository for the current status of the service and instructs Request Processing & Activation to initiate the de-activation process.	User & Access Management, Service Catalog & Repository, and Request Processing & Activation
3	Request Processing & Activation instructs Resource Pool Manager to initiate the release of resources.	Request Processing & Activation and Resource Pool Manager
4	Resource Pool Manager instructs Resource Provider Manager to stop virtual machines and to release IP addresses, vLANS, etc. Storage is released and data may be scrubbed from storage devices.	Resource Provider Manager
5	Resource Pool Manager marks resources as available in Resource Pool Catalog & Repository.	Resource Pool Manager, and Resource Pool Catalog & Repository
6	Resource Pool Manager tells Request Processing & Activation that resources have been released.	Resource Pool Manager and Request Processing & Activation
7	Request Processing & Activation removes the service instance from the Service Model Repository.	Request Processing & Activation and Service Model Repository
8	Request Processing & Activation stops metering and monitoring of the service.	Request Processing & Activation, Service Usage, Service Monitoring, and Usage Metering
9	Service Usage triggers final cost/bill.	Service Usage and Billing & Rating
10	Request Processing & Activation tells User & Access Management that de-provisioning is complete and the service is removed from the Service Catalog & Repository.	Request Processing & Activation, User & Access Management, and Service Catalog & Repository.
11	User is notified that de-provisioning is complete via portal, email, or API.	User & Access Management and Portal & Service Access

Now that we have seen an example of service provisioning, use, and de-provisioning, we will provide, for reference, a more complete list of the functions provided by the main blocks in each layer.

Demand Layer

Service Offer Management

- Supports the process for the introduction of new services, modification of existing services, and retirement of services from the services presently active in the Service Portfolio

Demand Modeling

- Defines models for the expected demand of new and existing service offers

- Together with Service Capacity Modeling (delivery layer), predicts when demand will exceed current supply

User and access management

- Provides access, authentication, and authorization of users by using Identity Management functions supplied by the Security functional block in the governance and management plane

- Uses policy to determine the capabilities of each user role

Order Management

- Order Management receives an order through the portal or an exposed API, validates that the order is correct, and adheres to policy (including entitlement)

- Based on the service catalog, it deconstructs it into its service elements

- Determines which service elements are provided directly (through the delivery layer) and which are provided by external suppliers (through aggregation)

- Directs the requests for the service elements to the delivery layer or to external suppliers, provides status, and initiates remediation in case of failure

- Uses the Service Catalog to know what services can be offered and to maintain information on which services a customer has signed up for

Billing and rating

- Combines the information about service usage by a consumer/customer with the associated price, based on policies, negotiated pricing models and the Service Usage (from the delivery layer)

- Presents rated usage (billing) information to an external billing system

Usage reporting

- Translates internal usage data to customer/consumer usage data

- Maintains usage history

Quality of Experience

- Quality of Experience (QoE) monitoring is responsible for providing a view on how the services are performing from the customer/consumer perspective

- When service quality is below prescribed levels, QoE tools, in conjunction with Quality of Service (QoS) tools, should allow for identification of the root cause of the quality degradation

SLA Compliance

- SLA Compliance is responsible for maintaining the SLA Management Model. As Service Offer Management creates/renews SLA terms and conditions, SLA Compliance needs to inherit the SLA information. As Order Management agrees to new SLA contracts, SLA Compliance needs to begin compliance verification

- Validation or denial of customer complaints regarding SLAs

Service Catalog and Repository

- Contains information regarding offered services and their composition

- Includes information on the agreed-to terms (price, SLA, etc.) and the specific service elements that implement it

- Entitlement mapping (which services can be ordered by which user)

Delivery Layer

Request Processing & Activation

- Handles the service requests for the internally delivered services

- Interfaces to the demand layer (order management) to take the service request and process it based on SLA policies, availability and performance of resources, and the service configuration model

- Orchestrates the activation/de-activation, usage setup, and population of the service status into the repository

Service Usage

- Collects usage and metering data records and process into per consumer/customer, per-service usage records

- In addition to feeding billing and rating, could also provide fraud and risk information

Quality of Service

- Interfaces with service monitoring to receive service and resource health and performance data for continuous service level assessment and dynamic resource reassignments

- Provides near real-time and historical reporting of operational service levels and feeds data to customer SLA compliance

Service Configuration

- Defines how the service elements are combined to be delivered by the supply layer (using the information in the service model repository)

- Receives specific configuration from the resources provisioned in the supply layer

- Provides link between the demand layer services and the supply layer resources that implement the services

- Provides the information required to provision the necessary resources for providing the customer services

Service Monitoring

- Collects real-time event and performance data for service health management as well as aggregation into the QoS function for continuous service level assessment and dynamic resource reassignments

- If a supply layer is over-subscribed, can issue a request to Request Processing & Activation to consider re-provisioning services using different supply layers

- Real-time updates into the Service Model Repository

Service Health Management

- Collects resource events and identifies if they result in a service incident

- Maintains a view of the service status

- Records service events

- Correlates service events and identifies if they result in an incident

- Initiates an incident in the service desk (trouble ticketing)

Service Model Repository

- The service model contains information including defined service hierarchy, mapping between customer facing service and the underlying resources, configuration templates activation/deactivation and automation workflows, and service attributes

- Service real-time status updates are stored within the repository

Service Modeling & Design

- Defines how a service is implemented

- Design of the service templates and automation workflows

- Revision/Release management for the service

Service Capacity Modeling

- Receives the forecasting and trending of service capacity requirements (from the demand layer)

- Receives from the supply layers the resource inventory and projections

- Models whether the demand can actually be delivered by the supply layers

- Interfaces with the governance plane to make decisions on how to address present and future shortfalls

Supply Layer

Resource Configuration

- Receives resource capacity configuration information from the Resource Pool Manager

- Mapping of resource configuration information to the Resource Pool Catalog and Repository

- Configures and provisions resources via Resource Provider Manager

Dynamic Resource Management

- Orchestrates resource pool(s) components to service workload and manages load balancing in real-time, using pre-defined workflow logic

- Reports resource configuration changes as a result of dynamic resource management to Resource Pool Manager for resource tracking and Usage Metering

Resource Metering

- Provides resource pool(s) components usage report to the Service Usage and Service Monitoring modules in the delivery layer

- Monitors resource pool(s) components availability and consumption level, communicates with Resource Provider Manager if pool resources are or will be oversubscribed (could be used to trigger cloud bursting)

Resource Health

- Provides the delivery layer with information about faults within the resource pool(s), potentially affecting the delivery of services (Service Health Management)

- Upon resource failure, can trigger autonomous recovery through resource pool manager

- Monitors resource pool(s) components failure and initiates failover operations in the event of pool resource failure

Resource Provider Manager

- Discovery of resource pool components (servers, storage, network, software)

- Provides an abstract mediation layer for resource pool(s) physical components to be configured, provisioned, managed, and monitored by upper layer configuration and workload management

- Provides real-time update of resource pool physical hardware and software components status and consumption information to the Resource Pool Catalog, Usage Metering, and Resource Health modules

Resource Pool Catalog & Repository

- Service real-time updates to be captured by Resource Health and Resource Capacity Modeling modules

- Dynamic Workload Manager uses real-time resource status to balance workloads across the resource pool

- Mapping service delivery model(s) to resource pool components

Resource Template Design

- Responsible for infrastructure resource design and modification of specific resource pool type(s) based on the customer-facing service defined in the Service Design, Configuration, and Capacity Modeling modules from the delivery layer

- Design of resource pool management metrics to monitor resource pool health

Resource Capacity Modeling

- Resource pool(s) capacity and performance real-time and historical reporting

- Coordination of the supply layer components of resource configuration, provisioning, workload management, and monitoring, to model delivery requirement

- Mapping resource demand information with available resources in Resource Pool Catalog and Repository

Test Preparation Questions and Answers

The following questions will help you measure your understanding of the material presented in this chapter. Read all the choices carefully, as there may be more than one correct answer. Choose all correct answers for each question.

Questions

1. Which of the following is a step in the HP Cloud Services Lifecycle?

    a. Identify the hardware architecture

    b. Automate the provisioning and monitoring of applications and infrastructure

    c. Implement the network infrastructure and SAN environment

    d. Invest in training of users and support engineers

2. Which sources are used in the definition of the Functional Reference Architecture? (Select two.)

    a. ITIL

    b. ANSI

    c. CMIP

    d. TOGAF

    e. INTAP

3. Which portal is used for monitoring events?

    a. User self-service portal

    b. IT administrator portal

    c. Service designer portal

    d. Service manager portal

4. Which layer is responsible for monitoring and calculating service usage by consumer/customer?

    a. Demand layer

    b. Delivery layer

    c. Supply layer

    d. Infrastructure layer

5. Which layer is concerned with Quality of Service (QoS)?

    a. Supply layer

    b. Infrastructure layer

    c. Delivery layer

    d. Demand layer

6. When a user logs onto the system in search of a particular service, what is the next step after order initiation?

    a. Resource provisioning

    b. Service configuration

    c. Request a service

    d. Service composition

Answers

1. ☑ **B.** One step in the HP Cloud Services Lifecycle is to automate the provisioning and monitoring of applications and infrastructure.
   ☒ **A** is incorrect, because the hardware architecture is not relevant to the lifecycle. **C** is incorrect, because the cloud services lifecycle is independent of the network infrastructure implementation. **D** is incorrect, because training investment is not a core concept of the cloud model.

2. ☑ **A and D.** The HP Cloud Functional Reference Architecture leverages ITIL and TOGAF as sources.
   ☒ **B** is incorrect, because ANSI is the American National Standards Institute. **C** is incorrect, because CMIP is the Common Management Information Protocol. **E** is incorrect, because INTAP is the Interoperability Technology Association for Information Processing.

3. ☑ **D.** The service manager portal is used for monitoring events.
   ☒ **A** is incorrect, because the User self-service portal provides authorized users with access. **B** is incorrect, because the IT administrator portal is used by IT staff to manage resources such as servers, storage, and networks. **C** is incorrect, because the Service designer portal is where the service architect designs the services.

4. ☑ **B.** The supply layer is responsible for monitoring and calculating service usage.
   ☒ **A** is incorrect, because the demand layer focuses on the interaction with the user. **C** is incorrect, because the supply layer provides access to the infrastructure. **D** is incorrect, because the infrastructure layer includes the hardware and software.

5. ☑ **C.** The delivery layer is concerned with Quality of Service.
   ☒ **A**, **B**, and **D** are incorrect, because they are not concerned with QoS. The demand layer is concerned with Quality of Experience, but that wasn't the question.

6. ☑ **D.** The next step after order initiation is service composition.
   ☒ **A** is incorrect, because resource provisioning is the fourth step. **B** is incorrect, because service configuration is the fifth step. **C** is incorrect, because requesting a service comes before order initiation.

4 HP CloudSystem

EXAM OBJECTIVES

✓ Describe the components of each HP CloudSystem offering.

✓ Explain how HP CloudSystem integrates with non-HP infrastructure.

✓ Explain how to move to HP CloudSystem while leveraging existing HP Converged Infrastructure components.

ASSUMED KNOWLEDGE

You should be in possession of the HP APC - Converged Infrastructure Solutions (2010) certification.

INTRODUCTION

Based on HP Converged Infrastructure and HP Cloud Service Automation software, HP CloudSystem solutions combine servers, storage, networking, management, and security to deliver a flexible, agile cloud solution for private, public, and hybrid cloud environments.

In this chapter we will be providing an overview of each of the HP CloudSystem offerings. In subsequent chapters we will look in detail at each offering.

HP CloudSystem Offerings

The HP CloudSystem is available in three configurations: HP CloudSystem Matrix, HP CloudSystem Enterprise, and HP CloudSystem Service Provider (see Figure 4-1). Each of these offerings is based on a single unified architecture combining hardware, software, and services. Together, the HP CloudSystem solutions address all deployment models (private, public, and hybrid) and service models (IaaS, PaaS, and SaaS).

Chapter 6 of this book is devoted to HP CloudSystem Matrix, Chapter 7 to HP CloudSystem Enterprise, and Chapter 8 to HP CloudSystem Service Provider.

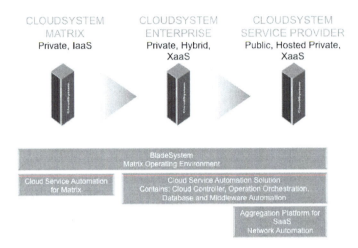

Figure 4-1. HP CloudSystem offerings

HP CloudSystem Matrix

HP CloudSystem Matrix is the base HP CloudSystem offering and includes HP BladeSystem with Virtual Connect, HP Matrix Operating Environment (Matrix OE), HP Cloud Service Automation for Matrix (CSA4M), and HP services. The main area of focus for HP CloudSystem Matrix is on delivering IaaS in a private cloud environment. It supports a limited set of third-party hardware and enables the rapid deployment of a private cloud solution that includes infrastructure and basic application provisioning. The optional HP CloudStart service delivers a fully functioning HP CloudSystem Matrix compute service in less than 30 days.

 Note

Do not confuse CSA4M in HP CloudSystem Matrix with the CSA that is part of the HP CloudSystem Enterprise and HP CloudSystem Service Provider solutions; they are different products. The differences will be covered in Chapter 7.

HP CloudSystem Enterprise

HP CloudSystem Enterprise is intended for clients wishing to deploy a private or hybrid cloud solution, using IaaS, PaaS, or SaaS (also known as XaaS) service models. HP CloudSystem Enterprise supports a large selection of third-party hardware, and supports full lifecycle management and advanced application provisioning. In its basic form it includes HP BladeSystem with Virtual Connect, HP Matrix OE, HP Cloud Service Automation (CSA), and HP services.

HP CloudSystem Service Provider

HP CloudSystem Service Provider has been designed for service providers and is focused on public cloud services—an aggregation of IaaS, PaaS, SaaS, and hosted private cloud.

HP CloudSystem Service Provider includes HP BladeSystem with Virtual Connect, HP Matrix OE, HP CSA, HP Aggregation Platform for SaaS (AP4SaaS), HP Network Automation, and HP services. HP CloudSystem Service Provider is HP CloudSystem Enterprise + HP Aggregation Platform for SaaS (AP4SaaS) and HP Network Automation.

 Note

There is an additional solution that does not require the use of the HP BladeSystem. It features CSA software running on hardware other than HP BladeSystem (such as HP ProLiant DL/ML and non-HP servers).

An Overview of the HP CloudSystem Offerings

Figure 4-2 shows a high-level overview and key use models for the three HP CloudSystem offerings. We will look at each of the three offerings in more detail over the coming pages.

	HP CloudSystem Matrix	HP CloudSystem Enterprise	HP CloudSystem Service Provider
Descriptor	• Private cloud environment, Infrastructure as a Service (IaaS), basic application deployment and monitoring	• Private and hybrid cloud; IaaS, PaaS and SaaS; advanced application to infrastructure lifecycle management	• Public and hosted private cloud; Software as a Service aggregation and management
Target Customers	• Enterprise	• Enterprise	• Service Provider
Key Use Models and Attributes	• Quick deployment of private IaaS • IT- based self service portal • Basic application deployment and monitoring • Tightly integrated Matrix resource pool • Bursting	• Private and Hybrid; IaaS, PaaS, SaaS • Role-based self service portal for IT and Line of Business • Advanced application to infrastructure lifecycle management • Multiple resource pools (Matrix, other HP, 3rd Party, bursting)	• Public cloud services – aggregation of IaaS, PaaS, SaaS, hosted private cloud • Role-based self service portal for public consumers, IT, and Line of Business • Advanced application and network lifecycle management • Multiple resource pools (Matrix, other HP, 3rd Party, bursting)

Figure 4-2. HP CloudSystem offerings

HP CloudSystem Sample Configurations

Each of the HP CloudSystem offerings (HP Matrix, HP Enterprise and HP Service Provider) can be built using small, medium, and large *base* building blocks (see Figure 4-3). These sizes are examples only, and should be modified and/or combined to meet customer requirements. The current building block sizes for HP CloudSystem with HP ProLiant Blades are:

- **Small:** 1 c7000, 8 servers (bl46xG7 blades), with optional P6300 EVA storage (27.9 TB raw)

- **Medium:** 1 c7000, 16 servers (bl46xG7 blades), with optional HP 3PAR F200 storage (51.8 TB raw)

- **Large:** 4 c7000s, 64 servers (bl46xG7 blades), with optional HP 3PAR F400 storage (145.4 TB raw)

Management servers are also required, and their number will vary depending on the offering (HP CloudSystem Matrix, HP Enterprise, or HP Service Provider) and scale of the HP CloudSystem solution.

A number of additional extensions are available for HP CloudSystem, including both hardware and software extensions, and these will be covered later in this book.

The light grey areas in Figure 4-3 represent key components that deliver the core value proposition of HP CloudSystem, and are included by default on every configuration.

The dark grey areas in Figure 4-3 represent additional components strategic to HP CloudSystem, leveraging the HP Software, Technology Services (TS), HP Software Professional Services (PS), and Enterprise Storage, Servers and Networking (ESSN) portfolios, and can be added to a configuration based on customer need. Some are loaded by default to promote key HP differentiation for cloud, and can be deselected if they are not required.

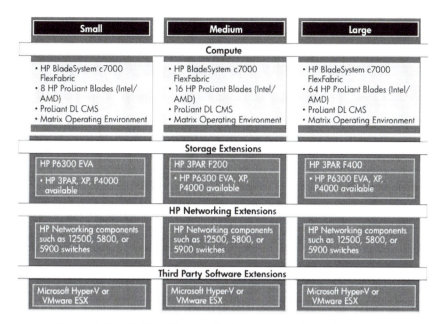

Figure 4-3. HP CloudSystem (ProLiant) example configurations

HP Integrity Blades running HP-UX are also supported with the HP CloudSystem, and Figure 4-4 shows the *base* building blocks for these systems. The current building block sizes for HP CloudSystem with HP Integrity Blades are:

- **Small**: 1 c7000, 4 servers (BL860c i2 blades), with optional EVA storage up to 5.4 TB

- **Medium**: 1 c7000, 4 servers (BL870c i2 blades), with optional HP 3PAR storage up to 55TB

- **Large**: 4 c7000s, 4 servers (BL890c i2 blades), with optional HP 3PAR storage up to 111 TB

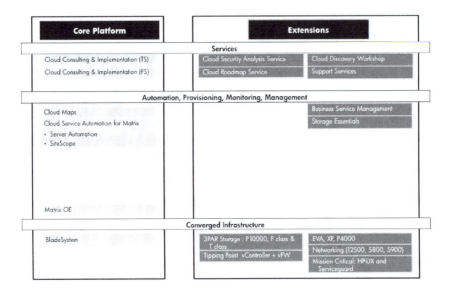

Figure 4-4. HP CloudSystem (HP Integrity) example configurations

Let us now take a closer look at each of the HP CloudSystem offerings.

HP CloudSystem Matrix

HP CloudSystem Matrix is the base offering and is intended for customers wishing to deploy a private cloud (for internal consumption) with a focus on Infrastructure as a Service (IaaS) (see Figure 4-5). This base configuration is built on the HP BladeSystem Matrix, which provides the means to create virtual pools of servers, storage, and networking. Included in the package is HP CSA for Matrix (a bundle containing HP Server Automation and SiteScope software products) that provides operating system provisioning, basic application provisioning, patching, monitoring, and compliance capabilities.

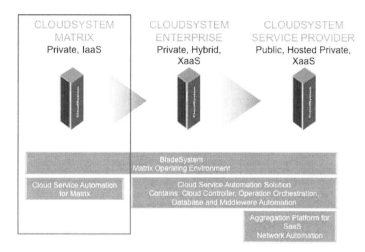

Figure 4-5. HP CloudSystem Matrix

HP CloudSystem Matrix Components

HP CloudSystem Matrix is an integrated offering of hardware, software, and services. It includes HP BladeSystem, HP Virtual Connect, HP Matrix Operating Environment, HP Cloud Service Automation for Matrix (CSA4M), HP Services and SAN storage (see Figure 4-6).

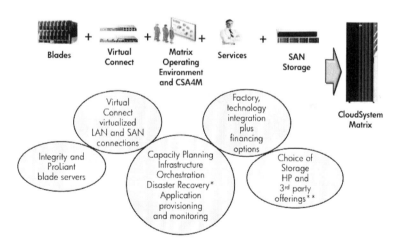

Figure 4-6. HP CloudSystem Matrix components

* Matrix recovery management is bundled for HP ProLiant systems. For HP-UX customers using HP Integrity blades, optional HP Serviceguard solutions are available.

** At the time of writing, Fibre Channel Storage Area Network (SAN) storage is required for physical and virtual environments. iSCSI SAN can be used for VM data stores, and support for iSCSI boot volumes may be added in the near future.

The light gray areas in Figure 4-7 represent *Core Platform* components that are mandatory and are included in all HP CloudSystem Matrix solutions. The dark gray areas represent optional extensions that add value to the solution.

We will provide a high-level overview of the core components and extensions in this chapter, leaving the detailed discussions for later chapters.

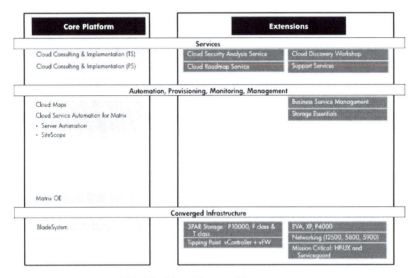

Figure 4-7. HP CloudSystem Matrix components

HP CloudSystem Matrix Core Components

Cloud Consulting and Implementation services: These services include racking, configuration, and cabling in the HP factory; and on-site implementation services, including system installation and deployment services from HP Technology Services (TS); and CSA4M software installation and configuration services from HP Professional Services (PS).

HP Cloud Services is covered in detail in Chapter 10.

HP Cloud Maps: HP Cloud Maps are building blocks for the creation of a service catalog, from which users can select a service for provisioning. Rather than customers having to build their cloud services from nothing, Cloud Maps can be downloaded from the HP website and used to define a specific set of infrastructure components (servers, network, and storage) to support a particular application workload.

Cloud Maps is covered in detail in Chapter 6.

HP Cloud Service Automation for Matrix: HP CSA4M is a bundle of HP Server Automation (HP SA) and HP SiteScope (HP SiS) software. HP SA provides policy-based provisioning, configuration, patching, and compliance management of servers, OS, and application infrastructure. HP SiS monitors the availability and performance of distributed IT infrastructures and applications, including servers, operating systems, network and Internet services, and applications.

CSA4M is covered in detail in Chapter 6.

HP Matrix OE: Matrix OE manages the automated provisioning, optimization, and recovery management capabilities of HP CloudSystem Matrix.

Matrix OE is covered in detail in Chapter 6.

HP BladeSystem: The HP BladeSystem c-Class architecture is a flexible infrastructure that integrates computing, network, and storage resources with common power and cooling. It is assumed that readers will already be familiar with HP BladeSystem, and it will not be covered in this book.

HP CloudSystem Matrix Extension Components

Cloud services: Cloud services are such an important part of a successful cloud engagement that we have dedicated Chapter 10 to them.

HP Business Service Management: Once the cloud service is deployed, whether private or public, it is critical to manage its availability and performance. HP Business Service Management (BSM) combines HP Application Performance Management, Network Management, and Systems Management to integrate application, system, network, and business transaction monitoring. HP BSM (previously known as Business Availability Center, or BAC) includes HP SiteScope and HP Operations Manager i (OMi) software, with HP ArcSight as an optional extra to enhance event management log analysis.

HP BSM utilizes a unique run-time service model, designed for highly virtualized environments, that enables the end-to-end monitoring of business processes. It helps IT teams pinpoint and repair system failures before they become business service problems. It can also help IT teams prioritize IT issues by making visible the links between technology and business services.

An in-depth discussion of HP BSM is outside of the scope of this book.

HP Storage Essentials: HP Storage Essentials is a HP CloudSystem extension that provides comprehensive storage resource management and storage automation for HP CloudSystem's physical and virtual infrastructures. It improves efficiency in managing, visualizing, and reporting on the HP CloudSystem storage environment and infrastructure.

HP Storage Essentials integrates with Operations Orchestration, applying pre-packaged storage operations and workflows to automate repetitive, time-consuming storage tasks. In conjunction with the uCMDB, HP Storage Essentials can record SAN changes and audit SAN configuration compliance, revealing the potential impact of changes before they occur.

HP Storage Essentials also works to monitor the health and availability of storage hosts, switches, and arrays, and it shows the impact of storage alerts on critical business services. HP Storage Essentials, along with HP Server Automation software, enables visualizing and reporting on servers and storage through a single pane of glass. It also includes storage compliance audits.

An in-depth discussion of HP Storage Essentials is outside of the scope of this book.

Converged Infrastructure: It is assumed that readers will already be familiar with HP Converged Infrastructure. A detailed discussion is outside the scope of this book.

HP CloudSystem Matrix Starter Kit

The method for purchasing HP CloudSystem Matrix is simple, and begins with ordering an HP CloudSystem Matrix Starter Kit. The starter kit contains the entire infrastructure needed for a fully-working environment supporting up to 16 HP ProLiant half-height server blades or 8 HP Integrity full-height server blades (or a mix of any of these blades). Additional infrastructure and blades can be added to the solution by ordering one or more expansion kits. When an expansion kit is added, the central management system (CMS) host implemented in the starter kit simply extends its domain to manage the additional infrastructure.

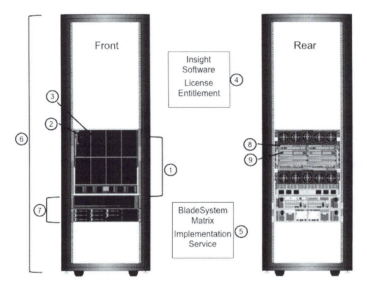

Figure 4-8. HP CloudSystem Matrix starter kit

The HP CloudSystem Matrix Starter Kit includes the following (see Figure 4-8):

1. One single phase HP BladeSystem c7000 enclosure

2. One Central Management Server (CMS). Figure 4-8 shows the optional HP ProLiant Blade-based CMS. The recommended option is the HP ProLiant DL360c G7 server CMS

3. 16 half-height device bays available for populating with server blades. (Only 15 half-height device bays will be available if the optional blade-based CMS is selected.)

4. Complete Matrix Operating Environment licenses (including Virtual Connect Enterprise Manager)

5. On-site HP CloudSystem Matrix Starter Kit Implementation service

6. An HP 10000 G2 Series rack is shown in Figure 4-8, but is not included with the Matrix Starter Kit.

7. Integration with an existing supported Fibre Channel SAN. The recommended option is to choose an HP 4400 Enterprise Virtual Array Starter Kit (EVA4400 controller pair enclosure with embedded switches, drive enclosure, eight 450-GB 10K- rpm 4-Gb dual-port FC EVA M6412 hard disk drives, CommandView and SmartStart media and 4x 1-TB Licenses)

8. HP Virtual Connect Flex-10 10Gb Ethernet modules (redundant pair) **or** HP Virtual Connect FlexFabric modules (redundant pair)

9. HP Virtual Connect 8Gb 24-Port FC modules (redundant pair) **or** Interconnect bays 3 and 4 available for additional HP Virtual Connect FlexFabric modules (redundant pair)

The HP CloudSystem Matrix Expansion Kit includes:

10. One single phase HP BladeSystem c7000 enclosure

11. 16 half-height device bays available for populating with server blades

12. Complete HP Matrix Operating Environment licenses (including Virtual Connect Enterprise Manager)

13. HP Virtual Connect Flex-10 10Gb Ethernet modules (redundant pair) **or** HP Virtual Connect FlexFabric modules (redundant pair)

14. HP Virtual Connect 8Gb 24-Port FC modules (redundant pair) **or** Interconnect bays 3 and 4 available for additional HP Virtual Connect FlexFabric modules (redundant pair)

 Note

All HP CloudSystem Matrix infrastructure ships with licensed disaster protection for both physical and virtual servers, in coordination with data replication provided by EVA or XP Continuous Access software. Disaster recovery protection can be achieved by implementing a secondary infrastructure at a remote location and enabling storage replication between the two sites.

For HP-UX installations, as part of the HP Matrix installation, HP will install Shared Logical Volume Manager (SLVM). SLVM is a mechanism that permits multiple systems in an HP Serviceguard cluster to share (read/write) disk resources in the form of volume groups. This is essentially a mini HP Serviceguard installation with a one-node cluster. The EULA (End User License Agreement) for the HP-UX Virtual Server Environment Operating Environment (VSE-OE) for Matrix has been extended to provide licensing to customers for use of this minimum HP Serviceguard configuration; this does not provide the full HP Serviceguard licensing. The EULA also restricts the customer and does not allow for reconfiguration of HP Serviceguard such as for a multi-node cluster, unless the customer also purchases the full HP Serviceguard product or upgrades from VSE-OE to Data center Operating Environment (DC-OE).

With all HP CloudSystem Matrix Starter and Expansion Kit orders, the following services are included:

- Factory services to rack, configure, and cable the infrastructure

- Firmware verification for the entire solution being purchased (the HP CloudSystem Matrix kits and the supported blades and options purchased with those kits) and updating to the latest current HP CloudSystem Matrix firmware release, if necessary. This ensures that the entire HP CloudSystem Matrix solution leaves the factory with the latest firmware revisions and eliminates any potential firmware revision mismatch issues.

- Coordination of solution hand-off to HP Technology Services (TS) or authorized HP partner. A TS or partner project manager is assigned for managing pre-engagement and assigning a team of engineers to perform the implementation service at the customer site.

HP CloudSystem Enterprise

The HP CloudSystem Enterprise offering is intended for customers wishing to deploy private or hybrid cloud environments, and offers extended support for third party infrastructure (see Figure 4-9). HP CloudSystem Enterprise leverages the capabilities found in the HP CloudSystem Matrix offering, and offers unified management across private, hybrid, and traditional IT. It also provides advanced application-to-infrastructure lifecycle management and is highly customizable and scalable.

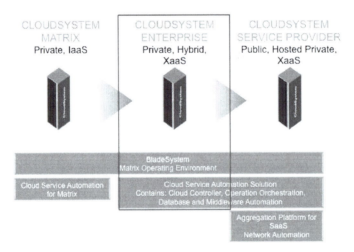

Figure 4-9. HP CloudSystem Enterprise

Differences between HP CloudSystem Matrix and HP CloudSystem Enterprise

The areas containing diagonal lines in Figure 4-10 illustrate the differences between the platforms of HP CloudSystem Matrix and HP CloudSystem Enterprise:

- **Core Platform:** HP CloudSystem Matrix includes CSA for Matrix whereas HP CloudSystem Enterprise includes CSA and Database and Middleware Automation (DMA).

- **Extensions:** HP CloudSystem Enterprise adds Hybrid Delivery Workload Analysis, IT Service Management, Network Automation, and Advanced Reservation Manager.

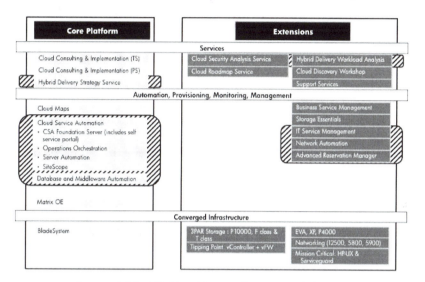

Figure 4-10. HP CloudSystem Enterprise definition

HP CloudSystem Enterprise Core Components

HP Cloud Service Automation: HP Cloud Service Automation (CSA) is a highly extensible cloud services solution, offering role-based portals for infrastructure and application provisioning. It is used for private, pubic, and hybrid cloud services, and for Cloud Lifecycle Management of the entire service lifecycle, from request, order, provisioning, and usage to a final retirement of the service, in alignment with business policies, cost, and performance goals. HP CSA provides: advanced provisioning and management of infrastructure and applications with industry best-practice templates, a highly flexible architecture with advanced workload optimization and metering, service assurance, application lifecycle management, security, and compliance.

HP CSA is covered in detail in Chapter 7.

HP Database and Middleware Automation (DMA): HP DMA provisions simple and complex application architectures onto existing infrastructure, and is the enabler of PaaS, because it provides the ability to provision middleware and databases, which are components that add significant value to a PaaS solution. After applications—including middle-ware and databases—have been provisioned and are up and running, DMA can manage those applications, providing pre-packaged workflows for application patching, compliance, and code release and eliminating the need for manual customization.

HP DMA is covered in detail in Chapter 7.

HP CloudSystem Enterprise Extension Components

HP IT Service Management (ITSM): HP ITSM is a software package that protects businesses from the risk of service disruptions, and from the consequences of failing to comply with regulations and audits. It ensures consistency, predictability, and reliability by leveraging standard IT Infrastructure Library v3 (ITIL v3) processes. It includes proven software for key service management functions, including service desk, change management, service catalog, and asset management.

HP Service Manager software is at the heart of the HP ITSM solution. It provides a scalable incident and problem management system while helping to optimize the quality of service delivery and support, leading to enhanced agent and end-user support.

An in-depth discussion of HP ITSM is outside of the scope of this book.

HP Network Automation: HP Network Automation software supports an exhaustive set of network devices from over 70 vendors. It helps to prevent errors before they occur and delivers measurable cost savings by using process-driven network automation. HP Network Automation automates the complete operational lifecycle of network devices, from provisioning to policy-based change management, compliance, and security administration.

When integrated with HP CloudSystem, HP Network Automation takes the automation of IT workflows beyond traditional network change and configuration management. It provides an integrated solution that unifies network fault, availability, and performance management with change, configuration, and compliance management, along with automated diagnostics.

HP Network Automation is covered in detail in Chapter 7.

- **Advanced Reservation Manager:** Advanced Reservation Manager software (based on MOAB from Adaptive Computing Enterprises Inc.) dynamically adapts cloud infrastructure to respond to changes in workload demand or resource conditions, optimizes utilization/capacity, and ensures quality of service and chargeback to the business. It dynamically adapts resources to meet changing IT service/resource demand or resource conditions, reducing risk and optimizing performance. It achieves this by taking data from HP CSA, using those data to make decisions, and then feeding data back into CSA.

A detailed discussion of Advanced Reservation Manager is outside of the scope of this book.

Mission-Critical Computing: With the Mission-Critical Computing extension for HP-UX and HP ServiceGuard failover clustering, HP CloudSystem Matrix optimizes IT capacity while ensuring predictable delivery and service levels for organizations. The HP-UX capabilities for Mission-Critical Computing are integrated into the HP Matrix OE level as well as the HP Cloud Service Automation level.

A detailed discussion of HP-UX and HP ServiceGuard is outside of the scope of this book.

HP CloudSystem Service Provider

HP CloudSystem Service Provider includes HP BladeSystem with Virtual Connect, Matrix OE, CSA, Aggregation Platform for SaaS, Network Automation, and HP services (see Figure 4-11). It is focused on enabling communications service providers (CSPs) to deliver public cloud services, including aggregation of IaaS, PaaS, SaaS, and hosted private cloud.

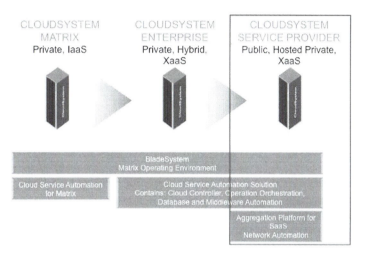

Figure 4-11. HP CloudSystem Service Provider

HP CloudSystem Service Provider Portals and Interfaces

In addition to the other portals and interfaces available in HP CloudSystem, the HP CloudSystem Service Provider offering adds other ways to interact with the system, including:

- An administrative portal to be used by service provider product management for product and offer creation and to register and manage SaaS providers

- A marketplace portal where the service provider's business customers can discover, order, and manage compute services, products, and bundles

These portals can be customized with the service provider's logo and other information.

Differences between HP CloudSystem Enterprise and HP CloudSystem Service Provider

The area containing diagonal lines in Figure 4-12 shows the major differences between the platforms of HP CloudSystem Enterprise and HP CloudSystem Service Provider:

- **Core Platform:** HP CloudSystem Service Provider adds Aggregation Platform for SaaS and moves Network Automation from *extensions* to *core*. In addition, the Hybrid Delivery Strategy Service has been removed.

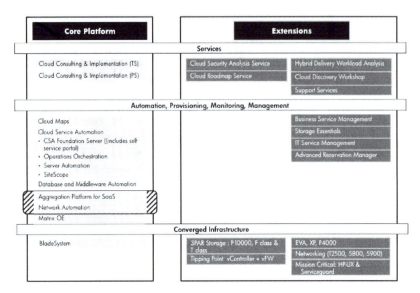

Figure 4-12. Differences between HP CloudSystem Enterprise and HP CloudSystem Service Provider

HP Aggregation Platform for SaaS (AP4SaaS)

The HP Aggregation Platform for SaaS (AP4SaaS) is a key component of the HP CloudSystem Service Provider offering. HP AP4SaaS serves as the single point of access for all applications (SaaS and hosted services), delivering a *one-stop shop* for cloud service providers.

This platform allows cloud service providers and large enterprises to manage the complete lifecycle of their compute services, and other cloud services products and bundles. The platform enables product creation based on service templates that are generated by utilizing the underlying HP CloudSystem software and hardware.

AP4SaaS enables the distribution, subscription, and consumption of IaaS, SaaS, and other on-demand cloud services. It also contains flexible charging functions that enable the service provider to offer a variety of pricing mechanisms for cloud services.

The AP4SaaS supports a variety of functions needed to create public cloud service offering, such as:

- Customer charging through leverage of the service provider's existing business support systems (BSS).

- Support for charging models relevant to a *compute services* business model—e.g., flat fee, pay-per-use, etc. Note that the term pay-per-use in this context refers to the service provider offering pay-per-use services to their customers, rather than HP offering pay-per-use services to the service providers.

- Reseller support that allows the service provider to manage revenue streams to reseller partners (of SaaS services).

- Monitoring of the availability of compute services to guarantee service level agreements.

Using this platform, a service provider's customers can discover SaaS and hosted services and bundles, run trials, and subscribe to and consume services. The platform also provides an environment for product managers to develop and price bundles and enable efficient lifecycle management of SaaS service and providers.

HP AP4SaaS is covered in more detail in Chapter 8.

HP Network Automation

We introduced HP Network Automation earlier in this chapter, in the "HP CloudSystem Enterprise Extension Components" section, and cover it in more detail in Chapter 7.

HP CloudSystem Infrastructure

Now that we have looked at each of the HP CloudSystem offerings, we will summarize the differences between HP CloudSystem Matrix, HP CloudSystem Enterprise, and HP CloudSystem Service Provider.

Component	Description	CloudSystem Configuration		
		Matrix	Enterprise	SP
Matrix OE	• Operating environment, management for Matrix	●	●	●
HP BladeSystem	• Integrated infrastructure platform	●	●	●
3PAR Utility Storage: P10000, F-Class and T-Class	• Next generation thin provisioned storage optimized for hybrid cloud	○	○	○
EVA, XP, P4000 Storage	• Diverse portfolio of traditional architecture storage arrays	○	○	○
Tipping Point V-Controller and V-Firewall	• Security solutions for physical and virtual cloud domains	○	○	○
Networking (12500, 5800, 5900)	• High performance, flexible core to edge networking fabric	○	○	○
Mission Critical HP-UX	• Matrix with HP-UX for most demanding mission critical workloads	○	○	○

Key: ● Included ○ Extension

Figure 4-13. Differences in HP CloudSystem offerings

The core HP CloudSystem infrastructure can be expanded and scaled up with additional hardware, such as the following (see Figure 4-13):

- **Servers:** Add HP ProLiant or Integrity server blades. HP CloudSystem can also support virtual machines running on rack-mounted HP ProLiant servers as well as certain third-party servers.

- **Storage:** Add any HP Matrix-supported shared storage such as HP 3PAR P10000, F-class or T-class Utility Storage, HP EVA, or HP XP storage products. Third-party storage can also be added.

- **Networking:** For a cloud-optimized networking fabric, add HP Networking components such as the 5800, 5900, and 12500 switches. Third-party networking can also be added.

Cloud Storage Requirements

Cloud computing is driving new storage requirements. These include:

- Virtual servers can be created rapidly, but it is often much more difficult and time consuming to provide the necessary storage for the VMs, resulting in increased time-to-productivity. Service providers need to generate revenue as soon as possible, and expect storage to be quick and easy to provision.

- Storage systems have to be able to handle diverse and unpredictable workloads. Workloads applied to storage devices can be classified as either transactional or bandwidth intensive. If these two types of workloads are applied simultaneously to a traditional storage array, the packets are processed serially, which means small transactions line up and wait while large data payloads get processed. A single processing resource must do everything, and this can lead to small I/Os (like updating a single person's address in a database) waiting on large I/Os (like storing an X-ray image). This applies not only to writes, but to reads as well.

- Storage devices are likely to be shared between different organizations/companies (multi-tenancy), and data must be protected appropriately.

- Maintaining storage capacity that has no data on it is very expensive. Buying excess capacity up-front wastes money; not only in the cost of purchasing the storage capacity, but also in the additional cost of power and cooling.

- The need for continuous access to data means that storage systems must be always-on, always-available.

- In order to deliver the needs of cloud computing, storage systems must be integrated with virtualization, provisioning, and management software.

HP Storage for Cloud

Matrix OE supports the use of virtual and physical logical servers. Figure 4-14 lists the virtual server storage options. Explanations for the numbered annotations are provided later in this section.

Storage Type	VMware VM			Microsoft Hyper-V VM	HP Integrity VM[1,2]
	VM file system (VMFS)	Raw disk mapping (RDM)	Network file system (NFS)	NT file system (NTFS)	SLVM with Serviceguard[3]
Fibre channel	✓	✓[4]		✓	✓
iSCSI[5]	✓[6,7]	✓[8]		✓[7]	
DAS	✓[7]			✓[7]	
SAS	✓[7]			✓[7]	
NAS			✓[7]		

Figure 4-14. Virtual server storage options

The numbered annotations in Figure 4-14 are explained below:

1. Integrity VM virtual machine guests must have an HP-UX operating system type. Windows and Linux guests are not supported.

2. Only HP-UX 11v3 guests are supported by infrastructure orchestration.

3. Shared Logical Volume Manager (SLVM) with HP Serviceguard is currently the only storage solution supported by Insight Orchestration for Integrity VM.

4. Not supported by Insight Orchestration

5. To use iSCSI, you must provide connectivity to a compatible iSCSI SAN. As with Fibre Channel storage, end-to-end support for an iSCSI storage device is generally certified by the storage vendor.

6. Supported by VMware ESX 4.0 and later

7. Not supported by Insight Recovery

8. Not supported by Matrix OE

HP recommends Fibre Channel Storage Area Network (SAN) with boot-from-SAN capability (for physical blade deployments). HP Matrix OE supports any Fibre Channel storage solution that supports the Virtual Connect environment (including the ability to present storage to an initiator World Wide Name, or WWN, which is not yet visible on the fabric), N_Port ID Virtualization (NPIV), and boot-from-SAN capability (boot volume as a pre-presented logical unit number, or LUN). Matrix OE also supports Raw Disk Management (RDM) for cross-technology logical server operations.

For Fibre Channel SAN solutions, HP recommends HP EVA, HP 3PAR, and HP XP disk storage systems. Customer-supplied Fibre Channel switches to an external SAN must support boot from SAN and NPIV functionality.

To realize the benefits of Virtual Connect logical servers, including the ability to move logical servers and to easily repurpose server blades associated with inactive logical servers, any local, direct-connect disks must be removed or disabled.

At the time of writing, iSCSI is supported only as a virtual backing store (not a physical server iSCSI boot or virtual machine directly accessing raw iSCSI LUNs through RDM). Support for iSCSI boot volumes may be added in the near future.

For security and performance purposes, HP recommends a dedicated network for iSCSI traffic.

HP recommends the following iSCSI targets as backing storage for virtual machine guests:

- HP StorageWorks P4300 G2 and P4500 G2 SAN Solutions
- HP StorageWorks MSA2000i

HP 3PAR Utility Storage: A Storage Platform Built for the Cloud

HP 3PAR Utility Storage technology is a highly recommended extension for HP CloudSystem. This storage supplies highly scalable, thinly provisioned, multi-tenant storage optimized for cloud computing (see Figure 4-15). Customers who are currently using standalone 3PAR storage arrays can continue to use them in their transition to HP CloudSystem.

HP 3PAR storage is based on an architecture specifically designed for cloud security and includes resiliency features for constant data availability. HP 3PAR Utility Storage technology provides multi-tenant support and makes it possible to consolidate thousands of virtual machines onto a single storage system. It delivers the agility and efficiency required by virtual and cloud datacenters.

HP 3PAR storage employs policy-driven tiering technologies that balance cost and performance to meet service level requirements, while increasing business agility and helping to minimize risk.

HP 3PAR storage also features autonomic provisioning; that is, the storage is designed to handle volume provisioning and change management quickly, intelligently, granularly, and without administrator intervention. Moreover, host-based HP 3PAR software products reduce manual administration by offering autonomic performance and capacity utilization monitoring, and by establishing secure, autonomic communication channels between storage and hosts.

Figure 4–15. HP 3PAR storage

With HP 3PAR storage systems, customers can implement a storage platform built for the cloud. Regardless of whether they are a hosting provider, a customer who needs to respond to business demands, or a large enterprise needing to build a private cloud, HP has a 3PAR cloud computing solution to suit these needs.

HP 3PAR storage includes the following features:

- **Thin Provisioning:** When a Thinly-Provisioned Virtual Volume (TPVV) is created, only a fraction of the total size of the volume is actually provisioned, with additional storage space being automatically allocated on demand. By enabling a true capacity-on-demand model, thin provisioning maximizes storage utilization and reduces costs. It is also possible to migrate LUNs from external arrays onto 3PAR storage and make them thin.

- **Virtual Domains:** The HP 3PAR *Virtual Private Array* technology enables secure, multi-tenant storage, yet maintains the scale-out flexibility to continuously adapt to application, customer, and infrastructure demands.

- **3PAR Virtual Lock:** Prevents deletion of virtual volumes (including thin volumes created with HP 3PAR Thin Provisioning software) and volume copies (such as those created with HP 3PAR Virtual Copy or HP 3PAR Full Copy software) for a specified period of time.

- **Autonomic management:** Software that enables the automation of storage provisioning, monitoring, and data protection. Autonomic management enables the rapid provisioning of multiple volumes to multiple servers. The same process that with legacy storage could take several days can now be reduced by as much as 90% by autonomic management.

- **Optimized for Applications:** Helps optimize service levels and minimize storage TCO in key applications and operating environments including Oracle Database, Oracle Solaris, Microsoft Exchange, Microsoft SQL Server, Microsoft Windows, Linux Server, and Veritas Storage Foundation by Symantec.

Storage in VMware Cloud Infrastructure

Integration between VMware and HP Converged Storage enables customers to deploy VMware vSphere-based servers in the same physical blade infrastructure as shared storage, delivering high density and low power footprint. Features include:

- HP SAN portfolio Replication Adapters for VMware vCenter Site Recovery Manager 5 can be used to automate the recovery of virtualized applications in the event of a disaster.

- Protect access to data using multi-site SAN capabilities within HP P4000 Storage Systems. This pioneering capability has led to collaboration with VMware to enhance resiliency and certify best practices for deploying fault tolerant solutions across multiple sites.

- HP reference configurations for virtualizing Microsoft Exchange and SAP applications with VMware vSphere 5 deliver optimized storage for popular application environments. These configurations, based on industry best practices, allow clients to accelerate deployment by taking the guesswork out of sizing and performance for infrastructure resources.

- Improved capacity utilization and performance of certain VMware functions by over 90 percent via support for VMware vSphere 5 and VMware vSphere Storage API for Array Integration capabilities.

- Accelerated VM provisioning with the HP 3PAR Utility Storage *Thin Built In* ASIC's zero-detect algorithm. This feature runs as a hardware service to achieve maximum performance and non-disruptively reclaims space from deleted VMs.

- Simplified orchestration of resources across the virtual stack

- Management capabilities, resulting from the integration of HP Converged Storage with the VMware cloud infrastructure suite, enable customers to reduce the expense and complexity of managing storage resources from within VMware vCenter Server with a single HP Insight Control plug-in that spans servers, storage, and networking. This includes integration of HP storage with VMware vSphere Storage Awareness and Discovery APIs, enabling VMware administrators to view detailed information about storage resources. The management capabilities also help to reduce costs by consolidating both mission-critical and general-purpose applications on the same server and storage hardware with the upgraded HP P9000 Application Performance Extender (APEX). This capability allows customers to assign specific service-level targets to VMs and to prioritize all storage system resources to meet them.

HP CloudSystem Security

HP CloudSystem takes advantage of all of the elements of the HP Security Intelligence framework, which lets customers:

- **Visualize IT infrastructures and their vulnerabilities:** Vulnerability and incident data can be gathered from all key infrastructure components of a business process—existing security controls at endpoints, IT infrastructure, and applications—and a view across the entire process (not just for a specific layer) can be presented. Points of attack are highlighted and, in addition, potential security issues can be identified and rectified before they become problems. The Security Intelligence framework also provides the ability to set metrics, such as risk scores and risk level agreements, which can be communicated with business and process owners.

- **Prioritize risks, events, and incidents:** Cutting-edge threat and vulnerability research, proactive pattern detection, and advanced algorithms identify and correlate items from both security and IT system sources to provide advanced security analysis, saving time and money.

- **Respond intelligently to threats:** Security Intelligence enables proactive and automatic response to the most important security issues and compliance requirements, so that vulnerabilities in critical applications can be eliminated before the applications are deployed. Also, attack sources can be identified from worldwide threat data and blocked automatically.

The HP Cloud Security service provides an onsite review and analysis of 15 domains of cloud security, resulting in a cloud computing security and compliance remediation roadmap. This analysis is coordinated with the broad set of HP security products and services.

HP CloudSystem solutions leverage core HP security technologies that are part of the framework:

- **HP ArcSight**: The HP ArcSight Security Information and Event Management (SIEM) system consolidates all event and log information to a single point, allowing for automated compliance and incident reporting across the entire security lifecycle. It provides complete visibility and critical insights into IT infrastructure across all users, networks, data centers, and applications and provides rules-based correlation (for example, the number of transactions within a certain time period) and identity-based correlation (for example, unusual activity for a specific employee when compared to others in that role).
  HP ArcSight IdentityView monitors user activity across all accounts, applications, and systems. This enables organizations to understand who is on the network, what data they see, and which actions they take with that data.
  Event correlation is used to eliminate the high level of false alarms that are generated by a security infrastructure and to focus the attention of the security staff on true threats and attacks, while helping them to avoid being overwhelmed by too much data.
  HP ArcSight receives and stores vulnerability information from popular vulnerability scanning tools including Nessus/Tenable, eEye Retina, McAfee Foundscan, Qualys, ISS Internet Scanner, nCircle IP360, Harris STAT scanner, AppDetective, and others.

- **HP TippingPoint:** HP TippingPoint delivers solutions for physical, virtual, and cloud environments that address today's sophisticated security threats. HP TippingPoint Intrusion Prevention System (IPS) platforms achieve high levels of real-time protection. With the Core Controller, Security Management System (SMS), and Digital Vaccine Service, they deliver a best-of-breed foundation for comprehensive network security, proactively addressing data center needs. The IPS solution delivers automated, in-line traffic inspection designed to protect the most demanding 10 Gbps network environments.

- **HP Fortify**: HP Fortify helps protect companies from the threats posed by security flaws in software applications. The HP Fortify solution addresses security risks by automating key processes of developing and deploying secure applications. The solution helps to make critical business software more secure and resistant to attack by addressing security risks at the application code level during the software development phase, meaning that application vulnerabilities can be detected and rectified before the application is deployed into the cloud.

HP-UX Compatibility with HP CloudSystem

As shown in Figure 4-16, HP CloudSystem with HP-UX is fully supported.

HP-UX Feature/ Supportability	CloudSystem Matrix	CloudSystem Enterprise	CloudSystem Service Provider
Physical Deployment	Yes*	Yes	Yes
Virtual Deployment	Yes*	Yes	Yes
Application Deployment	Yes	Yes	Yes
Patching	Yes	Yes	Yes
Compliance	Yes	Yes	Yes
Management	Yes	Yes	Yes

Figure 4-16. HP-UX Compatibility with HP CloudSystem

* In HP CloudSystem Matrix with HP-UX, infrastructure provisioning is delivered through the HP Matrix interface, while application provisioning and management is delivered through the HP Server Automation interface.

HP CloudSystem Matrix Platform Differences

The HP CloudSystem Matrix is available with HP ProLiant Blades, HP Integrity Blades, or a mix of both. Figure 4-17 shows the HP CloudSystem Matrix differences between HP ProLiant blades and HP Integrity blades.

Note

Mixed HP ProLiant/Integrity blade environments are fully supported.

	HP ProLiant	HP Integrity
Licensing	16 ProLiant blades	8 HP-UX sockets
Max number of managed nodes per CMS	10000	800
Server Automation integration	Yes	No, Server Automation accessed outside of MOE
Operating System	Not included	HP-UX VSE-OE included
Hypervisor	ESX and/or Hyper-V supported, not included	HPVM included
Infrastructure provisioning technology	Insight Control server deployment (RDP)	Ignite-UX
Service continuity protection	Recovery management included; HA clustering software must be purchased separately	Neither DR nor HA support included; HP-UX upgrade from VSE-OE to DC-OE adds support for both via ServiceGuard
Workload management	No	Yes, via gWLM

Figure 4-17. HP CloudSystem Matrix platform differences

 Note

The maximum number of nodes that can be managed by one CMS is 2,500. This number can be increased to 10,000 by using a *federated* CMS configuration, in which four CMS systems are combined.

HP Serviceguard

HP Serviceguard enables the creation of high-availability clusters using a networked grouping of HP Integrity servers running HP-UX. These servers are typically configured with redundant hardware and software components to reduce single points of failure (SPOFs). HP Serviceguard is designed to keep application services running in spite of hardware failures (for example, CPU, disk, or LAN) or software failures (for example, operating system or user application).

HP Serviceguard uses packages to group application services together, and are typically configured to run on several nodes in the cluster, one at a time. In the event of a service, node, network, or other monitored package resource failure on the node where the package is running, HP Serviceguard can automatically transfer control of the package to another node in the cluster, thus allowing the services to remain available with minimal interruption.

Note

HP CloudSystem Matrix does not include licensed disaster recovery protection for HP-UX but HP Serviceguard for automated failover and/or HP Metrocluster for disaster recovery can be added as options, if required. Implementing a secondary infrastructure at a remote location, and enabling storage replication between the two sites, can achieve protection against catastrophic events at one location.

HP Global Workload Manager

HP Global Workload Manager (gWLM) for HP-UX is a goal-based policy engine that manages resource allocation across multiple HP Integrity logical servers. The policy engine facilitates controlled sharing of system resources by moving processing resources to where they are needed. In addition, gWLM provides both real-time and historical monitoring of the resource allocation.

HP CloudSystem Matrix Extended Infrastructure

HP Matrix OE extends its software functionality beyond HP CloudSystem Matrix and can manage VM host pools across select HP ProLiant, HP Integrity, and third party servers from the same CMS that is used to manage HP CloudSystem Matrix (see Figure 4-18). HP CloudSystem Matrix support for this extended infrastructure includes most of the capabilities of HP Matrix OE, with the exception of some physical server deployment and management capabilities. Capabilities include:

- Infrastructure provisioning of VM guests on BL/ML/DL, Integrity blade and rack-mount, and certain third party servers

- Capacity planning

- Recovery Management (on HP servers only)

Support and licensing for HP Matrix extended infrastructure is handled in the same way as HP Matrix OE standalone software.

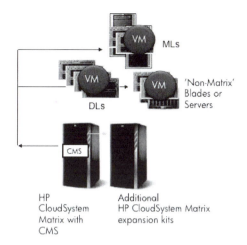

Figure 4-18. HP CloudSystem Matrix Extended Infrastructure

HP CloudSystem Software

This section is intended to provide a reference for the HP CloudSystem software products (see Figure 4-19). The individual software products will be discussed in more detail in later chapters.

Component	Description	CloudSystem Configuration Matrix	Enterprise	SP
Cloud Maps	• Pre-defined templates for enabling infrastructure, popular applications, database, and middleware	●	●	●
SiteScope	• Agent-less infrastructure and application performance monitoring, alerting, and reporting.	●	●	●
Server Automation (Starter Edition)	• Policy-based provisioning, configuration, patching and compliance management of servers, OS and application infrastructure. 1000 VM per OS limit.	●		
Server Automation (Enterprise Edition)	• SA Starter Edition plus: Application Deployment Manager, Multimaster Mesh, Satellite, and unlimited VM/OS scale		●	●
Cloud Service Automation	• Full lifecycle management and automation for building and managing hybrid cloud environments • In addition to SiteScope and Server Automation Enterprise Ed., includes: • CSA Foundation Server (self-service portal, cloud controller, resource management, uCMDB) • Operations Orchestration		●	●
Database and Middleware Automation	• Best-practice automation for database and middleware		●	●
Business Service Management	• Performance and availability management solutions for virtualized and cloud based services	○	○	○
Storage Essentials	• Deep, performance and availability management of HP disk arrays and multi-vendor SANs	○	○	○
Network Automation	• Lifecycle management for globally distributed heterogeneous networks		○	●
Aggregation Platform for SaaS	• A single point of access that integrates and aggregates multiple SaaS and hosted services offerings			●

Key: ● Included   ○ Extension

Figure 4-19. HP CloudSystem software

HP Cloud Maps are, strictly speaking, not software but an easy-to-use navigation system, and include pre-defined templates that can be used to architect infrastructure for applications and services.

HP SiteScope provides agentless monitoring of an infrastructure platform and an application's key performance indicators, such as CPU, disk, and memory usage. It includes out-of-the-box monitoring for over 100 different applications.

HP Server Automation provides policy-based provisioning, configuration, patching, and compliance management of servers, OS, and application infrastructure. HP Server Automation Starter Edition is included with HP CloudSystem Matrix, while HP Server Automation Enterprise Edition is included with HP CloudSystem Enterprise and HP Service Provider.

HP Server Automation with HP Application Deployment Manager (ADM) provisions simple and complex application architectures, including DMA content, onto the existing infrastructure. The HP ADM combined with the Database and Middleware Automation solution packs enable the deployment of an entire application stack—from the infrastructure to the database and middleware layer to the application itself.

Note

HP CloudSystem Matrix integrates with several deployment services to enable seamless application provisioning and lifecycle management. These services are:

- HP Server Automation (SA), for HP ProLiant targets running Solaris, Linux, and Windows

- HP Ignite-UX, for HP Integrity targets running HP-UX

- Insight Control server deployment (otherwise known as RDP – rapid deployment pack), for HP ProLiant targets running Windows, Linux (Red Hat and SUSE) and VMware

---

HP Cloud Service Automation provides advanced provisioning and management of applications and infrastructure (including extensive support for third-party hardware), a highly flexible architecture with advanced workload optimization and metering, service assurance, application lifecycle management, security, and compliance. The **HP Universal Configuration Management Database** (uCMDB) provides advanced configuration management that models configuration items (CIs) for the service architecture that has been built, allowing them to be shared with other applications.

HP Database and Middleware Automation (DMA) provides a content library for database and middleware management. DMA provisions simple and complex application architectures, including DMA content, onto existing infrastructure. After applications—especially middleware—have been provisioned and are up and running, DMA can manage those applications, providing pre-packaged workflows for application patching, compliance, and code release, and eliminating the need for manual customization.

HP Business Service Management (BSM) combines HP Application Performance Management, Network Management, and Systems Management to integrate application, system, network, and business transaction monitoring. Business Service Management helps with managing application performance to address issues before they impact customers and connects dynamic cloud and virtualized services to underlying infrastructure to prioritize by business impact, fix issues cost-effectively, improve quality, and provide better visibility into onsite and cloud services.

HP Storage Essentials provides a central console for managing all aspects of storage operations, including assets, configuration, topology, capacity optimization, performance management, charge-back, provisioning, and compliance.

HP Network Automation software automates network change, configuration, and compliance management, and provides real-time network visibility, automation and control for both virtual and physical environments.

HP Aggregation Platform for SaaS (AP4SaaS) solution serves as the single point of access for all applications (SaaS services). It enables service providers to create a SaaS marketplace portal where customers can discover SaaS products and bundles, run trials, subscribe to services, and consume them.

HP CloudSystem Services

Services are a critical component of a successful HP CloudSystem solution and are discussed in detail in Chapter 10. Figure 4-20 provides a summary of the HP CloudSystem services.

Component	Description	CloudSystem Configuration		
		Matrix	Enterprise	SP
Cloud Discovery Workshop	• Build consensus on cloud vision and components • Review cloud opportunities and implications • Detail key considerations for the business	○	○	○
Hybrid Cloud Delivery Strategy	• Learn about Hybrid Delivery Strategy • Develop a hybrid provisioning strategy	○	●	○
Cloud Consulting and Implementation	• Consulting, implementation, integration services for CloudSystem	●	●	●
Cloud Roadmap Service	• Develop strategic cloud architecture • Conduct gap analysis and program planning • Build multi-year roadmap for cloud adoption	○	○	○
Cloud Security Controls Assessment Service	• Analysis of the CSA control areas of cloud security • Security control maturity and compliance state • Security and compliance remediation roadmap	○	○	○
Hybrid Delivery Workload Analysis	• Run analysis on targeted workloads		○	○

Key: ● Included   ○ Extension

Figure 4-20. HP CloudSystem services

HP CloudSystem in a Heterogeneous Environment

While it is optimized for HP infrastructure, the HP CloudSystem solutions support servers, storage, and networking from third-party manufacturers. Virtual machines running on servers from non-HP x86 vendors such as IBM and Dell can be managed from a single portal.

> **Note**
>
> For information relating to supported hardware, operating systems, and hypervisors, see the HP Insight Software Support Matrix available at http://www.hp.com/go/matrixoedocs.

HP Cloud Service Automation (CSA) software (included with HP CloudSystem Enterprise and HP Service Provider) offers heterogeneous support through HP Server Automation (SA), which is used as a resource manager for HP CSA. All heterogeneous environments supported by HP SA can be supported in HP CSA. For example, if a customer wants to deploy on non-HP hardware (for instance, Dell, IBM, Oracle/Sun, etc.), or wants to deploy non-Windows/Linux/HP-UX operating systems (Solaris, AIX, etc.), then HP CSA will leverage the deployment capabilities of the SA component in the HP CSA architecture. HP CSA can also use VMware vCenter as a resource manager, and all virtual infrastructure supported by vCenter can be a deployment target in HP CSA as well.

HP CloudSystem integrates seamlessly into an existing environment. HP CloudSystem works with the common technologies and processes used in data centers, enabling it to integrate seamlessly into existing environments. It integrates with most storage and network fabrics, including EMC and Cisco. It connects to industry-leading IT service management platforms so it aligns with existing processes. It is integrated with the leading virtualization technologies from VMware, Microsoft, and HP. It also includes best practice templates (via HP Cloud Maps) for infrastructures supporting common applications such as SAP, Oracle, Microsoft Exchange, and SharePoint.

The HP CloudSystem solutions support:

- A choice of operating systems, hypervisors, and compute platforms, including Windows and Linux on x86 and HP-UX on HP Integrity

- Hypervisor integration, including VMware ESX and Microsoft HyperV

- Management platforms, including VMware Virtual Center, Microsoft System Center, and HP Software Business Service Automation (BSA)/Business Service Management (BSM)

- Any c-Class/Virtual Connect-certified FC SAN is supported, including HP Storage, EMC, IBM, Network Appliance, NetApp, and Hitachi

- Any network switching infrastructure (Cisco Catalyst/Nexus, Brocade, etc.)

Paths from Converged Infrastructure to HP CloudSystem

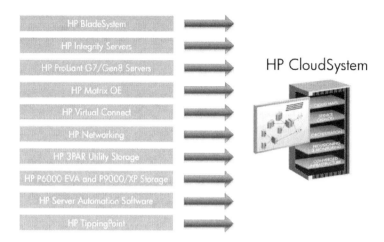

Figure 4-21. Paths from Converged Infrastructure to HP CloudSystem

Implementing HP CloudSystem is not a rip-and-replace exercise; much of the customer's existing infrastructure can be used with the HP CloudSystem. Customers who already have started the journey towards a converged infrastructure and who have existing HP technology (see Figure 4-21) installed in their data center can leverage that technology with HP CloudSystem. Converged infrastructure technology that can be leveraged includes:

- HP BladeSystem: For customers who have already invested in HP BladeSystem solutions, HP CloudSystem Matrix Conversion Services, delivered by HP Services experts, transforms the HP BladeSystem into a complete, fully supported HP CloudSystem Matrix environment.

- HP Integrity Blade servers with mission-critical HP-UX 11i v3: The world's first scale-up blades with an operating system for demanding, mission-critical workloads.

- HP ProLiant G7/Gen8 servers: Provide 3x more performance, 2x improved availability, 20:1 greater consolidation, 8x faster remote management, and a 96% reduction in power and cooling over previous generations.

- HP Matrix Operating Environment: A common platform for advanced infrastructure lifecycle management for rapid drag-and-drop provisioning of complex, multi-tier infrastructure

- HP Virtual Connect: A common, virtualized network fabric that connects servers to networking and storage while simplifying and increasing flexibility from the data center to the network edge

- HP Networking (5800, 5900, and 12500 switches): High-performance, flexible core-to-edge networking fabrics

- HP 3PAR P10000, F-Class and T-Class storage: Thin provisioned storage optimized for hybrid clouds with multi-tenancy capability

- HP P6000 EVA and P9000 XP storage: Traditional architecture storage arrays that bridge to traditional storage technology

- HP Server Automation software: Provides policy-based provisioning, configuration, patching, and compliance management of servers, OS, and application infrastructure.

- HP TippingPoint: vController + vfW: Security solutions for physical and virtual clouds, providing security for entire data center attack protection, including the hypervisor

Test Preparation Questions and Answers

The following questions will help you measure your understanding of the material presented in this chapter. Read all the choices carefully, as there may be more than one correct answer. Choose all correct answers for each question.

Questions

1. Which architecture is aimed at being an aggregation system for SaaS?

    a. HP Cloudsystem Enterprise

    b. Superdome 2

    c. HP Cloudsystem Service Provider

    d. HP Cloudsystem Matrix

2. What is the HP Cloud Roadmap Service?

    a. a building block for the creation of a service catalog

    b. a central console for managing storage operations

    c. a service for monitoring the infrastructure components

    d. a service for conducting gap analysis and program planning

3. Which service is standard only on the HP Cloudsystem Enterprise?

    a. Cloud Roadmap Service

    b. Hybrid Delivery Strategy Service

    c. Cloud Consulting and Implementation

    d. Hybrid Delivery Workload Analysis

4. Which functionality differentiates HP Cloudsystem Service Provider from HP Cloudsystem Enterprise? (Select 2.)

    a. Aggregation Platform for SaaS

    b. Matrix OE

    c. CSA

    d. Hybrid Delivery Strategy Service

    e. CSA4M

5. Which feature eases the deployment of the HP Cloudsystem in a heterogeneous environment?

    a. industry standard processor architecture

    b. Cloud Service Automation software

    c. leading edge technology

    d. implementation of blade systems

6. Which technology cannot be leveraged in the transition from converged infrastructure to HP CloudSystem?

    a. HP 3PAR Utility Storage

    b. HP 9000 Servers

    c. HP Virtual Connect

    d. HP Integrity Servers

Answers

1. ☑ **C.** The HP Cloudsystem Service Provider is aimed at being an aggregation system for SaaS.

   ☒ **A** is incorrect, because HP Cloudsystem Enterprise is aimed at the enterprise user. **B** is incorrect, because the Superdome 2 is not a HP Cloudsystem. **D** is incorrect, because HP Cloudsystem Matrix is aimed at private cloud.

2. ☑ **D.** The HP Cloud Roadmap Service is a service for conducting gap analysis and program planning.

   ☒ **A** is incorrect, because this describes HP Cloud Maps. **B** is incorrect, because the HP Cloud Roadmap Service does not provide a central console. **C** is incorrect, because the HP Cloud Roadmap Service is not a service for monitoring infrastructure components.

3. ☑ **B.** The Hybrid Delivery Strategy Service is standard only on the HP Cloudsystem Enterprise.

   ☒ **A** is incorrect, because HP Cloud Roadmap Service is an available extension on all HP Cloudsystems. **C** is incorrect, because it is standard on all HP Cloudsystems. **D** is incorrect, because it is an extension on HP Cloudsystem Enterprise and Service Provider.

4. ☑ **A and D.** The Aggregation Platform for SaaS is included, and Hybrid Delivery Strategy Service is excluded from HP Cloudsystem Service Provider.

   ☒ **B** is incorrect, because all HP Cloudsystems utilize the Matrix OE. **C** is incorrect, because HP Cloud Service Automation is standard on both definitions. **E** is incorrect, because CSA4M is only used on the HP CloudSystem Matrix.

5. ☑ **B.** Deployment of the HP Cloudsystem in a heterogeneous environment is eased by Cloud Service Automation software.

   ☒ **A** is incorrect, because standard processor architecture is not unique to the HP Cloudsystem definition. **C** is incorrect, because leading edge technology is not relevant to heterogeneous environments. **E** is incorrect, because the use of blade systems is not critical to heterogeneous infrastructures.

6. ☑ **B.** HP 9000 Servers cannot be leveraged in the transition from converged infrastructure to the HP CloudSystem.

   ☒ **A** is incorrect, because HP 3Par Utility Storage is part of the Converged Infrastructure. **C** is incorrect, because HP Virtual Connect is part of the Converged Infrastructure. **D** is incorrect, because HP Integrity Servers are part of the Converged Infrastructure.

5 Networking for Cloud

EXAM OBJECTIVES

✓ Explain cloud-specific networking challenges.

✓ Define the components of HP FlexFabric Networks.

✓ Describe the features and benefits of the HP Intelligent Resilient Framework.

✓ Describe the features and benefits of the HP Intelligent Management Center.

✓ Describe the features and benefits of the HP Secure Virtualization Framework.

ASSUMED KNOWLEDGE

You should be in possession of the HP APC - Converged Infrastructure Solutions (2010) certification.

INTRODUCTION

Cloud computing, with its inherent extensive use of virtualization, places great demands on data center networking infrastructure. In this chapter we will first look at the challenges for networking in a cloud environment, and then we will look at the HP technology that provides the solution.

Networking Challenges

The traditional approach of hosting only one or two applications per physical server often led to poor utilization of resources, as systems were routinely over-provisioned to cope with workload peaks that seldom occurred. One of the benefits of server virtualization is increased utilization of processing resources, and moving to one application per virtual server, with multiple virtual servers hosted on one physical server, certainly makes more use of the available processing resources and increases utilization ratios. Many enterprises have recognized the benefits of server virtualization, and the use of server virtualization technology is growing.

One of the negative consequences of the growth of server virtualization is that network traffic that used to be flowing to and from multiple physical servers over multiple network links is now consolidated into a single link (or a set of links if link aggregation is used)—to a virtual machine host system. With a virtual machine host system configured with ten virtual machines, network traffic could be as much as 900% greater than previously experienced with multiple physical servers. This places great pressure on the server edge connections, which will be expected to deliver extremely high-bandwidth.

Another effect of the growth of virtualization and cloud computing is that the direction of traffic flow is changing. In the traditional client-server model, data is processed on the server and is subsequently delivered over the network to the client. This is referred to as *North-South* traffic, where data travels from the servers, through the access, aggregation, and core layers, and into the WAN.

In emerging cloud data centers an increasing amount of application traffic is actually confined to within the rack in which it was generated. Some estimates suggest that this traffic—referred to as *East-West* traffic—can be up to 75% of total network traffic. To meet the demands of the business, this traffic must follow a high-speed, low-latency path through the network across the data center. In a traditional, three-tier data center network, there are often a large number of switches with a large number of cables connecting them all together. In addition, there is an aggregation layer that is used to connect the access switches to the core switches. The network performance between server A and server B (see Figure 5-1) may be adequate, as it only has to pass through one switch in the access layer. The performance between server A and server C may be less than adequate, as data has to travel up through the access and aggregation layers to the core, and then down through the aggregation and access layers to get back to the server.

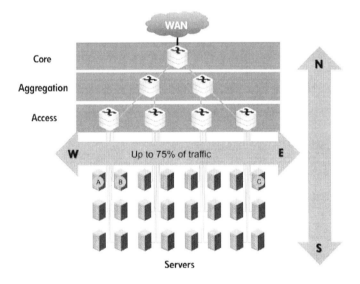

Figure 5-1. Traditional three-layer network

Flattening the network architecture and eliminating the aggregation, and possibly even the access layers, can improve the performance and the ease of management of the network. To understand how this can be achieved, we will now turn our attention to HP FlexFabric Networks technology.

Note

Every enterprise network will require one or more of the core networking services such as DHCP, NTP, DNS, firewalls, load balancers, and intrusion protection systems. Discussion of these core services is outside the scope of this book.

HP FlexFabric Networks

HP FlexFabric is a next-generation, highly-scalable data center network fabric architecture and is one of the pillars of the HP Converged Infrastructure. FlexFabric networks are designed with the reduction of the number of switches and cables in mind, and enable the rapid, efficient, and secure provisioning of network resources, which are characteristics that are essential for accelerating the deployment of virtualized workloads. FlexFabric supports the latest emerging industry standards, including high-speed Ethernet links, Virtual Ethernet Port Aggregation (VEPA), Fiber Channel over Ethernet (FCoE), and Converged Enhanced Ethernet (CEE).

FlexFabric Networks are simpler, flatter, and more highly-scalable than traditional networks, which means that they are also easier to manage. FlexFabric Networks comprise four key components:

- Intelligent Resilient Framework

- Virtual Connect

- Intelligent Management Center

- Secure Virtualization Framework

Let us now look at these key components and see how they work.

 Note

HP Virtual Connect technology is covered in the Converged Infrastructure training that supports the **HP APC - Converged Infrastructure Solutions (2010)** certification, and is outside of the scope of this book.

The HP Intelligent Resilient Framework (IRF)

Data centers have traditionally been designed with multiple layers—core, aggregation, and access. This can lead to a great deal of operational complexity, as each device in the network has to be configured, deployed, and managed individually. Spanning Tree Protocol (STP) is commonly used in data center networks and is effective at preventing loops (multiple Layer 2 paths between two network switches), but does so by blocking certain ports, thereby reducing the effective bandwidth of the network. In the event of a network failure, network convergence (recovery) can be slow—typically, several seconds—and this, of course, impacts applications and users, and ultimately has a negative effect on business results.

Later versions of STP, known as Rapid Spanning Tree Protocol (RSTP) and Multiple Spanning Tree Protocol (MSTP), converge more quickly than the original STP, but in a large network these protocols can be difficult to configure properly. Each switch must be managed individually, and spanning-tree instances must be set up on each switch in turn. Figure 5-2 shows an example of the traditional network using two layers—core and access—and illustrates the active/standby nature of the STP design.

Notice that even when the aggregation layer has been eliminated—reducing the complexity and management overhead of the network somewhat—the poor convergence time of STP may still be an issue.

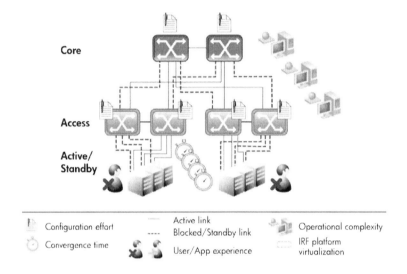

Figure 5-2. Topology with conventional network switch protocols

Intelligent Resilient Framework (IRF) is a virtualization technology that creates a logical switch by grouping together several physical switches into an IRF *domain* (or *stack)*. This simplifies the network as in the IRF logical switch; up to nine discrete switches can be stacked and managed as an IRF domain that has a single IP address. In this domain, one switch operates as the primary system switch, and is responsible for updating forwarding tables for all associated switches. The associated switches operate as secondary backups in the event of primary switch failure.

IRF's loop-free, non-blocking architecture keeps all links active, enabling highly efficient, high-bandwidth connectivity throughout the switching plane. IRF also provides a performance benefit, because all network links can be aggregated (using Link Aggregation Control Protocol or LACP), thereby giving users and applications access to the bandwidth of multiple switches. For example, if we have four links that are 1 Gb per second, IRF and link aggregation users have access to the bandwidth of those four links, which is 4 Gb per second. IRF also provides for a more resilient network; unlike STP-based solutions, whose recovery time is measured in seconds, recovery time with IRF is measured in milliseconds (see Figure 5-3).

Note

The HP 12500, 9500, 7500, 5900, 58XX, and 55XX products all come with HP IRF technology built in, at no additional cost.

Another consideration in the design of modern data center networks is the fact that modern switches have higher port density and bandwidth capabilities than their older counterparts; this provides the foundation for reducing the number of layers in the network.

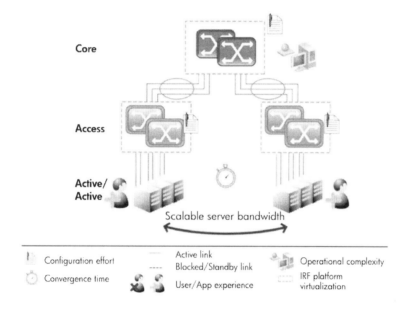

Figure 5-3. HP IRF

IRF configurations can be created for any layer of the network; for example, at the core or access layers. Indeed, multiple top of rack (TOR) switches can be transformed into a single logical switch (IRF domain). This logical switch will benefit from higher resiliency than a disparate collection of individual switches experiences. IRF configurations can be created using switches in a local data center and in geographically remote data centers that are up to 70 km (43 miles) apart.

In IRF configurations, one switch device acts as the primary (master) device, and all other switches act as slave devices. The primary device is responsible for collecting and distributing configuration information between all of the devices in the configuration. This results in simplified management, as the only device that needs to be managed is the primary device. When a new device is added to an IRF configuration, the primary device checks the software version on the newly added device, compares the version with other devices in the configuration and, in the event that there is a newer software version available, the master initiates the software update on the new device. Once the software update has completed, the new device is added to the IRF configuration and the other devices in the configuration are notified.

IRF delivers a network-based In-Service-Software-Upgrade (ISSU) capability that allows an individual IRF-enabled switch to be taken offline for servicing or software upgrades without affecting traffic going to other switches in the IRF domain.

Many data centers have a mix of rack-mounted servers and blade servers and are keen to simplify their networks. Figure 5-4 shows an example of a flattened, two-tier network design—using IRF—that completely eliminates the aggregation layer. The rack servers communicate with each other using an IRF logical switch (containing several top of rack switches), the blade servers communicate with each other using Virtual Connect, and the virtualized core (an IRF logical switch containing several core switches) is used for communication between the blade servers, the rack servers, and the outside world.

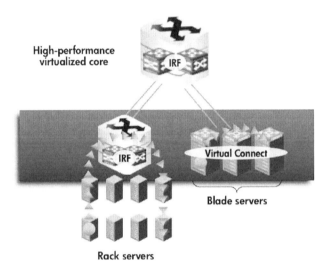

Figure 5-4. Two-tier network design

In data centers that make exclusive use of BladeSystem/CloudSystem, it may even be possible to eliminate the aggregation *and* access layers. Take another look at Figure 5-4 and imagine what it would look like without the rack servers and their top of rack switches. Figure 5-5 shows the logical view of this single-tier network, where the blade servers communicate with each other using Virtual Connect and with the outside world using the IRF logical switch.

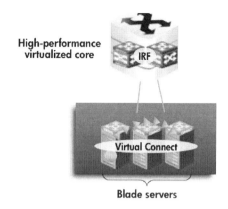

High-performance
virtualized core

IRF

Virtual Connect

Blade servers

Figure 5-5. Single-tier network

This flattened Layer-2 (L2) single-tier network design delivers high performance and ease-of-management and is ideally suited to highly-virtualized environments. It allows virtual machines to be moved without having to change IP addresses, and also supports vMotion over extended distances—the IRF fabric is capable of supporting dark fibre connectivity between switches up to 70 kilometers (43 miles) apart—using Virtual Private LAN Service (VPLS). It also reduces the number of devices that need to be provisioned and managed when setting up vLANs for virtual machines and, through its use of IRF, eliminates the need for STP (although STP can remain enabled if desired).

 Note

While it is possible to design CloudSystem solutions around a single-tier network, it may not always be entirely practical. For example, the number of vLANs in any L2 environment is limited to 4094 ($2^{12} - 2$ reserved), and in a multi-tenant environment, where it is important to keep the different tenants' network traffic in separate vLANs, this effectively limits the number of tenants to a maximum of 4094, which may not meet the customer's business needs. Several vLANs will also be required for management, so the practical maximum will be closer to 4000.

Figure 5-6 shows a physical rack view of a two-tier network incorporating two HP 5820 (TOR) and two HP 12518 (core) Switch Chassis.

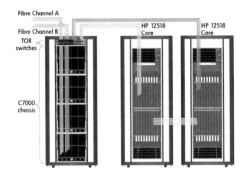

Figure 5-6. BladeSystem/CloudSystem two-tier network (rack view)

 Note

Figure 5-6 shows only one rack of servers. A two-tier network configuration using 12518 core switches is more appropriate when multiple racks of servers are present.

In this two-tier architecture, each C7000 enclosure has a 1:1 oversubscription ratio for traffic within that enclosure and to the TOR/core switch. The maximum configuration (based on each VM requiring 100Mb/s and each blade hosting 30 VMs) can be calculated as follows:

Maximum number of blades per enclosure	=	16
Number of VMs per blade	=	30
Number of VMs per enclosure	=	16 * 30 = 480
Bandwidth for each VM	=	100Mb/s
Total bandwidth for each enclosure	=	480 * 100Mb/s = 48,000Mb/s = 48Gb/s
Multiply by 2 for high-availability	=	96Gb/s
Number of 10Gbe connections required per enclosure	=	96 / 10 = 10 (rounded up)
Number of 10Gbe connections required per rack of four c7000 enclosures	=	10 * 4 = 40

In this example, the HP 5820 TOR switch will not be able to cope with the 40 cables emerging from the rack, as it has only twenty-four 10Gbe ports. The HP 5900 switch with its 48 10Gbe ports or the HP 12518 with its one hundred and twenty-eight 10 Gbe ports would need to be selected.

LAN/SAN convergence can be achieved by installing FlexFabric modules in the C7000 enclosures.

Table 5-1 summarizes the features and benefits of HP IRF.

Table 5-1. Features and benefits of HP IRF

Feature	Benefit
Devices no longer need to be configured and managed individually, simplifying network setup, operation, and maintenance.	Reduced management overhead and lower costs.
Unlike STP-based solutions, IRF keeps all network links active.	All network bandwidth that has been purchased is available, effectively reducing TCO.
IRF and Link Aggregation Control Protocol (LACP), used together, can boost performance by bundling several parallel links between switches and servers.	High-bandwidth, business-critical applications get the resources they need, leading to reduced risk of application unavailability.
Rapid recovery and network re-convergence in the event of a network failure.	Reduced risk of application unavailability and of the costs associated with downtime.
IRF can enhance disaster recovery by linking installations up to 70 kilometers (43 miles) apart.	Disaster-tolerant networking solutions protect the business against the risk of network downtime.
In-Service-Software-Upgrade enables devices to be serviced without negatively affecting network traffic.	Reduced cost of planned maintenance.

HP Intelligent Management Center (IMC)

Cloud computing, with its ubiquitous networking, magnifies the pressures that are being placed on network infrastructures. Challenges include the need to reduce costs, the need to align business and IT, complex architectures, virtualization, business continuity, and regulatory compliance. Enterprise networks are often too complex, rigid, costly, and unable to accommodate the changing needs of the business.

HP Intelligent Management Center (IMC) is a unified, single-pane-of-glass network management solution that provides visibility across entire networks, enabling complete management of resources, services, and users (see Figure 5-7). Unifying wired, wireless, and user management leads to increased performance, enhanced security, and reduced management complexity and costs.

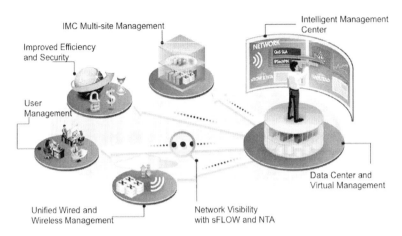

Figure 5-7. The HP Intelligent Management Center

IMC delivers business-centric network management with:

- Unified resource management across all network components

- Single pane visibility across networking and security

- Integrated access and user management

- Flexible, modular architecture to provide a tailored customer solution

The following paragraphs describe the capabilities shown in Figure 5-7, (moving clockwise around the figure):

- **Intelligent Management Center**: HP Intelligent Management Center (IMC) is a standalone, comprehensive management platform that delivers integrated, modular management capabilities across fault, configuration, accounting, performance, and security needs. IMC is designed on a service-oriented architecture (SOA), using a business application flow model as the core and featuring an on-demand, modularized structure. The combination allows the efficient implementation of end-to-end business management, while IMC software's modular design allows for the effective integration of traditionally separate management tools. Together, they provide complete management of resources, services, and users, and can manage HP and third-party devices.

Note

IMC has a library of over 1500 devices that are supported out-of-the box, including devices from HP, Brocade, Hauwei, Cisco, and others. IMC can identify third party devices that are not in the IMC library and will accurately display their topology as long as they are connected to HP products. Devices that are not in the library will be treated as generic SNMP devices and, as such, they will not benefit from backup/restore, software update, vLAN or ACL management, or other advanced monitoring and management functions.

- **Data Center and Virtual Management**: Rather than having separate management tools for physical and virtual resources, IMC provides management for both physical and virtual data center infrastructures.

- **Network Visibility with sFLOW and NTA**: The HP IMC Network Traffic Analyzer (NTA) Software Module is a graphical network-monitoring tool that provides network administrators with real-time information about users and applications consuming network bandwidth. It defends the network against virus attacks and applies varying levels of bandwidth traffic to different services and applications. The IMC NTA software module's network bandwidth statistics help plan, monitor, enhance, and troubleshoot networks, as well as identify bottlenecks and apply corrective measures for enhanced throughput. The software also monitors Internet egress traffic, helping administrators to analyze the bandwidth usage of specific applications and monitor the impact of non-business applications (e.g., network games) on user productivity. Granular, network-wide surveillance of complex, multilayer switched and routed environments helps rapidly identify and resolve network threats.
NTA uses capabilities embedded in switches/routers and has support for devices incorporating sFlow (HP), NetFlow (Cisco, Enterasys, Juniper), and NetStream (Huawei).

- **Unified Wired and Wireless Management**: The HP IMC Wireless Service Manager (WSM) software module provides unified management of wired and wireless networks, adding network management functions into existing wired network management systems. HP IMC WSM offers wireless LAN (WLAN) device configuration, topology, performance monitoring, RF heat mapping (for Wi-Fi Network Coverage analysis), WLAN intrusion detection and defense, and WLAN service reports. To help ensure network integrity, IMC WSM uses both wired and wireless network scans to identify and locate rogue access points (APs), including the detection of rogue APs that are not in range of your authorized APs or sensors. IMC WSM empowers your staff to take the necessary steps to counteract any threats by detecting wireless attacks and sending alerts about vulnerabilities. It facilitates centralized control over your wireless network, even if it is geographically dispersed

- **User Management**: The User Access Management (UAM) software module supports user identity authentication, based on access policies associated with infrastructure resources such as routers, switches, and servers. Integrated with the Intelligent Management Center (IMC) platform, the HP IMC UAM solution extends management to wired, wireless, and remote network users—enabling the integration, correlation, and collaboration of network device management and user management on a single, unified platform. This solution provides a full-featured Remote Authentication Dial-In User Service (RADIUS) server that supports centralized Authentication, Authorization, and Accounting (AAA) management of endpoints that connect and use network services. By furnishing authentication and authorization for endpoints accessing the network edge, the HP IMC UAM software module helps reduce vulnerabilities and security breaches. Policy management provides access control with tiered privilege levels.

- **Improved Efficiency and Security**: Endpoint Admission Defense (EAD) software minimizes network exposure by integrating security management and endpoint posture assessment to isolate risks and maximize uptime. EAD reduces the risk of malicious code infecting your network or other security breaches by detecting endpoint patches, viruses, Address Resolution Protocol (ARP) attacks, abnormal traffic, installation and running of sensitive software, as well as the status of system services. To ensure security, EAD provides continual monitoring of each endpoint's traffic, installed software running processes, and registry changes.

- **IMC Multi-site Management**: To manage large, distributed remote sites, multiple IMCs can be deployed. These additional IMCs feed alarms back to the top-level IMC, and enable multiple sites to be managed from a single console.

The features and benefits of HP IMC are summarized in Table 5-2.

Table 5-2. HP IMC features and benefits

Feature	Benefit
Provides automated features, default alerts, and a consolidation of tools and correlated information	Lower operating expenses and improved total cost of ownership
Provides automated configuration management and comprehensive auditing	Improved network availability and reliability that result in fewer trouble incidents
Improved network visibility leading to rapid problem recognition and troubleshooting	Network problems can be isolated and rectified rapidly, resulting in less downtime
Integrated management between wired and wireless networks, and even physical and virtual networks	Single pane of glass management for the entire network infrastructure reduces TCO
Automatic reconfiguration of network policies that remain tied to VMs and virtual workloads as they move within or across the data center	Security of VMs at rest, in motion, and in operation is assured, resulting in fewer security incidents and less downtime

HP Secure Virtualization Framework

Security of data center assets (hardware, software, and data) has long been a primary concern of CIOs. They are well aware that if an application—or its data—should become unavailable for some reason, bad things happen. They also know that there is an inevitable trade-off between security and usability; absolute security lockdown may secure assets adequately, but may be detrimental to the flexibility, performance, and usability on the IT systems. In a data center setting this means that flexibility and performance have to be considered when designing security systems. The challenge is further compounded by the growing complexity of the data center environment, where existing physical assets have to coexist, and be managed and secured, alongside their virtualized counterparts.

Three key areas need to be considered when designing data center security solutions—compliance, convergence, and consolidation.

Compliance

As previously mentioned, there are many regulations that aim to mitigate the risk of application unavailability and data loss. These regulations deal with data security and privacy, and neglecting these controls, and being found to be out of compliance, can have a devastating effect on the well-being of an organization. Regulatory compliance and industry controls include:

- The U.S. **Sarbanes-Oxley Act of 2002 (SOX)** requires CEOs and CFOs to attest to the accuracy of corporate financial documents, as well as provide IT and networking controls and their audit as per Section 404 of the Act.

- The **Payment Card Industry Data Security Standard (PCI DSS)** is a set of 12 requirements designed to secure and protect customer payment data. It covers the storing of sensitive authentication data, protecting the perimeter, internal, and wireless networks, securing applications, and monitoring and access controls.

- The **Health Insurance Portability and Accountability Act of 1996 (HIPAA)** applies to health plans, health care clearing houses, and those health care providers who use electronic methods to conduct certain financial and administrative transactions that are subject to the standards adopted by the Department of Health and Human Services.

- The **Gramm-Leach-Bliley Act of 1999 (GLBA)** applies to banking and financial industries and states that institutions must provide clients a privacy act that explains information collection, sharing, use, and protection.

- The **Federal Information Security Management Act of 2002 (FISMA)** requires each U.S. federal agency to develop, document, and implement programs to provide information security for the information and information systems that support the operations and assets of the agency.

- The **North American Electric Reliability Corporation (NERC)** provides standards and guidelines established for the national electric grid and its operation. IT and network controls are a major component of the guidelines for security.

- **BASEL III** is a global regulatory standard on bank capital adequacy, stress testing, and market liquidity risk, and largely supersedes its predecessor, Basel II.

All of these regulatory standards affect the design and operation of data center security systems. As virtualized systems and converged network infrastructure become more prevalent, identifying risks, weaknesses, and controls, and subsequent remediation and monitoring, becomes more and more complex.

As previously mentioned, being found to be out-of-compliance is usually associated with bad things happening to the organization and its management. To avoid the negative consequences of non-compliance, management should consider taking several proactive measures. These include:

- Identifying vulnerabilities and threats, and setting up the appropriate security controls

- Quantifying risk exposure, including identification of the vulnerabilities and threats, identification and definition of their compensating controls, and the calculation and documentation of risk

- Creating an IT risk management plan

- Ensuring that all IT compliance requirements are met

- Ensuring that all personnel receive training to enhance their awareness of IT security requirements

Convergence

Convergence, in the context of data center security, refers to the integration of various tools, such as firewalls, intrusion prevention systems, content security gateways, policy management systems, Security Information and Event Management (SIEM) tools, and Network Behavior Anomaly Detection (NBAD) tools into a single integrated tool. While this may simplify management and monitoring, care needs to be taken to ensure that security is not compromised.

This convergence means that data centers should not rely on a single network perimeter security device, as virtual machine hosts and their virtual machines also need to be adequately protected. To achieve this, intrusion protection systems need to be able to inspect all inbound and outbound traffic—not only from the physical network interfaces but also from the virtualized ones—and to block threats automatically.

Another important question to be considered is *who is responsible for security*? Some customers have a security team that spans server, storage, and network. They dictate what needs to be done and perform audits to ensure it is being done. For other customers, network security may fall under the remit of the network team, while operating system security may be the responsibility of the server team. So, who is responsible for securing the traffic that flows from one virtual machine to another within the same VM host and never actually emerges onto the physical network? It becomes clear that, for these customers, communication between the network team, the server team, and the security team is critical in order to ensure that all aspects of security are adequately dealt with.

Consolidation

The never-ending quest for reduced total cost of ownership (TCO—an abbreviation that could also mean *take cost out*), coupled with the ever-increasing power of computer systems and the widespread adoption of virtualization, has introduced some new security challenges that would not have been apparent in the legacy, non-virtualized data center. These challenges include:

- **Hypervisor security**: Neglecting to provide adequate security at the hypervisor layer could permit attackers to cause damage; either by accessing individual guest operating systems and their workloads, or by disrupting the hypervisor itself, which would have implications for all virtual machines.

- **vSwitch security**: A virtual switch is a software component that enables communication between VMs and other systems. We have already mentioned that VM-to-VM communications may never emerge onto the physical network and, as a result, may not be adequately secured.

■ **VM security:** VMs may migrate from one VM host (physical server) to another under conditions such as failure of the VM host system or a need by the VM for more resources than the VM host it currently resides on can provide. This VM mobility needs to be considered when designing and implementing security policies, and care should be taken to provide adequate security for workloads at rest, in motion, and operating normally.

The HP Secure Virtualization Framework is designed to provide a single consolidated, yet flexible, solution for extending the excellent threat protection of the HP TippingPoint IPS Series into the virtualized data center.

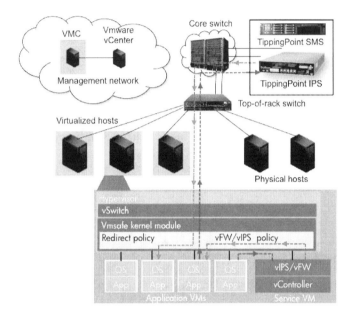

Figure 5-8. The HP Secure Virtualization Framework

The HP Secure Virtualization Framework includes the following components (see Figure 5-8):

■ **TippingPoint N-series IPS appliance**: This is a physical in-line device that inspects packets as they flow through the appliance and blocks malicious packets. It also includes security filters from DVLabs, which is the security research organization that keeps customers' IPS devices updated with the latest security vaccines.

■ **Virtual Controller (vController)**: The vController extends security protection from physical to virtual networks by routing traffic from VMs through an HP TippingPoint N-Platform Intrusion Prevention System (IPS) appliance. The vController inspects all VM traffic as it moves through the network, either between VMs or from VMs to traditional servers. Traffic is redirected through the physical IPS appliance based on a *redirect* security policy defined within the Virtual Management Center (vMC). The HP TippingPoint vController security solution is completely managed by vMC, which is fully integrated with the HP TippingPoint Security Management System (SMS).

- **Virtual IPS (vIPS) and Virtual Firewall (vFW)**: The vIPS is a virtual appliance that provides the same IPS capabilities as the hardware-based IPS appliance. The vFW is a virtual firewall that provides additional security capabilities for controlling traffic that will be allowed or blocked based on common firewall rules. The vIPS and vFW use the resources of the VM host system and can provide security in cloud environments or added security in virtualized environments, in combination with the physical IPS appliance. The vIPS and vFW are used to secure traffic between VMs based on the vIPS/vFW security policy. This vIPS/vFW policy, like the Redirect policy used by the vController, is configured using the vMC.

- **Security Management System (SMS)**: The TippingPoint Security Management System is a hardened appliance responsible for discovering, monitoring, configuring, diagnosing, and reporting for multiple TippingPoint systems. It features a secure Java client interface that enables analysis with trending reports, correlation and real-time graphs on traffic statistics, filtered attacks, network hosts and services, as well as IPS inventory and health.

- **Virtual Management Center (vMC)**: The vMC is used to automatically discover every VM in the data center and deploy the vController and virtual firewall on each VM host. This ensures that appropriate security policies are dynamically applied to and enforced by the vController and IPS Platform for all deployed/discovered VMs.

Table 5-3 shows a summary of the features and benefits of the HP Secure Virtualization Framework.

Table 5-3. HP Secure Virtualization Framework feature and benefits

Feature	Benefit
IPS and DVLabs security research capabilities can be extended into the virtual data center.	Existing security processes, methodologies, tools, and knowledge can be extended to secure virtual infrastructure, resulting in enhanced security for both virtual and physical infrastructure.
The HP TippingPoint Security Management System (SMS) makes it easy to keep all security management functions contained and available only to IT security personnel.	Security personnel gain visibility of all security domains, virtual and physical, leading to fewer security incidents and less downtime.
Automated policy enforcement across physical and virtual data center infrastructure virtually eliminates the need for reactive response to alerts.	IT security costs are reduced by eliminating ad hoc patching and alert response.
The vController and vMC provide visibility into the location and state of every VM, so that the appropriate security policies are applied, regardless of the VM state (on, off, or in motion).	Virtualized infrastructure is always protected, resulting in fewer security incidents and less downtime.

Test Preparation Questions and Answers

The following questions will help you measure your understanding of the material presented in this chapter. Read all the choices carefully, as there may be more than one correct answer. Choose all correct answers for each question.

Questions

1. What is the primary cause of challenges for networking in a cloud environment?

   a. increased number of users

   b. faster networking technologies

   c. increased use of virtualisation

   d. increased North-South traffic

2. What is the best way of improving the performance of networks?

   a. implement new switch technology

   b. use single pane monitoring functionality

   c. limit the number of users

   d. eliminate the aggregation layer

3. What technique is used in CloudSystem networking to implement flatter, more highly-scalable networks?

   a. a single entity, logical switch

   b. 10Gb networking

   c. consultative design and planning

   d. workload planning and management

4. Which feature of IRF enables high-bandwidth, business-critical applications to get the resources they need?

   a. In-Service-Software-Upgrade capability

   b. Infrastructure as a Service

   c. bundling several parallel links between switches and servers

   d. enhance disaster recovery by linking installations up to 70 kilometers apart

5. What is a feature of the TippingPoint Security Management System in the HP Secure Virtualisation Framework?

    a. compliance with Sarbanes-Oxley

    b. security personnel gain visibility of all security domains

    c. integrated access and user management

    d. automatic discovery of every VM in the data center

6. What is a primary function of the HP Intelligent Management Centre?

    a. providing disaster recovery capability

    b. providing compliance with legal requirements

    c. providing enhanced networking

    d. providing physical and virtual datacenter management

Answers

1. ☑ **C.** The primary cause of challenges for networking in a cloud environment is the increased use of virtualization.
   ☒ **A** is incorrect, because the Cloudsystem does not predicate more users. **B** is incorrect, because networking speed is not a primary factor. **D** is incorrect, because East-West traffic increases, rather than North-South.

2. ☑ **D.** The best way of improving the performance of networks is by eliminating the aggregation layer.
   ☒ **A** is incorrect, because simply introducing new switches into a multi-tier network may provide some benefit, but it is not the best solution. **B** is incorrect, because monitoring may demonstrate the challenge but not solve it. **C** is incorrect, because the challenge is not solely caused by number of users.

3. ☑ **A.** A single entity, logical switch is used in CloudSystem networking to implement flatter, more highly scalable networks.
   ☒ **B** is incorrect, because the network speed is not the primary bottleneck. **C** is incorrect, because planning is not a solution in itself. **D** is incorrect, because it is not part of network implementation.

4. ☑ **C.** IRF bundles several parallel links between switches and servers to allow high-bandwidth, business-critical applications to get the resources they need.
   ☒ **A** is incorrect, because ISSU reduces cost of planned maintenance. **B** is incorrect, because this is not a feature of IRF. **D** is incorrect, because this protects the business against the risk of network downtime.

5. ☑ **B.** The TippingPoint Security Management System allows security personnel to gain visibility of all security domains.
   ☒ **A** is incorrect, because compliance is a benefit of all features of the Framework. **C** is incorrect, because these are generic benefits. **D** is incorrect, because this is a benefit of the vMC.

6. ☑ **D.** The HP Intelligent Management Centre provides physical and virtual datacenter management.
   ☒ **A** is incorrect, because this is not a primary function of IMC. **B** is incorrect, because this is not a primary function of IMC. **C** is incorrect, because this is not a primary function of IMC.

6 HP CloudSystem Matrix

EXAM OBJECTIVES

✓ Identify the major components of HP CloudSystem Matrix.

✓ Explain the features and functions of the HP Matrix Operating Environment.

✓ Describe how HP Cloud Maps are used to build cloud services.

✓ Describe the main components and functionality of HP CSA for Matrix.

ASSUMED KNOWLEDGE

You should be in possession of the HP APC - Converged Infrastructure Solutions (2010) certification.

INTRODUCTION

We have seen that HP CloudSystem is available in three configurations: CloudSystem Matrix, CloudSystem Enterprise, and CloudSystem Service Provider; and that each of these offerings is based on a single unified architecture combining hardware, software, and services. We have also seen that together, the HP CloudSystem solutions address all deployment models (private, public, and hybrid) and service models (IaaS, PaaS, and SaaS).

In this chapter, we will look in detail at the HP CloudSystem Matrix and at the included HP Matrix Operating Environment and HP CSA for Matrix software components. We will also look at how HP Cloud Maps are used to build cloud services.

HP CloudSystem Matrix

HP CloudSystem Matrix is focused on private clouds and Infrastructure-as-a-Service (IaaS) and includes basic application deployment and monitoring. Built on HP Converged Infrastructure and HP Cloud Service Automation for Matrix, CloudSystem Matrix offers a self-service infrastructure portal for auto-provisioning and built-in lifecycle management to optimize infrastructure, monitor applications, and increase uptime for cloud and traditional IT. The major components of the base configuration include HP BladeSystem, HP Matrix Operating Environment (Matrix OE), Cloud Service Automation for Matrix (CSA for Matrix, or CSA4M), and implementation services. The base configuration should also include a server for the SIM CMS, onto which Matrix OE will be installed. Customers wishing to add CSA for Matrix to their environment will require separate servers for both Server Automation and SiteScope.

 Note

CSA for Matrix is an optional component and is not included with the base CloudSystem Matrix package. HP marketing text highlights the fact that CloudSystem Matrix should always include CSA for Matrix capability. When it comes to ordering the solution we need to remember to include CSA for Matrix part numbers.

As can be seen in Figure 6-1, the HP Matrix OE is responsible for infrastructure provisioning, and HP CSA for Matrix, which includes HP Server Automation and HP SiteScope software, is responsible for application provisioning and monitoring.

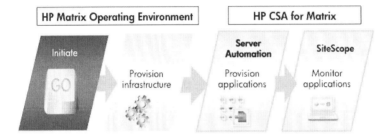

Figure 6-1. HP CloudSystem Matrix software components

Before we take a closer look at Matrix OE and CSA for Matrix, let us first do a quick review of the HP Insight Management software product structure and features, so that we can see where Matrix OE fits in.

HP Insight Management Software

HP Insight Management Software consists of three layers (see Figure 6-2):

- HP Insight Foundation

- HP Insight Control

- HP Matrix Operating Environment

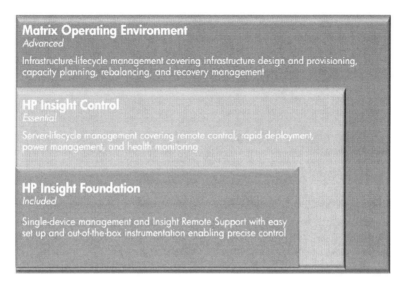

Figure 6-2. HP Insight software

As can be seen in Figure 6-2, the foundational component of HP Insight Management software is HP Insight Foundation. HP Insight Control includes the functionality of Insight Foundation, and HP Matrix OE includes the functionality of HP Insight Control (which as we just said includes the functionality of HP Insight Foundation).

HP Insight Foundation

HP Insight Foundation is included with most HP ProLiant and Integrity servers and provides core system management functions. These include the tools to configure single systems and install operating systems from CD and USB devices. To assist with multi-server deployments, a scripting toolkit is provided, and this makes it possible to create server configuration scripts that automate many of the steps in the server configuration process.

HP Systems Insight Manager (HP SIM) software is installed on a dedicated server known as the Central Management System (CMS), and it is this CMS that manages the automatic discovery, identification, and continuous monitoring of the discovered servers. HP SIM provides an intuitive graphical user interface that can be used to view the status of systems using a traffic light system, where green means that everything is working normally, amber means that a non-critical event has occurred, and red means that something has failed.

HP SIM has an *action on events* feature that can respond to alerts by automatically sending an email notification or a message to a pager, by launching a script, or by forwarding the alert as an SNMP trap. This feature of SIM makes it easy to select the exact set of devices and events for which notification should occur, and to automatically respond to those events.

HP Version Control Repository Manager is an HP Insight Management Agent that automates software and firmware distribution to managed systems. HP SIM also integrates with HP Software Update Manager (HP SUM) to provide agentless distribution of firmware for iLO, Onboard Administrator (OA), Virtual Connect (VC), and servers.

Insight Foundation includes Insight Remote Support Standard, which enhances system availability by automatically sending a notification to HP in the event that a system failure occurs.

HP iLO

HP Integrated Lights-Out (iLO) is a management processor that enables remote control for ProLiant and Integrity servers. iLO virtualizes system controls to help simplify server setup, engage health monitoring and power and thermal control, and enable remote administration of HP servers. HP iLO functions out-of-the-box without additional software installation and works regardless of the servers' state of operation; as long as chassis power is present, iLO is alive. Basic system management functions, diagnostics, and essential Lights-Out functionality is included as standard with HP ProLiant 300/500/700 and HP Integrity servers, all HP BladeSystems and select HP ProLiant Scaleable Systems (SL). HP iLO incorporates a dedicated LAN port that can be accessed via a web browser or terminal emulator and works alongside HP Systems Insight Manager, Insight Control, and Matrix OE to provide advanced remote management capabilities.

Advanced functionality, such as graphical remote console, multi-user collaboration, and video record/playback can be activated with the optional HP iLO Advanced or HP iLO Advanced for BladeSystem licenses. The HP iLO Advanced licenses can be purchased stand-alone or they can be acquired by purchasing Insight Control, Insight Control for BladeSystem, or Insight Control for Linux. The Advanced licensed features offer sophisticated remote administration of servers in dynamic data centers and remote locations and can help significantly reduce cost associated with IT-related travel and unplanned downtime.

HP Insight Control

Insight Control enables the proactive management of the health of physical and virtual servers and can be used to deploy servers rapidly, to optimize power consumption, and to control servers remotely. Insight Control also includes warranty and contracts reporting functionality that automatically retrieves warranty and support contracts details and sends a notification 30, 60, and 90 days before service agreements expire.

Server Deployment

Insight Control server deployment facilitates the installation, configuration, and deployment of high volumes of servers using either a GUI-based or a web-based console, using either scripting or imaging technology.

A common question is *HP CloudSystem Matrix includes Insight Control server deployment and HP Server Automation Standard Edition; which one should be used?* We will discuss how to choose between the two later in this chapter, after we have introduced HP Server Automation.

Server Migration

HP Insight Control provides a way to migrate under-performing or over-provisioned servers to a new physical or virtual server in an automated, accurate, and affordable way. Without Insight Control server migration, customers wanting to move workloads off of an existing server would have to deploy a new server from scratch by installing an operating system, loading drivers, installing and configuring applications, and finally transferring the data to the new server. Doing this manually using vendor provided CDs or DVDs could take days, weeks, or even months depending on the number of servers, operating systems, and number of applications.

Off-the-shelf ghosting products are available, but the process of capturing the image from an existing server and loading it onto a new server may result in errors that could take several hours to troubleshoot. Insight Control server migration eases the complexity by automating the migrations from old servers to new ProLiant servers or virtual servers. Insight Control includes unlimited migrations to each Insight Control-licensed server and offers Physical to ProLiant (P2P), Virtual to ProLiant (V2P), Physical to Virtual (P2V) and Virtual to Virtual (V2V) migrations. Insight Control can detect pre-failure hardware alerts on HP ProLiant servers and initiate the relocation of virtual machines to other host servers before any downtime occurs.

Performance Management

HP Insight Control performance management continuously monitors the performance of HP servers and compares the results with the known capabilities of each component and determines which components are having performance issues. It provides an interactive, online debugging tool that delivers precise indications of what the issue is, why it is of concern, and what can be done about it.

Power Management

HP Insight Control power management is an integrated power monitoring and management application that provides centralized monitoring and control of data-center power consumption and thermal output. Insight Control power management provides the tools needed to increase datacenter capacity by reducing power and cooling requirements of HP servers.

HP Thermal Logic technology enables the HP BladeSystem to pool and share power and cooling resources. The solution utilizes Insight Control management software to efficiently deliver those resources based on the performance level required.

All HP BladeSystem ProLiant blades (G6 and later) include an embedded technology called HP Power Regulator. HP Power Regulator constantly monitors the utilization of the processors, and will auto-throttle the processor input power and frequency to match the application load. The customer benefits from increased energy efficiency, without sacrificing any performance as the processors are automatically returned to full capacity whenever necessary.

HP Dynamic Power Saver mode enables more efficient use of power in the server blade enclosure. During periods of low server utilization, the HP Dynamic Power Saver places power supplies in standby mode, incrementally activating them to deliver the required power as demand increases.

HP has implemented Enclosure Dynamic Power Capping, which enables one power cap to be set for an entire BladeSystem enclosure that will dynamically adjust to changes in workloads between individual blades. This means that the enclosure power consumption will never exceed the designated power cap, but the enclosure will re-allocate power capacity between blades when necessary based on changing workloads.

Virtual Connect Enterprise Manager

HP Virtual Connect Enterprise Manager (VCEM) is HP's primary application for managing Virtual Connect environments across the data center, helping organizations streamline their IT operations, increase productivity, and reduce costs. While VCEM is present on the Insight Software media, it is, strictly speaking, not part of Insight Control. All HP CloudSystem solutions include licenses for HP Matrix Operating Environment (for 16 servers) and for VCEM (for the c7000 enclosure).

From a single console, customers can manage network connections and workloads for hundreds of Virtual Connect domains and thousands of blade servers. A Virtual Connect domain is a BladeSystem environment configured with Virtual Connect Ethernet and Fiber Channel modules, and can be either a single enclosure domain with up to 16 servers, or a multi-enclosure domain consisting of up to 4 local physical enclosures wired together as a single logical domain with up to 64 servers in total.

 Note
HP Virtual Connect is covered in detail in HP Converged Infrastructure training and is outside of the scope of this book. More information can be found at http://www.hp.com/go/virtualconnect.

Programmatic administration of MAC addresses and worldwide names to establish server connections to LANs and SANs is achieved via the central VCEM repository that is an extension of the HP SIM database. Rather than managing network addresses using a spreadsheet, which is labor intensive and prone to errors, especially in large environments, using VCEM reduces manual management overheads and eliminates the risk of address conflicts, which can be a real concern for customers. Within the VCEM repository, administrators can use the unique HP defined addresses, create their own custom ranges, and establish exclusion zones to protect existing MAC and WWN assignments.

A single VCEM console supports up to 250 Virtual Connect domains and can administer a total of 256,000 network addresses (128,000 MAC and 128,000 WWN). The maximum number of blade servers supported with Virtual Connect multi-enclosure domain configurations can be calculated as follows:

One Domain	=	Up to 4 enclosures in a VC multiple enclosure configuration
250 domains x 4 enclosures	=	1,000 enclosures
Each c7000 enclosure contains 16 servers		
1,000 enclosures x 16 servers	=	16,000 servers

HP Matrix Operating Environment (OE)

The HP Matrix OE for ProLiant and Integrity servers includes all of the functionality of HP Insight Foundation and Insight Control and is an integrated command center that manages the automated provisioning, optimization, and recovery management capabilities of HP CloudSystem Matrix.

HP Matrix OE provides advanced infrastructure management capabilities that enable enterprises to instantly adjust to dynamic business needs. It is the ideal tool for dynamic provisioning of infrastructure, energy-aware capacity planning, and infrastructure consolidation. The Matrix OE software is installed on a Central Management Server (CMS) alongside SIM, and the CMS provides a browser-based user interface for managing the infrastructure. Matrix OE integrates tightly with SIM, and many of its features are accessed via the SIM GUI.

Infrastructure Provisioning

The infrastructure orchestration (IO) capability of HP Matrix OE can automatically activate physical and virtual servers, storage, and networking from pools of shared resources. It finds available resources, initiates an approval process, and automatically provisions and configures the instances using the available infrastructure resources. It also enables the creation of a shared service catalog containing service templates that have been created by a system architect and provides an infrastructure portal to instantiate individual services. Infrastructure orchestration is discussed in more detail later in this chapter.

Storage Provisioning

HP Storage Provisioning Manager (SPM) is a software tool that manages storage provisioning within the HP Matrix Operating Environment. It enables storage requests to be fulfilled with available storage services contained within an SPM catalog, provides a secure service-centric management interface to storage, and automates storage management tasks by interfacing directly with storage arrays. SPM supports the use of HP EVA, XP, and 3PAR storage systems. SPM is discussed in more detail later in this chapter.

Infrastructure Optimization

Matrix OE provides a capacity-planning tool (also known as *Capacity Advisor*) that measures system utilization and captures key data points such as power, CPU, storage, and network I/O utilization, and provides easy-to-use workload simulation and ongoing capacity planning to ensure that workloads are optimally balanced across virtual servers. Historical data for virtualization configuration scenarios and utilization is captured and viewed through an intuitive graphical interface.

Matrix OE for HP-UX (HP Integrity Systems only) uses the HP Global Workload Manager (gWLM) intelligent policy engine to monitor service levels in real time and automatically adjusts server resource allocation among applications according to pre-defined policies so that resource utilization is improved, and service levels are maintained.

Service Continuity Protection

Matrix OE offers a wide spectrum of high-availability and recovery solutions. These range from server-aware and application-aware availability solutions, to disaster recovery solutions for both physical and virtual server environments.

Workloads running on HP ProLiant systems can be protected by the included Matrix recovery management capability (also known as *Insight Recovery*), while the optional HP Serviceguard portfolio can be used to protect workloads running on HP Integrity systems running HP-UX.

Let us now take a closer look at the orchestration capabilities of HP Matrix OE.

HP CloudSystem Matrix Operating Environment

Dynamic provisioning is achieved through the infrastructure orchestration capabilities of Matrix OE that are integrated with HP System Insight Manager (SIM). HP infrastructure orchestration, included with Matrix OE, contains a limited-functionality, embedded version of HP Operations Orchestration that can be used to extend the orchestration capabilities of IO.

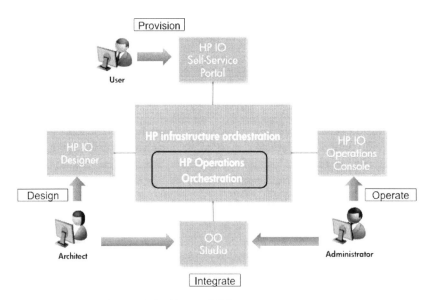

Figure 6-3. Matrix OE four main activities

HP Matrix OE supports four main activities to automate the deployment of infrastructure services: Design, Provision, Operate, and Integrate (see Figure 6-3). Let us now look at each activity in turn.

Design

The Matrix OE graphical designer interface enables a system *architect* to create infrastructure templates that, when tested, are published to a service catalog. Once published to the catalog, authorized users can select the service using the self-service portal to create infrastructure services.

Figure 6-4 shows the IO Designer interface. In order to design a service, the system architect would drag infrastructure components from the *components* pane (top-left of the interface) and drop them onto the whiteboard on the right side of the interface. The architect would then connect the components together before configuring other parameters such as cost per server, minimum and maximum number of servers, number of processors per server, memory size, processor speed, and processor architecture.

 Note

Before the architect can use the infrastructure components to design templates, the server and storage administrators must first define the logical server and storage configurations.

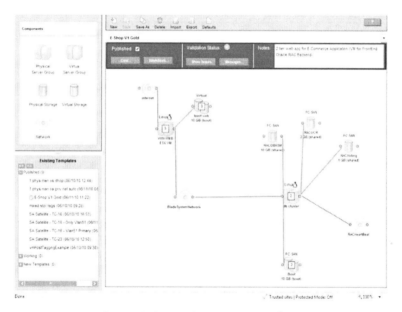

Figure 6-4. HP IO Designer interface

Provision

A *user*, using the self-service portal, selects an existing template and requests an instance of the service. Resources (server, storage, and networking) will be drawn from an assigned pool of resources and will be used to create the service instance. An approval request will be generated, and an administrator can approve or deny this request, and monitor its progress. The approval process may consist of simply pausing the user's request until an administrator approves it from within the HP IO operations console (within SIM), or if a ticketing system is in use in the customer's environment, the approval request could be forwarded to it, whereupon a support request would be generated.

Figure 6-5 shows the IO self-service portal with four services available for ordering. The user would select the required service and click **Create Service**. The user would then be prompted to supply information such as service name, hostname completion, and lease start and end dates before finally submitting the request.

Figure 6-5. HP IO self-service portal

Figure 6-6 shows an overview of the IO service creation process. The numbers in the circles correspond to the following steps:

1. A user logs in to the self-service portal and requests the creation of a service. This service may have been created by a service designer from scratch, or more likely, from an imported Cloud Map.

2. The **createService** operation creates the service from a template using parameters such as the name of the new service, the name of the template to use in order to create the service, the lease period, and optionally a list of servers pools to be used to create the service. If the list of server pools is not specified, the pools currently available to the requesting user will be used.

3. The request is validated to make sure that no errors exist.

4. Relevant server, storage, and networking components will be reserved. If free servers or networks are not available, the request fails. If free storage does not exist, the process will pause for manual storage allocation.

5. The user request is sent to an administrator for approval or rejection. If approved, the provisioning begins. If refused, the resources are released and the user is informed.

6. Provisioning of the new service (or extension of an existing service) will proceed. Servers, storage, and networking will be added and activated.

7. The final action is to return to the user either the reject notification and justification, or an email containing information on how to access the new service.

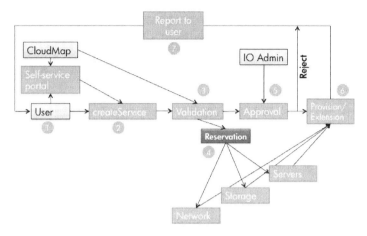

Figure 6-6. IO service creation

In order for the IO service creation process to succeed, reservation of server, storage, and networking resources must succeed. Let us now look at how storage can be provisioned using HP Storage Provisioning Manager.

Storage Provisioning Manager

Storage Provisioning Manager (SPM) is a software tool for managing storage provisioning that is installed automatically during the installation of Matrix OE, and runs on the same CMS as Matrix OE. SPM provides a secure service-centric management interface to storage, securely automating storage management tasks by interfacing directly with storage arrays, and enabling storage requests to be fulfilled using storage services listed in the SPM catalog.

SPM supports a variety of storage systems including HP P6000 EVA, HP 3PAR, and HP XP arrays. HP P6000 EVA and HP 3PAR arrays are managed using SMI-S, while HP XP arrays are managed using infrastructure orchestration and its integrated OO workflows. A reference implementation of OO workflows for the XP array is included with Matrix OE, and can be customized as appropriate.

There are three main SPM use models:

- **Pre-populated (proactive):** In this model, storage services to be exposed to infrastructure orchestration are added as storage pool entries to the SPM catalog by a storage administrator prior to the services being needed. The storage administrator must create LUNs and presentations, and set up zoning, and must also configure access rights for the services to control which users can perform specific SPM actions such as browsing and selecting services from the catalog. The pre-populated catalog will ensure that there will be candidate matches for the storage requests that are created as the server administrator defines logical server storage pool entries. The benefit of this approach is rapid logical server storage provisioning with no manual intervention by the storage administrator.
  This model, while being proactive and being performed in advance of storage services being requested, requires the use of several different interfaces and several manual steps.

- **Request-based (reactive):** In this model, when a server administrator requests provisioning of a service, the storage administrator must add the appropriate storage arrays and volumes to the SPM catalog in order to fulfill the service request. The service provisioning process will pause until the storage administrator has manually configured the necessary storage pool entries.

- **On-demand (automatic):** SPM has the ability to talk directly to SAN fabrics and storage arrays and perform tasks such as automatically creating new zones and LUNs. SPM storage templates are selectable in the IO Template Designer, and SPM storage template restrictions, guidelines, and defaults are shown when defining storage in IO. A storage definition in an IO template links directly to the storage template inside of SPM, and at server provisioning time, SPM will automatically create LUNs, and set up presentation and zoning.

 Note
If customers do not want to use SPM for storage provisioning, they can still use the Matrix OE Logical Server Management Storage Pool Interface to define and configure storage pool entries in advance without using SPM.

Operate

Administrators manage server, storage, and network pools, define virtual machine images and software deployment jobs, and monitor the health and utilization of the managed environment. Many of these tasks can be performed using the HP IO Operations Console (HP SIM). It is assumed that readers are familiar with HP SIM, so no more detail is provided here.

Integrate

The term *integration,* at its simplest, means providing a way to pass data in to and out of a system—CloudSystem Matrix and infrastructure orchestration in our case. Integration provides a way for external systems to control the actions of CloudSystem Matrix. These mechanisms enable customers, partners, and integrators to integrate the orchestration capabilities of Matrix OE into their business and IT operations processes.

Matrix OE integration interfaces include Web Services Interfaces, customizable OO workflows, and software deployment technology integration. Let us now take a look at each in turn.

Web Service Interfaces

There are several types of Web Service Interfaces, and the two main ones are the Web Service API and the Command Line API. These interfaces are made available when Matrix OE is installed, and can be used to perform actions such as creating and deleting services, and viewing or modifying an existing service.

The Web Service API is a Simple Object Access Protocol (SOAP) interface, which uses a simple XML-based protocol to let applications exchange information over HTTP or HTTPS. The Web Service API can be accessed via HTTPS from any installed IO system using a web browser. Typing the following URL into the browser's address bar will display the formal XML definition of the Web Service Interface, and developers can use this information to develop applications that interact with the API:

https://<IP_Address_of_CMS>:51443/hpio/controller/soap/v2?wsdl

 Note

Replace the string <IP_Address_of_CMS> with the IP address of the CMS on which Matrix OE is installed.

Examples of supported operations include retrieving a list of IO templates, importing, exporting, and deleting templates, retrieving a list of services, retrieving details of a specific service, creating an infrastructure service from a template, activating all logical servers in an infrastructure service, and many more.

These operations are also accessible via command line tools. Installing Matrix OE on a CMS automatically installs the **ioexec** command, and this can be used to access the IO Web Service via the command line interface (CLI). The CLI may be useful for scripting web service invocations and for testing purposes when developing a web service client. The CLI operations and data model mirror the Web Service Interface. The **ioexec** command may be copied from an IO (Matrix OE) installation to a different system to operate on the CMS remotely.

OO Workflows

Architects and administrators can integrate infrastructure orchestration with existing IT processes by using the included OO Studio application to create or modify the pre-built standard **Operations Orchestration** (OO) workflows to customize the infrastructure orchestration automation. They can link to approval processes, extend operating system deployment and server configuration, and integrate the SAN management processes with server deployment.

OO Studio is a standalone authoring program in which flow authors can:

- Create, modify, and test flows, including flows that run automatically, as scheduled

- Create new operations

- Specify which levels of users are allowed to run various parts of flows

Figure 6-7 shows a screen capture of Operations Orchestration Studio (OO Studio) displaying an OO workflow called *DeploySitescopeMonitor*, which, as its name suggests, can be used to deploy the SiteScope monitor on newly created server instances.

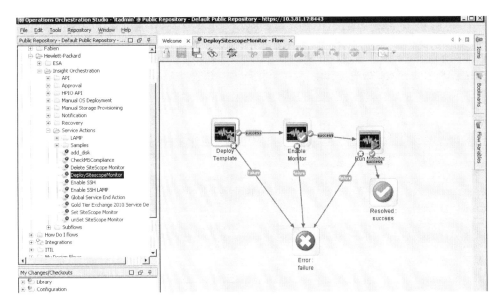

Figure 6-7. HP Operations Orchestration Studio

There are several integration (execution) points at which OO flows can be executed. These execution points are at the beginning and end of the create service, add servers, add data disk, change lease, standby servers or service, resume servers or service, and delete service operations. Figure 6-8 shows a workflow being selected and attached to the beginning of the **create service** operation. Examples of workflows that could be useful when creating a service are those that add the new servers into monitoring, backup, inventory, or other management applications.

Figure 6-8. HP IO OO flow execution points

The standard matrix OE solution provides out-of-the-box support for HP BladeSystem C-class with Virtual Connect, as well as a variety of virtual machine hosts. OO workflows extend that support with reference implementations for both servers and storage.

The server workflows included with Matrix OE provide support for HP ProLiant servers that do not use virtual connect, such as ML and DL servers. These workflows support (via iLO 2 or later) discovery, information retrieval, and powering on and off of HP servers. The storage workflows included with Matrix OE provide support for XP arrays and can be customized for other vendors' storage (for example, EMC). Storage OO workflows support device discovery, device information retrieval, enumeration of pools and volumes, retrieval of volume information, LUN presentation and un-presentation, and the setting of host mode.

 Note

For information relating to supported hardware, operating systems, and hypervisors, see the HP Insight Software Support Matrix available from http://www.hp.com/go/matrixoe/docs.

Software Deployment Technology Integration

The standard installation of Matrix OE provides out-of-the-box integration with HP server deployment technologies such as Insight Control server deployment, HP Server Automation, and Ignite/UX. It also provides integration with VMware and Microsoft Virtual Machine deployment technologies.

In simple terms, these integrations mean that Matrix OE infrastructure orchestration calls upon HP Server Automation, for example, to install and configure operating systems and applications on its behalf. In order to do so, Matrix OE passes the relevant data to HP SA, and then lets SA get on with installing the software. Upon completion, HP SA reports back to Matrix OE with status information.

HP Server Automation is covered later in this chapter.

Note
A full discussion of Matrix OE integration interfaces is outside of the scope of this book, and readers who want to know more are encouraged to read the *HP BladeSystem Matrix/ Insight Dynamics Integration Interfaces* white paper available from http://www.hp.com/ go/matrixoe/docs.

Comparing IO and OO

We will cover HP OO in detail in Chapter 7, but for now, let us compare the functionality of IO to that of OO. Figure 6-9 shows the differences between IO and OO—the most notable being that IO is focused on template-driven provisioning of infrastructure services, whereas OO is focused on the automation of tasks relating to business services.

	Function	HP infrastructure orchestration (IO)	HP Operations Orchestration (OO)
Business Services	Automate simple and complex IT tasks other than automated provisioning	No	Yes
	Seamlessly direct complex IT workflows and coordinate information sharing across disparate systems and teams (ITIL Incident management)	No	Yes
Infrastructure Services	Template driven infrastructure services (one or more servers (physical or virtual), storage, OS	Yes	No
	Provision infrastructure consistently and automatically from pools of shared resources through a web-based portal tracking lease periods	Yes	No
	Custom workflows to automate pre and post-provisioning actions on IO managed servers	Yes	Yes

Figure 6-9. Comparing HP IO and HP OO

Matrix OE Installation

The installation of Matrix OE on a CMS is a multi-stage process, and HP recommends that the first action after reading all of the related documentation (including the HP Insight Software Installation and Upgrade Release Notes, HP Insight Software Support Matrix, HP Insight Software Getting Started Guide, HP Insight Software Pre-installation Worksheet, and the HP Insight Software Installation and Configuration Guide) is to run the Insight Software Advisor that can be found on the Insight Software installation DVD. The advisor will test the current CMS environment to make sure that all requirements are met, and if any requirements are not met, the advisor will recommend remedial action.

The Insight Software documentation previously mentioned runs to several hundred pages, and it is beyond the scope of this book to document the steps. All of the necessary documentation can be accessed at http://www.hp.com/go/matrixoe/docs, and should be followed carefully in order to achieve a successful installation.

HP Cloud Maps

HP Cloud Maps are a building block for the creation of a service catalog, and enable customers to create their own pre-defined services for CloudSystem Matrix. Cloud Maps define and deliver a suggested state of infrastructure (servers, network, and storage) to support a particular application workload and enable one-touch infrastructure provisioning including the OS and may additionally provide for initial application layer deployment.

HP Cloud Maps consist of tested engineering components such as:

- Customizable templates for hardware and software configuration that can be imported directly into an HP CloudSystem Matrix

- Sizers to help with capacity and performance planning

- Customizable workflows and scripts designed to automate installation in a repeatable fashion

- Reference white papers to help customers customize an HP Cloud Map for a specific implementation

At the time of writing, there are many Cloud Maps available for CloudSystem Matrix, (and also one for CloudSystem Enterprise). The Cloud Maps available at http://www.hp.com/go/cloudmaps are shown in Table 6-1.

Table 6-1. Cloud Maps available from www.hp.com/go/cloudmaps

Company	Application
Citrix	XenApp
Ericsson	BSCS iX, iX Collections
F5 Networks	BIG-IP
IBM Software	Informix on HP-UX, WebSphere Message Broker on Linux WebSphere MQ on Linux DB2 on Linux DB2 on HP-UX WebSphere Application Server for HP-UX
McAfee	Management for Optimized Virtual Environments (MOVE) AntiVirus (AV) Total Protection for Server (ToPS)
Microsoft	Exchange Server 2010, Office Communications Server 2007 R2 SharePoint 2010, Office SharePoint Server 2007, SQL Server 2008
OpenText	Media Management
Oracle	Oracle Retail Predictive Application Server on Linux Oracle Single Instance Database for CloudSystem Oracle RAC for HP-UX and Oracle Fusion Middleware SOA Suite for Linux Oracle Fusion Middleware SOA Suite for Linux Oracle E-Business Suite on HP-UX PeopleSoft Enterprise Applications Oracle Fusion Middleware SOA Suite for HP-UX Oracle Fusion Architecture Oracle RAC Oracle Single Instance Database PeopleSoft Enterprise Human Capital Management (HCM)
PTC	Windchill
QAD	Enterprise Applications EE
Red Hat	JBoss
SAP	BusinessObjects NetWeaver on Microsoft Windows NetWeaver on Linux NetWeaver on HP-UX
SAS	Enterprise BI
Symantec	NetBackup on Windows
TIBCO	iProcess Suite ActiveMatrix BusinessWorks Enterprise Message Service
Trend Micro	Deep Security
WordPress	LAMP Reference Implementation

The HP Cloud Map Validation Service provides AllianceONE Independent Software Vendor (ISV) and System Integrator (SI) partners hands-on engineering assistance to create HP CloudSystem Matrix Cloud Maps. AllianceONE members can start the Cloud Map validation process by visiting the AllianceONE site http://www.hp.com/go/cloudmapvalidation, logging in, and submitting their application for review. Validated solutions will be posted on http://www.hp.com/go/cloudmaps, and will be included in HP campaign promotions specific to Cloud Maps. Validated solutions will also receive a Converged Infrastructure Ready insignia. This insignia demonstrates expertise in delivering solutions that are Converged Infrastructure compliant. The Converged Infrastructure Ready testing and validation procedures leverage HP best practices and extensive experience in delivering secure, best-in-class applications and solutions.

Building a Service Catalog Using Cloud Maps

Cloud Maps include an infrastructure service template and workflows. The infrastructure service template specifies the requirements for an application infrastructure. Workflows are logically linked sequences of steps that are used to perform tasks in an automated fashion. A workflow can perform any task that can be programmed.

A Cloud Map defines an application infrastructure and can:

- Describe server, storage, and network resources and their interactions

- Help with template creation; no training is required to develop basic templates

- Represent simple and complex infrastructures

- Apply cost information to infrastructure components

- Deploy applications; many Cloud Maps provide workflows for application deployment

Cloud Map Infrastructure Service Template

A drag-and-drop interface is used for designing service templates (see Figure 6-10). The infrastructure service template specifies the requirements for an application infrastructure and is where a system architect can specify server type (physical/virtual), cost per server (used for reports or charge-back), number of servers, processors, memory, processor speed, and architecture (32 bit/64 bit/Itanium). Built-in validation rules check templates for errors, and when template creation is complete, they are published to a self-service portal, from where they can be ordered by other authorized users.

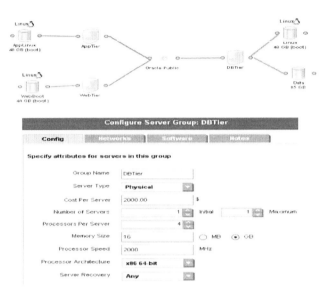

Figure 6-10. Cloud Map infrastructure service template

In addition, storage assignments, redundant networks, network assignment type (DHCP/Automatic/Static), and virtual IP addresses can be specified.

Cloud Map Workflows

Cloud Map workflows are logically linked sequences of steps that are associated with operations and capture the steps required to automate simple or complex tasks. Workflows enforce a repeatable, standard process.

Let us now see an example to demonstrate how Cloud Maps can be used to create a service. In this example we will use the Cloud Map for Oracle Single Instance Database.

The *HP Cloud Map for CloudSystem - Oracle Single Instance (SI) Database* provides a template to deploy the infrastructure for a single instance Oracle Database (DB) on a single server with a 40 GB boot disk and a 10 GB data disk. In order for the template to work properly, storage pool entries for the boot and data disks must be configured before attempting to deploy the template.

Having downloaded the template from http://www.hp.com/go/cloudmaps/oracle, it must be imported using the Insight Orchestration Designer portal by selecting the **Import** button on the main taskbar. Browse to the location where the template is saved and press **Open**. The template will now be imported into IO (see Figure 6-11). Notice that the Validation Status indicates that there is a problem. This is because the network that was defined in the template does not match the network that exists in this particular data center. In addition, the boot image specified in the template does not exist either. The **Edit Network Configuration** option can be used to select the network that the application servers will use to connect to the database server. The **Edit Server Group Configuration** option can then be used to select the correct Linux deployment job. The **Edit Storage Configuration** option can be used to change the size of the data disk if required.

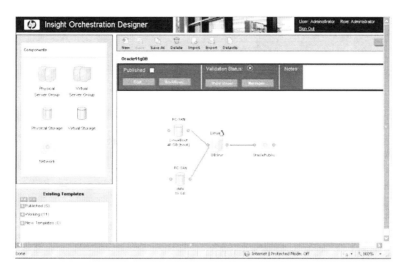

Figure 6-11. Oracle Single Instance Database template imported into IO Designer

The Validation Status should now be green and the template can be saved and published by clicking the **Published** checkbox and then clicking the **Save** icon.

Users will now be able to select and deploy this template from the HP IO User (self-service) Portal.

HP CSA for Matrix

HP CSA for Matrix (CSA4M) integrates HP Server Automation and HP SiteScope directly into the service catalog and orchestration engine of the Matrix OE. It enables customers to build an IaaS solution with advanced configuration lifecycle management, patching capability, compliance auditing, basic application provisioning, and service monitoring.

HP CSA4M enables application provisioning and monitoring for HP CloudSystem Matrix environments. It includes two HP software products, which integrate with the Matrix OE GUI and API:

- **HP Server Automation:** HP Server Automation is used in conjunction with HP Matrix OE to provision operating systems and applications on target systems created from the shared resource pool.

- **HP SiteScope:** HP SiteScope provides an agentless monitoring framework to monitor the health and performance of target systems, applications running on target systems, and the CSA4M infrastructure.

CSA for Matrix Architecture

CSA for Matrix enables the automated delivery and management of infrastructure services in a cloud computing environment. CSA for Matrix delivers monitoring templates for HP SiteScope, workflows for HP Operations Orchestration (OO), and specialized integration capability for HP Server Automation (SA) with HP infrastructure orchestration (IO).

HP is focused on designing infrastructure optimized for applications, and from a functionality standpoint, it is about managing the entire application lifecycle. CSA for Matrix gives customers the ability to not only provision infrastructure (servers, storage, and networking), but to include the applications with the infrastructure and to provision those applications from the same self-service portal that is used to provision the infrastructure.

CSA for Matrix can automatically configure and initiate monitoring when new services are delivered through Matrix OE, helping to ensure the availability and performance of distributed IT infrastructures and application components.

The fundamental principle behind CSA for Matrix is that it delivers complete lifecycle management for logical servers and applications. The lifecycle extends from establishing a baseline to provisioning, patching, configuration management, and compliance assurance.

The CSA for Matrix deployment consists of the following key systems (see Figure 6-12):

- HP CMS (which includes HP Matrix OE with infrastructure orchestration and a limited functionality embedded version of HP Operations Orchestration). The CMS also runs HP Insight Control.

- HP Server Automation server(s) (A single core installation may include one or more servers.).

- HP SiteScope server.

- Optional. HP Storage Essentials server. This is only necessary when the optional integration with SE is needed.

 Note

In many cases CSA for Matrix is sold with a full version of HP Operations Orchestration that should be installed on its own server. If the full version of OO is not included in the configuration, a separate OO server will not be required in the deployment.

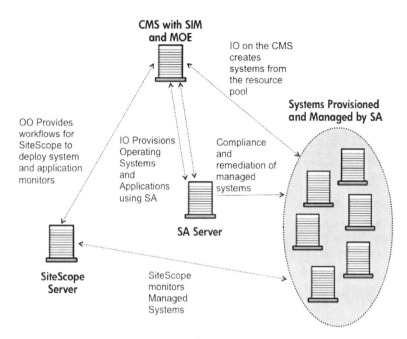

Figure 6-12. CSA for Matrix key systems

HP Server Automation (SA)

HP Server Automation (SA) provides a solution for end-to-end server and application lifecycle management. It can help automate compliance management by enabling users to set and enforce corporate standards for configurations, deploy OS and software patches regularly, and keep patch levels consistent with desired states. This could mean downgrading or removing software patches to be consistent with the standard and to remain compliant.

One challenge that server administrators face in a virtualized environment is virtual machine sprawl. SA enables administrators to manage the complete lifecycle of virtual machines with the same policies and processes that are used to manage physical servers. SA also enables administrators to map the relationships and dependencies between physical and virtual servers.

SA also helps streamline the application release process. It enables application updates to be deployed consistently and according to best practices. It can be used to coordinate the people, processes, and code across the quality assurance, staging, development, and production environments.

SA can also be used to enable centralized IT management. Its architecture is suited for highly available, large-scale distributed environments. It also provides users a way to share best practices and a consistent set of tools across heterogeneous systems. It provides administrators with the same level of visibility and control across the complete environment.

SA is completely integrated with Matrix OE. SA jobs are shown in the Infrastructure Orchestration interface under the **Select additional software** tab (see Figure 6-13) and can be selected as part of the automated deployment tasks carried out by IO. Note that SA is being used instead of Insight Control server deployment.

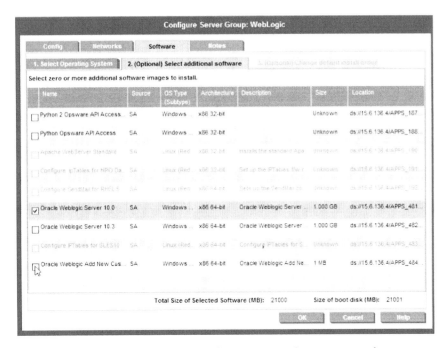

Figure 6-13. SA jobs in the infrastructure orchestration interface

As mentioned earlier in this chapter, the CloudSystem Matrix solution includes Matrix OE, which itself includes Insight Control and Insight Control server deployment. CloudSystem Matrix also includes CSA4M, which includes Server Automation Starter Edition. Which of the two software deployment tools should be used?

While Insight Control server deployment features are extensive, the functionality of Server Automation, with its ability to manage system configuration and application deployment, builds on the functionality of Insight Control server deployment and means that the consistency of software deployment and system configuration can be controlled, resulting in fewer errors and a reduction in the time and effort needed for management of infrastructure and applications. In addition, the auditing and compliance features of SA aid compliance with corporate security guidelines.

There are two versions of HP Server Automation:

■ **Starter Edition:** This is the version supplied with CSA for Matrix in CloudSystem Matrix. It is pre-integrated with Matrix OE and provides policy-based provisioning, configuration, patching, and compliance management of servers, OS, and application infrastructure (basic application provisioning). However, there is a limit of 1,000 physical and virtual servers (operating system instances).

■ **Enterprise Edition:** This version is supplied with CSA in CloudSystem Enterprise and CloudSystem Service Provider and builds on the functionality of the Starter Edition by adding:

  ■ Application Deployment Manager (ADM): For managing complex, multi-server, multi-tier applications.

  ■ Database and Middleware Automation (DMA) software: Provides a content library (delivered via solution packs) for database and middleware management.

  ■ Satellite: For managing remote facilities with a single SA core and one or more satellites; each satellite containing a small subset of SA core components.

  ■ Multimaster Mesh: For managing remote facilities by installing multiple SA cores.

  ■ Unlimited physical and virtual servers (operating system instances).

Note

In this chapter we will focus on the functionality of the starter edition of SA. In the following chapter on CloudSystem Enterprise, we will cover the functionality of the Enterprise Edition.

Let us now look at the functionality of SA using the four pillars of **Baseline**, **Provision and Upgrade**, **Change and Configure**, and **Compliance** (see Figure 6-14).

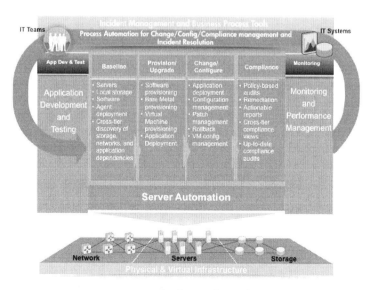

Figure 6-14. The four pillars of HP SA

Baseline

Servers that are not being managed by SA can be discovered by SA and have the SA agent installed on them, bringing them under the control of SA. A base configuration can then be established for servers, local storage, hardware, operating system, and software configurations, including installed software, patches, and packages. This baseline configuration, or snapshot, can be considered to be a *known good configuration* against which other configurations can be compared.

Server, network, storage, and logical application environments and dependencies and compliance state can be visualized with HP Service Automation Visualizer software, which is integrated with HP Server Automation and enables users to visualize cross-tier services, discover and dynamically draw maps of application, server, network, and storage infrastructure. These maps can help administrators to understand how changes might affect server configurations, quickly isolate the changes, and reduce the time it takes to resolve issues.

Provision and Upgrade

Build sequences—incorporating operating systems, patches, and software policies—can be defined for server provisioning.

Software code can be deployed on servers in single or multiple instances without proprietary packaging. Files, objects, and scripts can be imported to define configuration best practices. Remote server access uses a secure communications channel with audit logs and access control policies to provide direct connections to servers in any location. Remote desktop connections, Windows PowerShell, and all shells for UNIX and Linux environments are supported.

Change and Configure

Server vulnerabilities can be identified quickly and easily and the time needed to patch multiple servers can be dramatically reduced. Patching policies can be created and flexible patch deployments enabled. The can be of massive benefit in a large-scale cloud environment, where a large number of systems may have been installed over a period of time. With SA, if a vulnerability becomes apparent, rather than the system administrators having to write patching scripts that would need to be run and monitored (or even worse, having to patch each system one by one), the issue can be dealt with by patching all of the systems at once.

Native patch formats for all major operating systems are supported, and out-of-the-box integration with Microsoft Patch Network and Red Hat Network is provided.

The functionality of Server Automation can be extended by creating Automation Platform Extensions (APXs). APX extensions provide a framework that allows programmers using script-based tools such as shell scripts, Python, Perl, and PHP, to extend the functionality of SA and create applications that are tightly integrated into SA.

HP Storage Essentials (SE) is not included with CloudSystem by default, but if it is in use in the customer's environment, Server Automation can collect data from storage arrays, fabrics, switches, and NAS devices, and server administrators can view storage capacity and utilization metrics, run compliance checks on SAN storage, and identify relationships and dependencies between SAN devices, servers, and applications.

Compliance

Enterprises realize the necessity for ensuring that hardware and software configurations comply with corporate standards. In order to achieve this, it is necessary to check the state of the configurations. Audit and remediation makes it possible to identify *which* objects need to be checked (files, directories, configuration values), *where* they need to be checked (servers and server groups), and *when* they need to be checked (one time or as a recurring job).

In SA, server configuration policies can be defined to ensure that servers meet policy standards. When servers are found to be out of compliance—not configured the way they need to be—remediation will change them to comply with the organization's standards. This capability is of great benefit in a cloud environment, owing to the potential for very large-scale deployments; where manual audit and remediation would be very time consuming and may expose the customer to an unacceptable level of risk (of non-compliance).

SA provides a comprehensive compliance dashboard with consolidated servers and cross-tier compliance views, along with the ability to audit local storage configuration settings.

Integration with HP Business Service Automation (BSA) Essentials security and compliance subscription service provides an ongoing feed of risk and security vulnerability content. BSA Essentials Subscription Services provide daily vulnerability alerts and also provide access to the most current regulatory compliance policies, including the Federal Information Security Management Act (FISMA), Sarbanes-Oxley (Sox), the Center for Internet Security (CIS), and Payment Card Industry (PCI).

SA reduces system administration overhead while increasing accuracy and compliance. It also provides a proven, scalable solution for establishing a baseline, provisioning, patching, configuration management, script execution, and automated application deployment.

SA Architecture

SA software includes a number of components—collectively known as a *core*—running on one or more physical or virtual servers, known as *core* servers. These components represent the server side of the SA server-agent architecture and work together to enable the discovery of servers on the network, add those servers to a Managed Server Pool, and then provision, monitor, configure, audit, and maintain those servers from a centralized SA GUI interface. The components are (see Figure 6-15):

- **Model Repository:** An Oracle database containing all of the data collected from the devices in the managed environment. Each core has one Model Repository.

- **Infrastructure component bundle:** Provides communications between satellites and other cores in a Multimaster Mesh. Each core has one infrastructure bundle.

- **Slice component bundle:** Provides services between the user interfaces, model repository, infrastructure components, and the devices in the managed environment. Each SA core must have at least one slice bundle, but can have more—installed on separate servers—if the number of managed devices is high.

- **OS Provisioning component bundle:** Provides OS provisioning services to the managed devices. Each core has one OS provisioning bundle.

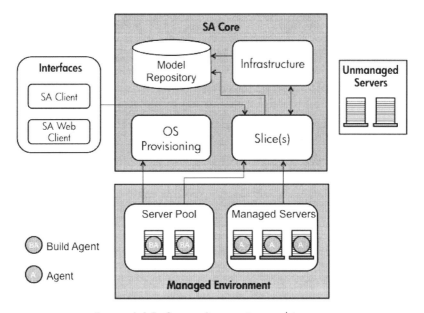

Figure 6-15. Server Automation architecture

 Note

The arrows in figure 6-15 represent the lines of communication between the different components in the core, the user interfaces, and the managed environment. The direction of the arrow indicates the connection initiation, not necessarily the flow of information.

Core components can all be installed on a single host or distributed across several hosts; however, the typical SA installation uses Core component bundling, which installs certain components together on the same server for performance and maintainability purposes. Core components, even if distributed to multiple hosts, are still considered part of a single SA core.

In order to communicate and perform certain server management activities, SA installs Server Agents on each Managed Server and communicates with the managed servers through *gateways* that are part of the SA core components. Server agents also perform certain actions on managed servers as directed by user input from the SA GUI.

In order to manage servers with SA, an SA core needs to be installed into the environment and SA agents need to be installed on the servers that are to be managed. In an SA managed environment, all managed servers either have an SA *Build Agent* or SA *Agent* that communicates with the SA core. The SA *Build Agent* is installed on a bare metal server that contains no operating system. The Build Agent runs in memory and communicates with the SA core and waits for provisioning instructions. The SA *Agent* is software running in an existing operating system on the server and is used to communicate with the SA core. After the Server Agents are deployed, they automatically contact the Core through the Agent Gateway and register their server with SA. The SA Client can then be used to manage the servers.

SA Topology

The three main SA topologies are known as *Single Core*, *Multimaster Mesh*, and *Satellite*.

The simplest topology is the *Single Core* (formerly called Standalone Core), which is ideal for managing a small network of servers contained in a single facility. Although a Single Core (see Figure 6-16) does not communicate with other SA Cores (because by its very nature, a single core has no other cores to communicate with), it has all of the components required to do so and can easily be converted into a core that is part of a *Multimaster Mesh*.

Texas
Core

Managed
Data
Center

Figure 6-16. SA Single Core installation

After the first SA Core is installed, subsequent SA Cores can be added to create a *Multimaster Mesh* in which two or more cores communicate with each other through management gateways and use the network to synchronize the managed server data contained in their respective model repositories.

A *Satellite* installation is typically installed for remote sites that do not have a large enough number of potential SA Managed Servers to justify a full SA Core installation. An SA Satellite contains a small subset of SA core components and enables management of remote servers from an existing core. An SA Satellite must be linked to at least one core.

Note
Multimaster Mesh and Satellite topologies are discussed in Chapter 7.

SA Interfaces

There are several Server Automation interfaces, each with their own features and functions. The choice of interface will depend on the tasks to be performed. The interfaces are:

- **SA Web Client:** The web-based user interface to SA through which users manage servers. Management operations include adding user accounts and assigning permissions, adding customers and facilities, changing SA configuration, and monitoring and diagnosing SA problems.

- **SA Client:** A Windows application (see Figure 6-17) whose features include discovery of unmanaged servers and deployment of SA agents; provisioning of operating systems onto bare metal and virtual servers; provisioning of applications on to Managed Servers; management of patches for Windows, UNIX, Solaris, and HP-UX; management of audit and remediation. The SA client also includes Server Automation Visualizer (SAV), which automatically discovers server, application, and network device dependencies and presents them in an easy-to-understand way using physical and logical drawings. SAV makes it easy to see what is connected to what, where performance problems might arise, what might be the result of any changes made in the environment, and also helps with troubleshooting and resolving problems.

- **Automation Platform Extensions (APXs):** APX extensions provide a framework that allows programmers using script-based tools such as shell scripts, Python, Perl, and PHP, to extend the functionality of SA and create applications that are tightly integrated into SA.

- **SA Command Line Interface (OCLI):** A command line interface used to upload packages into the Software Repository, and to perform batch commands and run scripts.

- **DCML Exchange Tool (DET):** Utility that enables users to export almost all server management content from any SA Core and import it into any other SA Core.

- **ISM Development Kit:** A development kit that consists of command-line tools and libraries for creating, building, and uploading ISMs. An ISM is a set of files and directories that include application bits, installation scripts, and control scripts.

- **SA APIs:** A set of APIs and a command-line interface (CLI) that enables the extension of SA and the integration with other IT systems—such as existing monitoring, trouble ticketing, billing, and virtualization technology—to exchange information with SA.

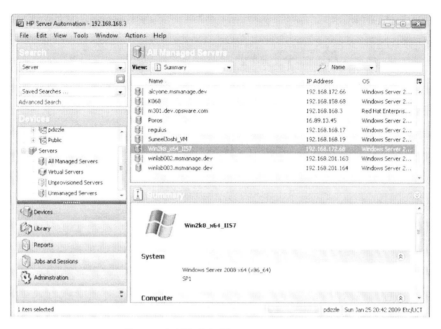

Figure 6-17. SA Client main screen

SA Installation Methods

There are four methods for installing SA, and the choice of method will be determined by the complexity of the proposed managed environment.

The first method is known as *single-host* installation and is supported on a single Windows physical host only—installation on a virtual server is not supported. This installation type uses an HP-supplied Oracle database (Model Repository), which must be installed on the same server as the SA Core.

The second method is known as *simple* installation. This installation enables the distribution of SA Core Components over multiple hosts and allows the use of a remote Oracle database (Model Repository).

The third method is known as *advanced* installation. This installation enables the SA Core components to be distributed over multiple hosts, enables the use of a remote Oracle database (model repository), and allows for Multimaster Mesh and Satellite installations.

The fourth method is known as *expert* installation, and allows for the customization of all SA configuration parameters. This is a highly complex undertaking and should only be used by HP technical support and services personnel.

Let us now take a closer look at the SA single-host installation process.

SA Single-Host Installation

An SA single-host installation has eight phases:

1. **Pre-installation:** This involves locating the SA installation DVDs (SA Product Software DVD, Agent and Utilities DVD and the Oracle_SA installation DVD), gathering information needed to complete the installation interview in step three, and making sure that the necessary permissions are gained.

2. **Install the HP-supplied Oracle database:** This database is used for the model repository and stores information about the SA installation and all managed servers.

3. **Installation interview:** This is where the SA administrator password is chosen, where the name of the SA managed environment (the *facility*, in SA parlance) is chosen, and where the location of the required Windows patch management files are specified.

4. **Install SA:** The installer prompts for a filename to which all responses given during the installation interview will be saved. After saving the response file, the installation can proceed using the information contained in the file. The file location should be noted as it may be needed for future installations and upgrades.

5. **Upload SA content:** In this phase, default content—required for SA functionality—must be installed from the SA Agent and Utilities DVD.

6. **Post-installation:** This phase involves setting up the SA web client and the SA client, and creating SA users.

7. **Discover servers on the network:** In this phase SA scans the network and discovers any servers not managed by SA. Once discovered, each server can be brought into the SA Managed Server Pool.

8. **Advanced post-installation tasks:** Depending on the SA features that are required, there may be additional advanced tasks that need to be performed. For more information about these tasks, *see the SA Simple/Advanced Installation Guide that comes with the Server Automation software.*

SA is now ready to be used for end-to-end server and application lifecycle management. Let us now summarize our discussion of SA with a look at the benefits.

HP Server Automation Benefits for the Cloud

HP Server Automation helps customers reduce their total cost of ownership by providing a single solution for automating the deployment of applications and the on-going management of the application stack across physical and virtual servers. The more complex the environment, the more benefit customers will realize as a result of using HP SA. In a cloud environment, there may be many logical servers, a variety of operating systems, multiple geographically-dispersed data centers, a complex mix of multi-tier applications, a complex network environment, and a requirement for regulatory compliance. Couple these characteristics with the fact that the operating systems and applications may need to be reconfigured and patched on a frequent basis, and the case for using SA becomes compelling.

The main features and benefits are shown in Table 6-2.

Table 6-2. Features and benefits of HP Server Automation for the cloud

Feature	Benefit
Easily detect vulnerable servers and patch-levels, apply patches to large numbers of servers at once, and create patch reports	Save time and money, and reduce risk of non-compliance and potential security weaknesses.
Automated configuration and compliance management.	Reduce time to deploy new infrastructure and minimize risk of human error.
Automated application deployment using a consistent set of deployment processes.	Accelerate the overall application deployment process and improve deployment results resulting in reduced time-to-productivity.
Reduce server and application downtime caused by misconfigurations.	Reduce risk and cost of downtime.
Establish a baseline of all server, local storage, operating system, installed packages, and configuration data.	Ensure that infrastructure complies with all corporate standards and policies, minimizing risk of noncompliance.
Achieve server-to-administrator ratios as great as 200:1 by automating time-consuming tasks.	Reduce administration overhead and focus resources on innovation rather than maintenance.
Improve visibility and control of physical and virtual servers and software.	Reduce administration overhead and gain insight.
Enforce processes and best practices for building and making changes to servers.	Reduce the risk of ad-hoc changes causing unforeseen breaches in overall system security.

HP SiteScope

HP SiteScope software monitors the availability and performance of distributed IT infrastructures and applications including servers, operating systems, network and Internet services, applications, and application components (see Figure 6-18).

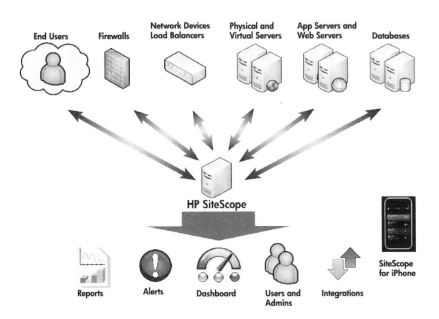

Figure 6-18. HP SiteScope

HP SiteScope is an agentless solution, which means that it is not necessary to install monitoring software on the servers to be managed. The result is a monitoring solution that is easy to deploy and configure.

A customizable dashboard is provided and enables users to apply filters, create their own favorite views, and to modify the look and feel of the interface (see Figure 6-19). Role-based views can also be created.

Figure 6-19. The SiteScope dashboard

Integration with other products, such as HP Operations Manager, enables the management of several SiteScope instances from a single pane of glass. Integration also makes it possible to transfer configuration information from one HP SiteScope instance to another and to synchronize settings between multiple HP SiteScope servers.

The features of HP SiteScope can be categorized into four main groups:

- **Monitoring:** *Monitors* are the heart of data collection—they collect performance and availability data about the systems, devices, and applications being monitored by SiteScope. This performance data is then used for the *alerting*, *reporting*, and *baselining* features of SiteScope. SiteScope continually monitors more than 100 types of components on Windows, UNIX, and Linux systems, through a web-based architecture that is highly customizable.

- **Alerting:** Based on user-defined thresholds (error conditions), alerts will be sent to system/ application administrators to notify them of failures. Alerts can also initiate automated corrective measures, such as restarting servers.

- **Reporting:** HP SiteScope's reporting system can generate daily, weekly, and monthly reports for single or multiple monitors. These reports enable detailed analysis of system and application performance over time.

- **Baselining:** Data is gathered over a period of time from monitor performance metrics and is used to provide a *baseline* comparison for establishing acceptable or expected threshold ranges. HP SiteScope then establishes dynamic thresholds and adjusts alerts accordingly, thereby reducing false alerts.

HP SiteScope Architecture

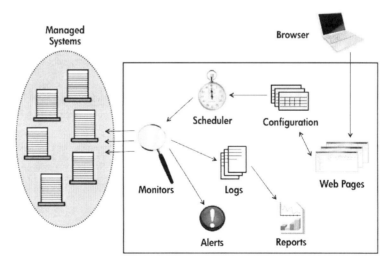

Figure 6-20. SiteScope architecture

The SiteScope architecture consists of several components that work together to provide a comprehensive monitoring solution. The main components are (see Figure 6-20):

- **Browser-based GUI:** The SiteScope user interface is a Java application that runs within a web browser and is used to view the status of the managed systems via various **web pages**, request changes to **configuration** parameters, and to perform other administrative tasks.

- **Scheduler:** The scheduler is responsible for running the SiteScope monitors, creating alerts, and generating reports.

- **Monitors:** The SiteScope monitors query the managed systems and collect performance and availability data for the systems, devices, and applications being monitored. Every monitor must be part of a **group** (not shown in Figure 6-20), which acts as a container for SiteScope assets such as monitors and alerts.

  SiteScope Server monitors can be used to monitor server resources (for example, CPU, disk space, memory, and services) on Windows NT/2000/2003/2008/XP Pro/Vista/Windows 7, Sun Solaris (Sparc and x86), Linux, AIX, HP-UX, SGI IRIX, SCO, and FreeBSD. SiteScope web monitors provide monitoring details about a website's performance, including web-related processes, web services, and can even use a synthetic transaction to model end-user experience.

- **Alerts:** In the event of an incident or failure (based on configured thresholds and defined schedules), administrators will be notified by e-mail, SNMP trap, pager, or SMS. Alerts can also be used to initiate corrective actions.

- **Logs:** SiteScope stores performance data—not in a database—but in log files. These log files are aggregated and analyzed and are used to generate reports.

- **Reports:** The data collected by the monitors and stored in the logs is formatted and presented in a way that can help with visualizing operational performance, trends, and with troubleshooting of problems.

SiteScope Monitors

The SiteScope monitoring model consists of four main objects: *groups*, *monitors*, *alerts*, and *reports*. *Groups* are containers for monitors and help with keeping the monitors organized in a logical way. Monitors must be contained within a group, so at least one group must exist before the first monitor is created.

Once the group has been created, *monitors* can be added to it. These monitors will be checking the status of server components, application processes, log files, and network devices.

Alerts can then be created that will notify administrators in the event of a failure.

Reports can be generated from the data collected by the monitors.

SiteScope uses two methods for monitoring systems, servers, and applications:

1. **Standards-based network protocols:** This category includes HTTP, HTTPS, FTP, SMTP, SNMP, and UDP. These types of monitors are generally independent of the platform or operating system on which SiteScope is running. For example, SiteScope installed on Linux can monitor Web pages, file downloads, and SNMP data on servers running Windows, HP-UX, and Solaris.

2. **Platform-specific network services and commands:** This category includes monitor types that log in to a remote machine as a user and request information. SiteScope must be configured with a username and password to allow it to log in to remote servers. It can then use Telnet or SSH to log in to a remote server and use command line tools to request information regarding disk space, memory, or processes. On the Microsoft Windows platform, SiteScope also extracts performance data from the Windows performance counter libraries and displays it.

SiteScope provides many different monitors out-of-the-box, ranging from server metrics to database metrics and application systems monitors (see Table 6-3).

Table 6-3. SiteScope out-of-the-box monitors

Server Monitors	Network Monitors	Application Systems Monitors
CPU, Disk Space, Memory, Service, IPMI, Unix Resources, Web Server, NonStop Resources/Event Log. MS Windows: Performance Counter, Event Log, Resources, Services State	Formula Composite, SNMP, SNMP by MIB, SNMP Trap, DNS, FTP, Port, Ping, Mail, MAPI, Network Bandwidth, MS Windows Dialup, IPv6	Apache Server Broadvision Application Server MS ASP Server Check Point, Cisco Work, Citrix ColdFusion Server, COM+ Server
Database Monitors Database Counter, Database Query, IBM DB2, Oracle Database, Microsoft SQL Server, Sybase Database	**Web Monitors** e-Business Transaction, WebScript, Link Check, URL, URL Content, URL List, URL Sequence	MS Exchange, MS IIS Server F5 Big-IP, News, Radius WebSphere MQ Server Oracle Application Server SAP, SAP CCMS, Java web application server, work process Siebel Application server, Siebel log, Siebel web server SunOne Web Server, Tuxedo, UDDI Server WebLogic Application server WebSphere Application Server WebSphere Performance Servlet
Streaming Monitors MS Windows Media Player, MS Windows Media Server, Real Media Player, Real Media Server	**Virtualization Monitors** VMware Performance (ESX Server, Virtual Center, ESXI, VSphere, Vmotion), Solaris Zones, Microsoft Hyper-V, Amazon CloudWatch	
Generic Monitors XML Metrics, Composite Directory, File, JMX, Log File, Script, Web Service	**Integration Monitors** Technology Database, Log File, SNMP Trap, Web Service Integration HP OM Event, HP Service Manager, NetScout Event	

SiteScope monitoring capabilities include:

- Amazon Web Services monitor that enables monitoring of Amazon Web Service cloud resources.

- Microsoft Hyper-V monitor that enables monitoring of Microsoft Hyper-V hosts and virtual machines.

- HP iLO (Integrated Lights-Out) monitor which enables monitoring of hardware health on supported HP ProLiant servers. The HP iLO monitor supports monitoring HP iLO 2 and 3 versions.

- Connection Statistics monitor collects data on SSH and Telnet connection behavior and statistics for the Perfex and Perfex_dispatcher pool.

- Apache Server monitor supports monitoring on Apache HTTP Server 2.2.

- Citrix monitor supports monitoring on Citrix XenApp 4.6.

- MAPI monitor supports monitoring on Outlook 2007.

- Microsoft Exchange monitor supports monitoring on Microsoft Exchange 2010.

- Microsoft IIS Server monitor supports monitoring on Microsoft IIS Server 7.0.

- Microsoft SQL Server monitor supports monitoring on Microsoft SQL Server 2008 R2.

- Microsoft Windows Resources monitor supports monitoring on Windows Vista, Windows 7, and Windows Server 2008.

- WebLogic Application Server monitor supports monitoring on WebLogic 11g.

- Virtualization support.

- Microsoft Hyper-V Monitor supports monitoring on Microsoft Windows Server 2008 R2 Hyper-V.

- SiteScope reports near real-time virtual server change topology to BSM for VMware Performance monitor and Solaris Zones monitor (moving of VMs between ESX servers; changes in zones configuration).

- SiteScope installations on UNIX servers include extended support for monitoring Microsoft Windows servers. The Windows server being monitored must be configured for SSH.

SiteScope Installation

Infrastructure monitoring relies on platform-specific services (NetBIOS, telnet, rlogin, Secure Shell, and so on). Being an agentless solution, SiteScope needs to log on and authenticate frequently to many servers in the infrastructure. For performance and security reasons, it is best to deploy SiteScope within the same domain and as close to the system elements to be monitored as possible. It is also best to have SiteScope in the same subnet as the applicable network authentication service (for example Active Directory, NIS, or LDAP). Avoid deploying SiteScope in a location where a significant amount of the monitoring activity requires communication across a Wide Area Network (WAN).

SiteScope is easy to install and configure with an intuitive, easy-to-learn user interface.

There are out-of-the-box templates and thresholds that are easy to configure and maintain. They provide simple, yet powerful customization capabilities.

With four basic steps, SiteScope can be set up to monitor systems and applications (see Figure 6-21):

1. Use the installation wizard to install the SiteScope software.

2. Create groups and monitors. As previously stated, groups are containers that are used to organize monitors and alerts. Monitors then need to be created—not just for standard metrics such as CPU utilization or ping time—but for cloud-specific metrics such as SLAs, quality of experience (QoE), and quality of service (QoS).

3. Create monitor thresholds. These are used to determine the conditions under which warnings and errors are generated.

4. Configure alerts. Alerts are triggered when there is a change in the status of a monitor; for example, when a specific monitor transitions from *good* to *error* state. The alert can trigger an action such as sending an email or SMS, adding an entry to a log file, or updating a table in a database.

With these four steps complete, monitoring can begin.

Figure 6-21. SiteScope installation

HP SiteScope Integration With HP Operations Manager

While HP SiteScope can be deployed standalone, in many situations it is used in conjunction with HP Operations Manager (OM) or Operations Manager i (OMi). This approach provides a powerful combination of agentless and agent-based infrastructure management where a single console acts as a central repository for all discovered events (see Figure 6-22). Serving as an agent of Operations Manager, SiteScope targets are added automatically to Operations Manager Service View maps, which enables Operations Manager to seamlessly display SiteScope data and monitor status. SiteScope alerts and monitor metric status changes are sent directly to Operations Manager.

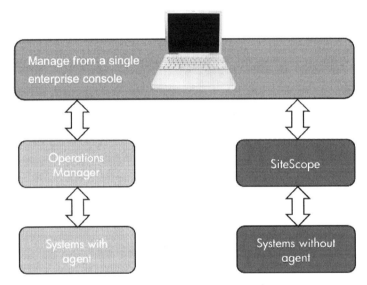

Figure 6-22. SiteScope integration with HP OM

HP SiteScope can be managed centrally from the HP Operations Manager console, allowing the transfer of configuration information from one HP SiteScope instance to another and synchronization of settings between multiple HP SiteScope servers. In addition, HP SiteScope tools can be launched directly from the HP Operations Manager console.

The combined functionality of agentless and agent-based monitoring provides a highly-scalable, powerful, and in-depth monitoring solution.

Not only can SiteScope be integrated with OM/OMi, but the additional HP ArcSight integration with OMi provides a mechanism for root-cause analysis of problems. When OMi receives an alert from SiteScope, it can use the centralized logging capability of ArcSight to correlate the alert with the contents of a log (or a set of logs) to drill down to the root cause of the problem.

OMi is used with OM to add new capabilities designed for next-generation data centers and complex cloud environments. Reasons to add OMi to OM include:

- Simplification of the process of building and maintaining service maps that show the relationships between IT elements and business services.

- Improvement of efficiency across multiple different IT groups as a result of OMi cross-domain event correlation.

SiteScope Failover For High Availability

SiteScope can be configured in an HA configuration with automated *mirroring* and *failover* functionality. SiteScope Failover automatically transfers the functions of the primary SiteScope system to a standby system in the event that the primary system becomes unavailable. In addition, configuration data from the primary SiteScope system are automatically and periodically *mirrored* (copied) to the failover system so that the failover system stays current with any changes to the monitoring configurations. This means that any transition to the failover system will provide the same monitoring content and services to users as the primary system.

 Note
Previous versions of SiteScope Failover were called SiteScope High Availability (SiteScopeHA).

SiteScope Failover needs be installed on a standby server with similar system resources (processor speed and memory) as the primary SiteScope server. Since the failover is not intended to store monitor data for extended periods of time, the available disk space does need not be as large as that of the primary SiteScope server.

An additional method for protecting SiteScope monitoring is to configure the SiteScope server on a VM in an ESX cluster, and let the ESX cluster provide the high availability for SiteScope.

SiteScope Solution Templates

SiteScope solution templates are preconfigured templates designed to monitor popular enterprise applications and systems. The use of solution templates enables the rapid deployment of a combination of standard *and* solution-specific monitors with settings that are optimized for monitoring the availability, performance, and health of the application or system. Solution templates can be customized to meet specific requirements if required.

Solution templates are supplied with a best practices guide that specifies the most important key performance indicators (KPIs), troubleshooting tips, such as where performance problems typically occur, and gives the description and recommended threshold for each metric.

Table 6-4 lists the solution templates available for SiteScope.

Table 6-4. SiteScope solution templates

Solution Template Name	Description
Failover Monitoring	Monitors the availability of primary and failover SiteScope machines when using SiteScope Failover Manager.
Active Directory	Monitors performance, availability, and health for AIX host machines.
AIX Host	Monitors performance, availability, and health for AIX host machines.
HP Quality Center	Monitors performance, availability, and health for HP Quality Center 9.x and 10.x application servers on Windows and UNIX, HP Quality Center license usage and expiration time on an Oracle Database server, and HP QuickTest Professional license server application and system availability.
HP Service Manager	Monitors HP Service Manager application servers availability and system status on Windows and UNIX platforms.
JBoss Application Server	Monitors performance, availability, and health for JBoss environments.
Linux Host	Monitors performance, availability, and health for Linux host machines.
Microsoft Exchange	Includes individual solution options for monitoring application health, message flow, and usage statistics for Microsoft Exchange 5.5, 2000, 2003, 2007, and 2010 servers.
Microsoft IIS	Monitors performance, availability, and health for IIS 6.0 and IIS 7.x environments.

Solution Template Name	Description
Microsoft Lync server 2010	Monitors performance, availability, and health for the following Microsoft Lync Server 2010 Servers: A/V Conferencing Server, Archiving Server, Director Server, Edge Server, Front End Server, Lync Server Event Log, Mediation Server, Monitoring Server, and Registrar Server.
Microsoft SharePoint 2010	Monitors performance, availability, and health for Microsoft SharePoint 2010.
Microsoft SQL Server	Monitors performance, availability, and usage statistics for Microsoft SQL Server 2005 and SQL Server 2008, and for Microsoft SQL Server 2008 R2.
Microsoft Windows Host	Monitors performance, availability, and health for Microsoft Windows 2000, Windows XP, and Windows Server 2003 host machines.
.NET	Monitors performance, availability, and health of .NET applications and environments on Windows 2000, Windows XP, and Windows Server 2003.
Oracle Database	Monitors performance, availability, and usage statistics for Oracle 9i and 10g databases.
SAP	Monitors performance, availability, and usage statistics for SAP system components.
Siebel	Monitors performance, availability, and usage statistics for Siebel Application Server installed on Windows and UNIX operating systems.
Solaris Host	Monitors performance, availability, and health for Solaris host machines.
VMware host	Monitors CPU, memory, storage, state, and network performance and usage statistics for the VMware Host server and on guest virtual machines on the host server.
WebLogic	Monitors performance, availability, and usage statistics for Oracle WebLogic application servers.
WebSphere	Monitors performance, availability, and usage statistics for IBM WebSphere Server 5.x application servers.

HP SiteScope Benefits for the Cloud

HP SiteScope can drive down the total cost of ownership of infrastructure performance and availability monitoring.

SiteScope features and benefits are shown in Table 6-5.

Table 6-5. Features and benefits of HP SiteScope for the cloud

Feature	Benefit
Monitor cloud-specific SLAs, QoE, and QoS	Rapid detection and rectification of problems, resulting in SLAs being met, and enhanced user experience
Integration with HP Operations Manager enables agent-based and agentless monitoring	Manage the entire infrastructure from a single pane of glass, resulting in reduced administrative overhead
Agentless, enterprise-ready architecture	Reduce total cost-of-ownership by removing the need to install and maintain server agents
Monitor critical health and performance characteristics of systems and applications	Centralized management reduces administrative overhead and reduces time-to-repair
Generate alerts using customizable thresholds	Problems can be resolved before end-users are affected, resulting in improved end-user experience
Solution Templates provide specialized monitors, default metrics and thresholds, proactive tests, and best practices for applications and components being monitored	Reduce time to deploy monitoring solution, resulting in shorter time-to-productivity
Follow monitored VMware virtual machines as they move from one server to another with vMotion and generate an alert if the VM does not return to normal operation	Rapid detection of vMotion issues leading to reduced VM downtime

HP CloudSystem Matrix Product Mapping

Now that we have described the individual components of the CloudSystem Matrix solution, let us finish this chapter by seeing which software products are responsible for providing the functions in the Demand, Delivery, and Supply layers of the HP Cloud Functional Reference Architecture, and in the Design/Deploy, Provision, Use, and Assure phases of the cloud services lifecycle. Mapping the software products to the Reference Architecture is done to ensure that we have deployed the capabilities required by the customer. Figure 6-23 shows a high-level overview of the product mapping, and Figure 6-24 shows a more detailed view.

 Note
Care should be taken when using the detailed product mapping information, as the names of the products may change over time.

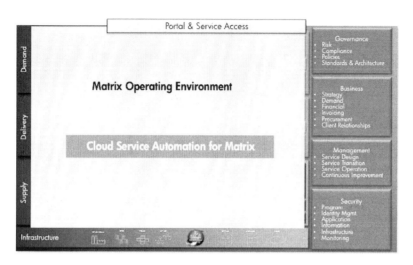

Figure 6-23. HP CloudSystem Matrix product mapping overview

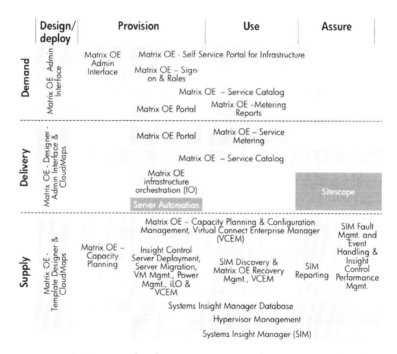

Figure 6-24. HP CloudSystem Matrix product mapping detail

 Note

The features in light grey are provided by Matrix OE and the features in dark grey are provided by HP CSA for Matrix.

Test Preparation Questions and Answers

The following questions will help you measure your understanding of the material presented in this chapter. Read all the choices carefully, as there may be more than one correct answer. Choose all correct answers for each question.

Questions

1. What is not a major component of CloudSystem Matrix?

   a. Matrix OE

   b. Database and Middleware Automation

   c. Cloud Service Automation for Matrix

   d. Implementation Services

2. Which statement best describes CloudSystem Matrix?

   a. It is focused on IaaS, PaaS, and SaaS.

   b. It is focused on IaaS and SaaS.

   c. It is focused PaaS.

   d. It is focused on IaaS.

3. Which statement best describes the capabilities of Matrix OE?

   a. It provides advanced infrastructure management capabilities.

   b. It provides a means of backing up customer data.

   c. It works with all third-party infrastructure.

   d. It dynamically adds and removes CPUs to/from x86 servers.

4. What is the main purpose of CloudSystem Matrix APIs?

   a. They provide a way to configure up to four local physical enclosures into a single logical domain.

   b. They provide a way for external systems to control the actions of CloudSystem Matrix.

   c. They enable CloudSystem Matrix to be upgraded to CloudSystem Enterprise.

   d. They provide a mechanism for controlling the amount of power that is consumed by CloudSystem Matrix.

5. What is the main purpose of HP Cloud Map infrastructure service templates?

    a. They are logically linked steps that are used to automate tasks.

    b. They specify the requirements for data center backup requirements.

    c. They are published to the service catalog by end-users, and can then be used by service designers.

    d. They specify the requirements for application infrastructure.

6. Which statement best describes HP Server Automation Starter Edition?

    a. It provides a server failover disaster recovery solution.

    b. It allows virtual machines to synchronise customer data.

    c. It provides a solution for server and application lifecycle management.

    d. It provides a solution for deploying and managing complex, multi-tier applications and databases.

7. Which statement best describes the main functionality of Sitescope?

    a. HP Sitescope assesses the expansion capabilities of an IT infrastructure.

    b. HP Sitescope monitors availability and performance of distributed IT infrastructures.

    c. HP Sitescope installs and configures Matrix OE.

    d. HP Sitescope is an agent-based monitoring solution.

Answers

1. ☑ **B.** Database and Middleware Automation in included with CloudSystem Enterprise and CloudSystem Service Provider, but not with CloudSystem Matrix.
   ☒ **A** is incorrect; Matrix OE is a major component of CloudSystem Matrix. **C** is incorrect because Cloud Service Automation for Matrix is a major component of CloudSystem Matrix. **D** is incorrect because Implementation Services are included with CloudSystem Matrix.

2. ☑ **D.** HP CloudSystem Matrix is focused on private clouds and Infrastructure-as-a-Service (IaaS).
   ☒ **A**, **B**, and **C** are incorrect; CloudSystem Matrix is focused on IaaS.

3. ☑ **A.** HP Matrix OE provides advanced infrastructure management capabilities that enable enterprises to instantly adjust to dynamic business needs.
   ☒ **B** is incorrect; Matrix OE is not concerned with backing up customer data. **C** is incorrect because Matrix OE supports a limited set of third-party hardware. **D** is incorrect because Matrix OE does not dynamically add CPUs to x86 servers. Matrix OE for HP-UX includes gWLM, which can add CPUs to HP Integrity partitions, but that was not the question.

4. ☑ **B.** Integration provides a way for external systems to control the actions of CloudSystem Matrix. Matrix OE integration interfaces include the Web Service API and the Command Line API.
   ☒ **A** is incorrect; this is a description of VCEM. **C** is incorrect; they do no enable CloudSystem Matrix to be upgraded to CloudSystem Enterprise. **D** is incorrect. They do not provide a mechanism for controlling the amount of power that is consumed by CloudSystem Matrix.

5. ☑ **D.** Infrastructure service templates specify the requirements for an application infrastructure and are where a system architect can specify server type, cost per server, number of servers, processors, memory, processor speed, and architecture.
   ☒ **A** is incorrect; this is a description of workflows. **B** is incorrect because they are not concerned with data center backup requirements. **C** is incorrect; they are published to the service catalog by service designers, and can then be used by end-users.

6. ☑ **C.** HP Server Automation Starter Edition provides policy-based provisioning, configuration, patching, and compliance management of servers, OS, and application infrastructure, and end-to-end server and application lifecycle management.
   ☒ **A** is incorrect; SA is not a server failover disaster recovery solution. **B** is incorrect because SA is not concerned with the synchronisation of customer data. **D** is incorrect; SA Starter Edition can manage basic application provisioning.

7. ☑ **B.** HP SiteScope monitors the availability and performance of distributed IT infrastructures and applications including servers, operating systems, network and Internet services, applications, and application components.

☒ **A** is incorrect; assessing the expansion capabilities of an IT infrastructure is not a function of HP SiteScope. **C** is incorrect because HP SiteScope is not involved in Matrix OE installation and configuration. **E** is incorrect because HP SiteScope is an agentless monitoring solution.

7 HP CloudSystem Enterprise

EXAM OBJECTIVES

✓ Define CloudSystem Enterprise.

✓ Describe the main Cloud Service Automation (CSA) components and concepts.

✓ Explain the purpose of HP Operations Orchestration.

✓ Describe the main components and functionality of Server Automation Enterprise Edition.

✓ Explain the purpose of HP Network Automation.

✓ Identify the main CSA installation and configuration tasks.

ASSUMED KNOWLEDGE

You should be in possession of the HP APC - Converged Infrastructure Solutions (2010) certification.

INTRODUCTION

We have seen that HP CloudSystem is available in three configurations: CloudSystem Matrix, CloudSystem Enterprise and CloudSystem Service Provider and that each of the offerings is based on a single unified architecture combining hardware, software and services.

In this chapter, we will look in detail at HP CloudSystem Enterprise and, in particular, at the HP Cloud Service Automation (CSA), HP Operations Orchestration (OO), and HP Server Automation Enterprise Edition software components that are included with the solution. We will also look at Network Automation, which is an extension for CloudSystem Enterprise (and is part of the core platform of CloudSystem Service Provider). The reason for looking at Network Automation in this chapter is that customers considering a CloudSystem Enterprise solution may have a complex heterogeneous datacenter, and would be well advised to automate as much of the management of the network as possible, thereby mitigating the risk of unplanned downtime owing to human error. We will also answer the question *what is the difference between CSA for matrix and CSA?*

What is the CloudSystem Enterprise?

CloudSystem Enterprise is built with HP Cloud Service Automation (CSA) software, which uses HP CloudSystem Matrix as a compute provider. The main differences between the CloudSystem Matrix and CloudSystem Enterprise platforms are:

- **Core Platform**: CloudSystem Matrix includes CSA for Matrix and Server Automation Starter Edition whereas CloudSystem Enterprise includes CSA, and Server Automation Enterprise Edition [which includes HP Application Deployment Manager (ADM) software] and Database and Middleware Automation (DMA) software.

- **Extensions**: CloudSystem Enterprise can add Hybrid Delivery Workload Analysis Service, IT Service Management, Network Automation and Advanced Resource Manager

CloudSystem Matrix excels at delivering IaaS (up to 10,000 VMs) in a single datacenter using the resources of the HP BladeSystem, and also has the ability to deploy VMs on a limited set of non-HP x86 servers (from Dell and IBM). CloudSystem Enterprise can scale across multiple, geographically-dispersed, heterogeneous datacenters and can deliver IaaS, PaaS, and SaaS to a scale far exceeding that of CloudSystem Matrix. The HP CSA *service lifecycle* (described later in this chapter) also provides that capability for integrating specific security solutions such as HP TippingPoint IPS into CloudSystem Enterprise.

HP CSA software is the primary enabler of CloudSystem Enterprise's extensive heterogeneity, massive scalability, and full cloud service management from infrastructure to cloud services. It also permits the independent management of the applications and infrastructure, unlike in CloudSystem Matrix, where they are managed as a single entity. Let us now take a closer look at HP CSA.

HP Cloud Service Automation (CSA)

HP CSA introduces the concept of the *service lifecycle*. Without HP CSA, every service that is built using HP Operations Orchestration (OO) has to be constructed out of raw *workflows* (also known as *ops flows* or *flows*) using HP OO studio (of which more later). HP CSA deals with all of the lifecycle actions required to build services, and simply passes instructions to OO, which in turn communicates with the providers. CSA includes out-of-the-box (OOB) designs that use Matrix templates that have been created in the IO designer. This removes the need to always build HP OO ops flows manually.

Providers are an essential part of the CSA cloud services lifecycle process, and are responsible for supplying the building blocks such as compute, application, monitoring and configuration management that combine to form a service. When CSA initiates a lifecycle action, the system can call upon the resources of one of several underlying service providers. Service providers include:

- **Compute Providers**—VMware vCenter and HP Matrix infrastructure orchestration (IO) manage the provisioning of compute resources within the system.

  - VMware vCenter provides virtualization management services, coordinating with vSphere for virtualized platform and infrastructure support.

- HP Matrix infrastructure orchestration (included with Matrix OE) is an integrated part of the HP CloudSystem Matrix solution, providing automated provisioning for blade servers. This means that CSA can pass requests for infrastructure resources (for example, logical servers with storage and networking) to CloudSystem Matrix, and CloudSystem Matrix uses IO to build the resources before delivering them back to CSA.

 Note
HP CSA does not have a direct integration out-of-the-box with Microsoft Hyper-V. However, Matrix OE provides out-of-the-box integration with Hyper-V, and CSA can directly leverage the Hyper-V capabilities of Matrix OE. A direct Hyper-V integration with CSA (without Matrix OE) could be created but is not shipped out-of-the-box.

- **Monitoring Providers**—HP SiteScope provides monitoring of resources and infrastructure.

- **Application Providers**—HP Application Deployment Manager (ADM) is a provider that manages the deployment and configuration of applications on the target platform. HP ADM is part of HP Server Automation Enterprise Edition software.

- **Runtime Configuration Management Providers**—HP Universal Configuration Management Database (uCMDB) stores and tracks infrastructure configurations required at runtime, such as configuration for server groups and the relationship between individual server configurations.

In addition to these providers, HP Server Automation adds server management and host administration capability. Other providers communicate with HP Server Automation to obtain server and platform configuration data used in the infrastructure provisioning process.

HP CSA software provides *orchestrated* deployment of compute resources and complex multi-tier applications. It provides several portals, including a *design portal* that Service Designers use to create offerings, a *provider console* that a Service Publisher uses to make those offerings available via a customer catalog, and a *customer* (also known as *end-user* or *subscriber*) *portal* that customers use to browse the catalog and to order the services. The catalog could contain anything from a simple VM with a predetermined number of CPUs, amount of memory, and a specific size of boot disk, all the way through to a complex multi-tier infrastructure complete with applications, database, high-availability clustering, and service level agreements for availability and/or performance.

 Note
CloudSystem Enterprise customers can (and often do) replace the supplied customer portal with a portal of their own design.

HP CSA supports a hybrid environment, meaning that services can use local resources (such as an HP CloudSystem Matrix) *and* resources provided by an external provider such as Savvis. In this case, the CloudSystem Matrix and the resources provided by Savvis are treated by CSA as compute *providers*. This concept of providers is central to the operation of CSA and will be discussed in more detail later in this chapter.

HP CSA software is delivered in a package known as *HP CSA Foundation*, which includes the HP CSA Controller, the HP CSA Database, and the HP Universal CMDB (uCMDB). Solution components and various service providers are added to manage the resources (such as compute, application, and monitor providers) required for service delivery.

One potential source of confusion lies in the comparison between CloudSystem Matrix with its CSA for Matrix software, and CloudSystem Enterprise with its CSA software. Is there a difference between CSA for Matrix in CloudSystem Matrix and CSA in CloudSystem Enterprise?

HP CSA for Matrix and CSA

HP Cloud Service Automation automates and manages the deployment of compute resources and *complex, multi-tier applications* in *heterogeneous*, private and hybrid cloud implementations for enterprise and service provider customers. HP CSA provides advanced provisioning and lifecycle management of databases, middleware, and applications as well as compliance and service management (through its integration with Server Automation **Enterprise Edition**, Application Deployment Manager (ADM), Database and Middleware Automation (DMA) and SiteScope). Operations Orchestration operates in an unrestricted mode, and can be called upon to automate *any* task throughout the *entire* service lifecycle.

As we saw in Chapter 6, CSA for Matrix is a packaging of HP Server Automation **Standard Edition** and HP SiteScope that is integrated directly into the Matrix service catalog and orchestration engine. It gives customers an easy, cost effective way to build IaaS solutions with configuration lifecycle management, patching capability, compliance auditing, *basic* application provisioning and service monitoring. Operations Orchestration operates in a restricted mode, and is called upon to automate a *limited* set of tasks at *specific* points in the service lifecycle. We will look in more detail at Operations Orchestration later in this chapter.

CSA Foundation Components

HP CSA calls upon the services of other software products during the lifecycle process to assist with tasks such as the installation and configuration of operating systems, applications, and databases (HP Server Automation and Application Deployment Manager), and the setting up of performance monitoring (HP SiteScope). HP CSA also calls upon the services of compute providers such as VMware vCenter and Matrix infrastructure orchestration. CloudSystem Matrix also acts as a compute provider to CSA, and manages the provisioning tasks for Converged Infrastructure. It includes standard automation flows provided by HP for the lifecycle actions supported in CSA.

The components of HP CSA, and the interactions between them, can be represented by three layers. These are:

- Service Interfaces
- Service Delivery
- Service Provider

Let us now look at each layer to find out what it does (see Figure 7-1).

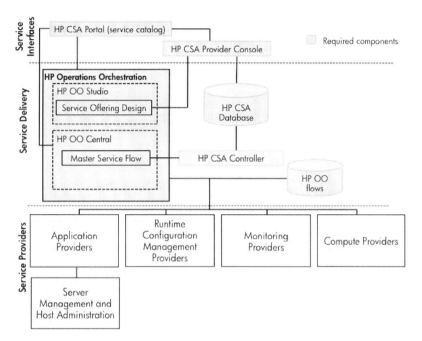

Figure 7-1. CSA Foundation components

Service Interfaces

Two interfaces are central to the operation of the CSA software:

- The **HP CSA portal** provides a simple graphical interface that enables *end-users* (also known as *subscribers* or *customers*) to subscribe to service offerings that are present in the Service Request Catalog.

- The **HP CSA Provider Console** is used by the *Service Publisher* to populate the Service Request Catalog with service offerings which end-users can then subscribe to. The HP CSA Provider Console also contains an interface for administrative functions, such as managing cloud resources and administering system settings.

There is a third interface that is not shown in the figure. CSA includes an API, and this provides a mechanism for passing data into and out of CSA.

Service Delivery

The middle layer of figure 7-1 shows HP Operations Orchestration, the HP CSA Controller, and the HP CSA Database. The interaction between these three components provides the main driving force of the CSA engine.

We will be looking in detail at HP OO later in this chapter, but to help with our understanding of the operation of HP CSA, we will provide a brief description of the major OO components now.

- **HP OO Central** and the **HP CSA Controller** work together to automate the service delivery process.

- The **HP CSA Controller** communicates with the **HP CSA Database** on an ongoing basis to access the information—such as lifecycle actions—required for completion of the lifecycle process. The database also stores information regarding service instances and their lifecycle states.

- **HP OO Studio** is used by the Service Designer to design service offerings, which are then made available to the Service Publisher.

Service Providers

The bottom layer of figure 7-1 shows the *providers* that, as the name would suggest, provide services during the lifecycle process. When a lifecycle action is initiated by the CSA controller, the resources of one or more of the Service Providers will be used. Included with HP CSA are sample service design flows for several types of Service Providers:

- **Compute Providers**: VMware vCenter and HP Matrix OE (included with CloudSystem Matrix) manage the provisioning of compute resources. HP CSA relies upon the intelligence inherent in the Compute Providers, which means that when an end-user requests a service, CSA does not have to concern itself with the detailed configuration and deployment tasks for the infrastructure (servers, storage, and network), it simply passes the request to the appropriate Compute Provider, which then builds the infrastructure as directed by CSA.

- **Application Providers**: HP Application Deployment Manager (HP ADM)—included with HP Server Automation Enterprise Edition—is the provider of choice for managing the deployment and configuration of applications on the target system

- **Runtime Configuration Management Providers**: The HP Universal Configuration Management Database (uCMDB) is a management system that stores configuration information relating to the service instances that have been built and enables this information to be shared with other applications such as Microsoft System Center Service Manager (SCCM/SMS), EMC Control Center, and IBM CCMDB.

- **Monitoring Providers**: HP SiteScope provides performance and health monitoring for infrastructure and resources.

HP CSA User Roles And Portals

Successful implementation of a CSA solution depends upon building a team of people with the necessary skills—including deployment experts, IT administrators, service designers, service publishers, and last but not least, the end-user (also known as the *subscriber*). The tasks necessary for successful implementation and operation of CSA can be categorized and assigned to specific *user roles* as shown in Figure 7-2.

CSA has a number of GUIs (portals) that have been designed to provide the most appropriate access to CSA features based on the specific user roles. There is no single *central portal,* as this would expose users to controls and functions that are not relevant to their role, and may negatively impact the user's experience. It is possible that a single person will be responsible for several user roles, and will have access to more than one of these portals.

One way of thinking about user roles and portals is that the user role represents the *who*, and the portal represents the *how*.

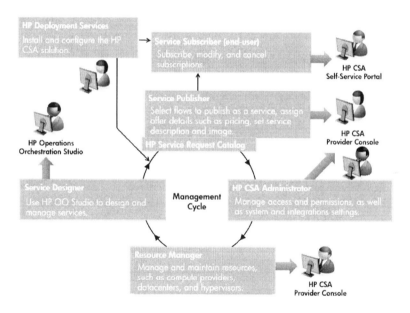

Figure 7-2. HP CSA user roles and portals

Let us now elaborate on the user roles, starting at the top left-hand side of Figure 7-2 and moving counter-clockwise.

HP Deployment Services

HP Software Professional Services Organization (PSO) is responsible for coordinating the installation of the CSA solution. They will work closely with IT professionals from HP partner organizations and from the customer's IT department to make sure that everything works as it should.

Service Designer

The Service Designer is responsible for designing service offerings using the graphical interface of the **HP Operations Orchestration Studio**. When the Service Designer has finished designing an offering, he/she places the OO *flow* into the HP OO Studio library, which makes it available to the Service Publisher.

When the Service Designer designs a service, they decide how much detail to expose to the end-user. For example, service inputs—number of CPU cores, amount of memory, etc.—can be presented in the catalog, which means that the end-user will be able to make a choice regarding the number of CPUs, amount of memory, etc. of their server. The alternative is that these parameters are hard-coded in the service design, which means that the user will not be given the ability to choose the size of their server.

Resource Management

HP CSA uses the concept of *providers*, and these represent the infrastructure on which the cloud services will be provisioned. The Resource Manager is responsible for populating the HP CSA database—which is used to maintain provider, compute, and lifecycle state information—by using the **HP CSA Provider Console** to access the Provider Creation Wizard.

Predefined service provider categories include application management platforms, compute/virtual infrastructure resources, runtime configuration management, and monitoring.

CSA Administrator

The HP CSA Administrator uses the **HP CSA Provider Console** to access a control panel to perform functions such as specifying system settings, viewing parameters for the CSA database, viewing integration settings for HP OO—including HP OO central server connectivity settings, and setting up access to remote servers—including Windows Remote Desktop, VNC and SSH settings—that are provisioned by HP CSA.

Service Publisher

The Service Publisher is responsible for making service offerings available to end-users. This is done by the Publisher locating service offering *templates*—created by the Service Designer—in the service library, and then *publishing* those service offerings to the HP Service Request Catalog. The Service Publisher uses the Service Offer Creation Wizard, via the **HP CSA Provider Console,** to select a template, and to give the service a name, category and price, before selecting the **Create** button (see Figure 7-3). In doing so, the service offering is made available for end-users to order.

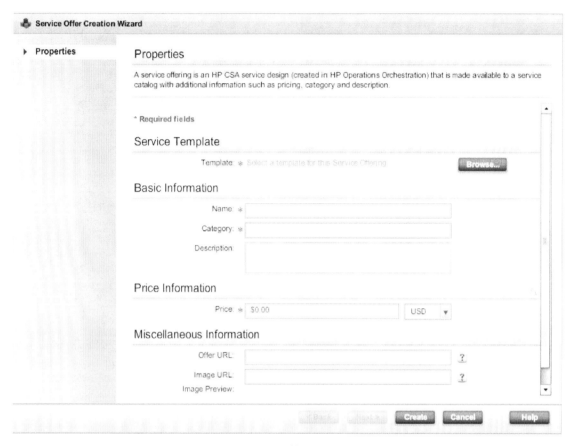

Figure 7-3. Service Offer Creation Wizard

Service Subscriber (End-User)

Service subscribers (end-users or customers) can use the **HP CSA Self-Service Portal**, which features an easy-to-use catalog-based ordering system that gives them the ability to order (subscribe) to services in the Service Request Catalog (SRC). The customer can opt to use a custom-built portal if desired.

Figure 7-4 shows an example of a user browsing the SRC and seeing that two services are available; the first being a simple IaaS service comprising a physical server, and the second being a more complex PaaS service consisting of Red Hat Enterprise Linux, Apache web server, MySQL, and the PHP programming language (LAMP). The user simply needs to click the **request** button to initiate the order for a particular service. When an end-user requests (subscribes to) a service offering, the lifecycle process is activated and provisioning begins.

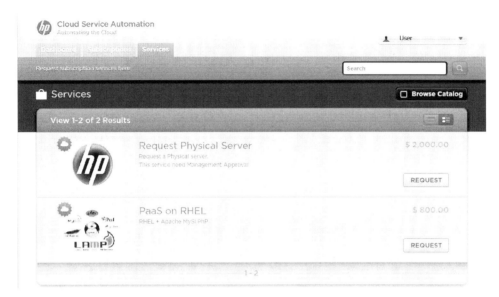

Figure 7-4. The CSA self-service portal showing available services

Having requested the service, the Subscriber will be given a subscription ID along with the status of the subscription (see Figure 7-5). The status of this particular service request is *pending*. This is because this particular service has been configured with an approval phase, which means that the request will sent to a resource manager who will need to authorize the request before provisioning can start.

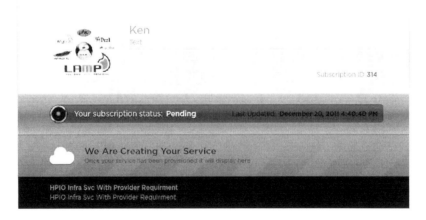

Figure 7-5. Subscription ID and status of requested service

The customer may be notified by email as each stage of the subscription process completes. The notification process is customizable, and can be configured according to the customer's needs.

After a subscription has been fulfilled, the customer will be able to view configuration details, and can also cancel or modify the service.

The HP CSA Service Lifecycle

We have seen how end-users can order a service from a catalog of service offerings—anything from a simple VM, all the way through to complex multi-tier environments complete with applications, database, and high-availability clustering. The process of service creation (and deletion) is known as the *service lifecycle* (see Figure 7-6), and it is this lifecycle that manages all phases of resource allocation and service delivery. As you can imagine, managing all of the tasks necessary to provision complex, multi-tier environments requires a great deal of coordination. HP CSA achieves this coordination through *lifecycle phases*.

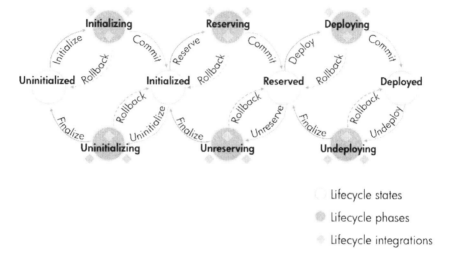

Figure 7-6. The CSA service lifecycle

When an end-user orders a service, the CSA Controller attempts to progress from the initial *uninitialized* state through to the final *deployed* state (updating the CSA database as it goes), at which time the end-user is notified that the service has been created and is ready for use.

Let us use an example of an end-user ordering a service and follow the lifecycle process from beginning to end to see what happens.

During the *initializing* phase, the available resources are evaluated to make sure that the resources required by the new service are actually available. Once the availability of resources has been confirmed, the process reaches the *initialized* state. If all resources are available, the *reserving* phase will attempt to reserve the resources. Assuming that all resources been successfully reserved, the process reaches the *reserved* state. From here, the process moves into the *deploying* phase and attempts to deploy all of the resources that have being reserved. The end-user will be able see the progression of the service lifecycle by viewing the status reports in the CSA self-service portal.

The process we have just described is the ideal scenario, but what happens if problems are encountered along the way?

The service lifecycle has been designed to provide *rollback* capability in all phases of the process. This rollback capability takes care of situations where, for whatever reason, there is a failure with resource allocation. It could be that the server we are trying to allocate has a hardware failure. Without the rollback capability, the process would continue to attempt to allocate the server forever, and would generate a series of error messages. Other resources required for the service may have been allocated successfully, and without the rollback capability, these resources would be held forever, even though the server failure has prevented the service creation from completing successfully. The rollback capability gives the lifecycle process an escape mechanism, allowing it to wind back to the previous state in the process, and to return any allocated resources back to the pool of free resources, where they can be used by someone else.

Let us now use the same example, but now we will introduce the rollback.

During the initializing phase, the available resources are evaluated to make sure that the resources required by the new service are actually available. Once the availability of resources has been confirmed, the process reaches the initialized state. If all of the necessary resources are not available, the process will roll back to the uninitialized state and an error message may be generated. If all resources are available, the reserving phase will attempt to reserve the resources. Again, if there is a problem with reserving any of the resources, the process will roll back to the initialized state, whereupon the reservation attempt may be repeated. If the reservation of resources fails again, the process will roll back to the uninitialized state and an error message will be generated and a trouble ticket may be generated. Assuming that all resources been successfully reserved, the process reaches the reserved state. From here, the process moves into the deploying phase and attempts to deploy all of the resources that have being reserved. If the deployment fails for any reason, the process will roll back to the reserved state whereupon the deploying phase may be retried. If it fails again, an error message may be generated and a trouble ticket issued.

When the end-user has finished with the service, or when the lease expires, the lifecycle process runs in reverse, from the deployed state back to the uninitialized state, freeing up resources and updating the CSA database as it goes.

HP CSA Lifecycle Integrations

The CSA service lifecycle can call upon the services of external functions by using *lifecycle integrations* as shown in Figure 7-6. These lifecycle integrations make it possible to perform actions such as sending an email message at a particular phase in the lifecycle, or integrating with an external monitoring product such as HP TippingPoint IPS. There are eighteen integration points in total; one before, one during, and one after each lifecycle phase.

HP Operations Orchestration

HP Operations Orchestration (HP OO) is a software solution that automates datacenter tasks and processes using *workflows* (also known as *ops flows* or *flows*) that help IT teams rapidly and consistently execute change in the datacenter.

HP OO is also known as a *run book* automation solution, in that it is used to take a series of individual tasks and assemble those tasks into an end-to-end process that can be executed at will. While HP OO can automate any task that can be programmed, its strength lies in managing a diverse range of activities in the cloud environment; everything from simple repetitive daily tasks like checking the status of a particular system—maybe using a command like **ping** or **uptime**, all the way through to highly-complex, end-to-end processes that integrate with other management systems. An example of a more complex process could be responding to events generated by system monitoring tools and executing scripts that automatically troubleshoot and repair problems with server, storage, and network devices, and providing status updates to an external ticketing system.

HP OO consists of two major components:

- **HP OO Studio**: A standalone authoring program used by flow authors to create, modify, and test flows. As previously mentioned, the CSA Service Designer uses OO Studio to design service offerings which are then made available to the Service Publisher. Figure 6-2 in Chapter 6 shows the OO Studio interface and an OO workflow called **DeploySitescopeMonitor**.

- **HP OO Central**: Contains the Master Service Flow, which is responsible for request verification, approval, and service activation. When an end-user subscribes to (requests) a service (from the Service Request Catalog), the request is sent to the Master Service Flow in HP OO Central, which determines whether the service instance should be created, modified, or terminated. The Master Service Flow activates the HP CSA Controller, which with OO Central drives the service lifecycle actions to launch task-specific flows (such as deploying a SiteScope monitor or cloning a virtual machine).
  OO Central also includes a web-based interface in which users can run flows, analyze data generated by run flows, and administer the system. Figure 7-7 shows an example of the available flows in the Flow Library.

Figure 7-7. HP OO Central

Earlier in this chapter we spoke of a potential source of confusion when comparing CSA for Matrix and CSA software. Another potential source of confusion presents itself when comparing the capabilities of Matrix OE infrastructure orchestration (IO) and Operations Orchestration. Why does it appear that we use two separate orchestration engines?

The Orchestration Engines

The HP CloudSystem uses Operations Orchestration (OO) engines in two places; the first is embedded in the Matrix OE infrastructure orchestration (IO), and the second is in Cloud Service Automation.

The CloudSystem Matrix Operating Environment includes IO, which includes an embedded OO operating in restricted mode, whereas CloudSystem Enterprise (and CloudSystem Service Provider) include CSA with a full version of OO. CloudSystem Matrix customers can purchase the full version of OO without having to upgrade to CloudSystem Enterprise.

Infrastructure orchestration is a core element of the Matrix OE and drives infrastructure provisioning by interpreting infrastructure templates, called IO templates. To deploy an instance, IO takes the templates created in the IO Template Designer and then calls upon underlying resource pool managers and configuration subsystems, such as Server Automation or RDP, to provision services. This is illustrated on the lower left side of Figure 7-8. (The dotted arrows in the figure signify the design phase, while the solid arrows signify run-time operations.)

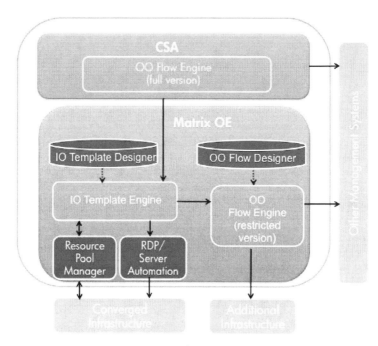

Figure 7-8. Orchestration engines

The Matrix OE embedded Operations Orchestration flow engine is supplied with a restricted use license (as shown on the right-hand side of Figure 7-8), and a set of pre-built OO flows. The restricted use license of the Matrix OE embedded OO engine allows for flows to be triggered only as pre- and post-provisioning flows related to IO provisioning tasks. The supplied pre-built OO flows represent a small infrastructure-relevant subset of the more than 4000 OO flows that comes with the full OO. During pre- and post-provisioning of infrastructure components, the IO system will call OO flows if they are defined. These flows can be used to perform extra configuration steps that cannot be performed by the standard IO templates. For example, after IO has provisioned a server an OO flow can be used to add the server's IP address to a load balancer. The OO flows also allow for integration with other management systems, for example, a change management system, and can perform actions such as updating an Asset Management system when a server is configured.

The full Operations Orchestration (OO) flow engine used in CSA is a fully generic workflow engine that requires no understanding of infrastructure templates but has automation flexibility for managing the service lifecycle in providers.

In CloudSystem Enterprise, HP CSA is used to orchestrate the overall service lifecycle flow. This lifecycle flow can call upon the Matrix compute provider, which uses IO for provisioning infrastructure, and then OO orchestrates other aspects of delivering the service such as provisioning complex, multi-tier applications and database packages and communicating with external management systems.

Out-of-Box Service Designs

As mentioned earlier, HP CSA includes out-of-box (OOB) service designs to manage orchestration activity for common services, and rather than having to create custom OO flows to drive each service, OO delegates much of the task-specific automation the specialist providers. To deploy services, CSA orchestrates the lifecycle actions (initialize, reserve, deploy, etc.) between multiple providers. Operations Orchestration (OO) is used to communicate between the CSA controller and CSA's supported providers, where the providers take on the responsibility for co-ordinating the tasks to deploy the services within their own domain. For example, VMware vSphere owns the execution of VM provisioning and HP MOE owns the execution of converged infrastructure provisioning.

Out-of-box CSA Service Designs support predefined flows specific to the provider and lifecycle action, and are located in the HP Operations Orchestration Studio Published Designs folder. They do not require customization. The HP CSA team maintains and supports the predefined CSA Controller/providers OO flows.

The Matrix OOB service designs make direct use of Matrix templates that have been created in the MOE IO designer tool. CSA understands MOE templates provided they fit with one of the OOB service designs shown below. For example, if the MOE template is pure IO then there is an OOB provider service that permits CSA to invoke the Matrix template entitled **Matrix Provisioned Cloud**. CSA can invoke any template that has been designed in the IO designer, (and can provide the necessary parameters for the instance). When CSA uses the OOB service design no additional OO work is required since this has already been provided in the IO standard flows.

Matrix OOB service designs are provided for two Compute Providers; HP IO, and VMware vCenter, and these are listed in Table 7-1 along with some of their attributes.

Table 7-1. Matrix OOB service designs

HP IO Compute Provider Service Designs	
Design Name	**Attributes**
Matrix Provisioned Cloud	HP IO Compute Provider Illustrates how to invoke a complex service design template through HP infrastructure orchestration (IO)
Matrix Provisioned Cloud (Compute and Applications)	HP IO Compute Provider One multi-tier application installed and managed by HP SA with ADM
Matrix Provisioned Cloud (Compute and Monitors)	HP IO Compute Provider SiteScope server monitoring template
Matrix Provisioned Cloud (Compute and uCMDB)	HP IO Compute Provider Infrastructure configuration items (CIs) provisioned into HP uCMDB
Matrix Provisioned Cloud (Compute Application, Sitescope and uCMDB)	HP IO Compute Provider One multi-tier application installed and managed by HP SA with ADM SiteScope server monitoring template. Infrastructure configuration items (CIs) are provisioned into HP Universal CMDB

VMware vCenter Compute Provider Service Designs

Design Name	Attributes
Managed Simple Compute - Linux on vCenter with uCMDB	VMware vCenter Compute Provider A simple Linux infrastructure with a configurable number of servers. Provides Stop, Start, Suspend, and Restart functionality for each server. Infrastructure CIs provisioned into HP Universal CMDB. Sends basic email notifications
Monitored and Managed Application - Linux on vCenter with ADM Sitescope and uCMDB	VMware vCenter Compute Provider A simple Linux infrastructure with LAMP stack application deployment and a configurable number of servers Provides Stop, Start, Suspend, and Restart functionality for each server One multi-tier application installed and managed by HP SA with ADM SiteScope server monitoring template is configured for each server Infrastructure CIs provisioned into HP Universal CMDB Sends basic email notifications
Monitored Simple Compute - Linux on vCenter with Site-Scope	VMware vCenter Compute Provider A simple Linux infrastructure with a configurable number of servers Provides Stop, Start, Suspend, and Restart functionality for each server SiteScope server monitoring template is configured for each server Sends basic email notifications
Simple Application - Linux on vCenter with ADM	VMware vCenter Compute Provider A simple Linux infrastructure with LAMP stack application deployment and with a configurable number of servers Provides Stop, Start, Suspend, and Restart functionality for each server One multi-tier application installed and managed by HP SA with ADM Sends basic email notifications
Simple Compute - Linux on vCenter	VMware vCenter Compute Provider A simple Linux infrastructure with a configurable number of servers Provides Stop, Start, Suspend, and Restart functionality for each server Sends basic email notifications

Provisioning of multi-tier applications and database packages can be very complex, and CloudSystem Enterprise calls upon the services of Server Automation Enterprise Edition to manage the process.

HP Server Automation (SA) Enterprise Edition

In Chapter 6, we stated that there are two versions of HP Server Automation; the Starter Edition that is supplied with CloudSystem Matrix, and the Enterprise Edition that is included with CloudSystem Enterprise and CloudSystem Service Provider. We also said that Server Automation Enterprise Edition builds on the functionality of the Starter Edition by adding:

- HP Application Deployment Manager (ADM): For managing complex, multi-server, multi-tier applications

- Satellite: For managing remote facilities with a single SA core and one or more satellites; each satellite containing a small subset of SA core components

- Multimaster Mesh: For managing remote facilities by installing multiple SA cores

- Unlimited physical and virtual servers (operating system instances).

We will now describe the functionality of ADM, Multimaster Mesh, and Satellite installations.

HP Application Deployment Manager (ADM)

Enterprise applications typically consist of one or more *tiers*; for example an application tier, a web tier, and a database tier. Each tier includes a number of *components* that implement the functions of the application. For example, an application may consist of components such as HTML files, JAR files, databases, configuration files, and Windows registry settings. Each application can have multiple *releases*, and each release, in turn, may have multiple *versions*. Applications may also be configured with *rollback* and *undeploy* options for each component. When rollback is enabled, a backup will be performed before a new version of the application is installed, and if the installation fails for any reason, rollback instructions will be used to return the application to its previous state. If undeploy is enabled, the application can be uninstalled easily using a predefined set of instructions.

In a software development environment, the development lifecycle typically sees an application release moving from the Development stage to the Quality Assurance (QA) stage, whereupon the application will go through several cycles of testing and fixing problems (in collaboration with the software developers). When the application has been approved by QA, it may be deployed in a pre-production environment for performance testing prior to being deployed into the production environment.

Managing the successful development and deployment of applications that include multiple tiers, each with multiple components, multiple releases and multiple versions, can be a major headache for IT administrators. This process often requires a great deal of communication and coordination between multiple different organizations, and when performed manually, the process can be very time-consuming and error-prone.

The inclusion of HP Application Deployment Manager (ADM) with CloudSystem Enterprise enables full application stack management and full application lifecycle management. HP ADM provides a central knowledge repository and a web-based user interface, through which everyone involved in the process can view or enter data that is relevant to their role. This makes it possible—even in large enterprises with lots of applications changing and new applications being required—to perform repeatable, consistent deployment across the lifecycle. Different teams can work on different applications, releases, and versions, and because the lifecycle status of each application is tracked for each stage and version, application performance and functionality are consistent from one stage to the next, and one environment to the next.

With ADM, software teams can model the application for each phase of its lifecycle and also model the deployment targets. In the event that a software update causes problems, the software can easily be rolled back to a previous version.

Best-practice provisioning and configuration of enterprise application server instances is provided, along with patching single or multiple application servers with single or multiple patches. Application teams are provided with self-service, audited access to process automation throughout the development cycle. J2EE web application archive (WAR) and enterprise application archive (EAR) deployments are supported.

ADM also integrates with other HP software technologies to further simplify the process. One of these other software technologies is HP Database and Middleware Automation, which we will cover later in this chapter.

HP SA Multimaster Mesh and Satellite Topologies

In Chapter 6, we described the three main SA topologies as *Single Core*, *Multimaster Mesh* and *Satellite*. We also said that HP SA software includes a number of components—collectively known as a *core*—running on one or more physical or virtual servers, known as *core* servers. A small network of servers in a single facility can easily be managed by a single core installation. However, large, geographically-dispersed networks will require a Multimaster Mesh installation—in which two or more cores work together, a Satellite installation—in which a small subset of SA core components are installed on remote sites, or a combination of both.

First we will look at the Satellite topology, then we will go on to the Multimaster Mesh, and then we will finish off by looking at a Multimaster Mesh installation with several Satellites.

Satellite Topology

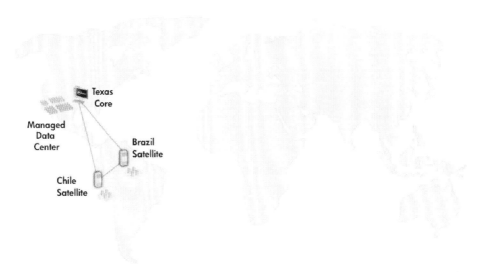

Figure 7-9. SA Satellite topology

Figure 7-9 shows a relatively simple installation with one SA core and its managed datacenter located in Texas, and two satellite installations; one in Brazil and one in Chile. The Texas data center has several hundred servers, and to manage the servers effectively, an SA Core installation is required.

This Single Core consists of several components (omitted from the figure for simplicity), including:

- **The Software Repository**: This is where the binaries/packages/source for software/application provisioning and remediation is uploaded and stored.

- **The Model Repository**: This requires either the SA-supplied Oracle database or an existing Oracle installation and stores an inventory of all managed servers, the hardware (including memory, CPUs, storage capacity) and software (operating system and applications) associated with these servers. This database also stores an inventory of operating system installation media (not the media itself; that is stored on the OS Provisioning Media Server), an inventory of software available for installation (again, not the media itself; that is stored in the Software Repository).

- **A Core Gateway and an Agent Gateway**: The Core Gateway communicates directly with Agent Gateways passing requests and responses to and from Core Components.

- **A Management Gateway**: Manages communication between SA Cores and between SA Cores and Satellites.

The branch offices in Brazil and Chile only have a few servers, and can be adequately managed by SA satellites. These satellites contain a small subset of SA core components including:

- **A Software Repository Cache**: This contains a local copy of the contents of the software repository from the SA Core. Having a local copy of the software repository on the Satellites can decrease network traffic and increase performance when software is being installed or updated on a satellite's managed servers.

- **A Satellite Agent Gateway**: This manages communications between the Satellite and the Core through the Core's Management Gateway

- **An optional OS Provisioning Boot Server and Media Server**: The operating system (OS) Provisioning Boot Server takes part in the OS provisioning process and enables network booting of Sun and x86 systems. The Media Server is responsible for providing network access to vendor-supplied OS media during the OS provisioning process.

Some of the remote branch offices may be connected to their Core installation using a low-bandwidth network link, and to make sure that Satellite network traffic does not interfere with other important network traffic, the Satellite's network bandwidth can be restricted to a specific bit rate.

Multimaster Mesh Topology

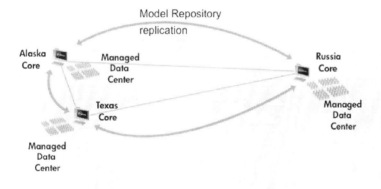

Figure 7-10. SA Multimaster Mesh topology

A Multimaster Mesh is a set of two or more SA Cores that communicate through Management Gateways and can perform synchronization of the data about their Managed Servers contained in their respective Model Repositories over the network.

Figure 7-10 shows a Multimaster Mesh installation with SA cores and their associated managed datacenters in Alaska Texas, and Russia. Each data center has several hundred servers, and to manage the servers effectively, an SA Core installation is required in each location.

Changes to the data in any Model Repository in a Multimaster Mesh are broadcast to all other Model repositories in the Mesh. This replication capability enables enterprises to maintain a blueprint of software and environment characteristics for each facility, making it easy to rebuild the infrastructure in the event of a disaster. It also provides the ability to easily provision additional capacity, distribute updates, and share software builds, templates and dependencies across multiple facilities.

Managed Servers in a Multimaster Mesh can be centrally administered from any facility with a Core installation. Administration is not locked into a single location or even restricted geographically. This means that an administrator could use the SA client at the Alaska facility and manage servers that belong to the Russia facility (assuming that he or she has the appropriate access rights).

Multimaster Mesh Plus Satellite Topology

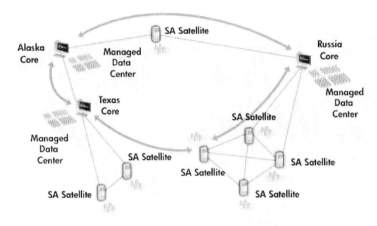

Figure 7-11. SA Multimaster Mesh with Satellites topology

In environments that have multiple datacenters *and* multiple branch offices, the Multimaster Mesh and Satellite topologies can be combined. Figure 7-11 shows SA cores in Alaska, Texas, and Russia—each managing their own data center, and Satellite installations in multiple locations—each managing their own small network of servers.

HP Database and Middleware Automation

HP Database and Middleware Automation (DMA) is included with CloudSystem Enterprise and provides a content library (delivered via solution packs) for database and middleware management. Solution packs are HP-tested and certified out-of-the-box automation content, including automation steps, workflows, reports, and configuration discovery. DMA solution packs can be deployed within minutes and are fully customizable to meet specific use cases. DMA solution packs can also be upgraded rapidly, which enables HP to deliver critical updates, such as support for new middleware platform versions and changes in platform patching processes.

DMA provisions simple and complex application architectures onto existing infrastructure, and effectively is the enabler of PaaS, as it provides the ability to provision middleware and databases; components that add significant value to a PaaS solution. After applications—including middleware and databases—have been provisioned and are up and running, DMA can manage those applications, providing pre-packaged workflows for application patching, compliance, and code release—eliminating the need for manual customization.

DMA solution packs are updated frequently to support new versions and configurations. Packs are available for Oracle Database, Microsoft SQL Server, IBM DB2 Universal Database (UDB), Sybase, IBM WebSphere Application Server and Oracle WebLogic. Current packs include:

- App Server Patching Solution Pack: Enables customers to quickly identify and roll out patches to heterogeneous application servers.

- App Server Provisioning Solution Pack: Provides point-and-click application server build operations that deploy, install and configure application server binaries and components.

- App Server Release Management Solution Pack: Streamlines application server code deployments by providing configuration of application server settings, deployment of application components and rollback of deployments and configurations.

- Database Compliance Solution Pack: Provides end-to-end database compliance, including compliance auditing, comprehensive compliance reports, and resolution of non-compliant database configurations.

- Database Patching Solution Pack: Enables customers to quickly identify patch candidates, stage patch binaries and roll out patches to various databases. Patch rollback is also included.

- Database Provisioning Solution Pack: Provides four types of point-and-click database build operations; deploy and install database binaries, configure database components, create golden master configurations from any existing database and clone to any target server, and database upgrades.

- Database Release Management Solution Pack: Streamlines database code deployments by providing process governance and version validation. The syntax of code is checked prior to deployment to avoid potential problems.

HP Network Automation (NA)

Back in Chapter 1 when we described the fundamentals of cloud computing, we said that resources are made available over a network (intranet or Internet) and are accessed through client systems. It should be fairly obvious that without ubiquitous, highly-available, high-performance networking, cloud computing simply would not be possible.

In a cloud environment the network needs to be configured for each tenant. The configuration will include basic switches and routers, and network services like firewalls and load balancers. HP Network Automation (NA) understands the interfaces to these devices, which means that a cloud service designer is free from the need to have product-specific knowledge. HP NA enables the management of the client network in a heterogeneous network.

In order to provide such a networking infrastructure, telecommunications service providers need to deal with four primary challenges:

- **Visibility**—Keeping track of device inventory, configurations, and software versions in a geographically-dispersed network infrastructure of hundreds or thousands of devices can be a major headache. In addition, there may be software dependencies that, unless adequately understood, have the potential for disrupting business-critical applications. For example, it may be that traffic for a particular critical application is dependent upon a particular switch port. If this port becomes unavailable for any reason—either from a hardware or software failure, or perhaps more likely, as a result of a misconfiguration—the business will suffer.

- **Compliance**—The consequences of audit failures are rarely pleasant, and businesses often invest a large amount of time and money in order to remain compliant. Out-dated equipment and security vulnerabilities conspire to compound the challenge of remaining compliant.

- **Growth**—The term *ubiquitous networking* alludes to the fact that networks need to be omnipresent (everywhere), and cloud computing's need for ubiquitous networking is leading, amongst other factors, to explosive growth in the number of networking devices being deployed. Not only are the networks growing, but telcos are under pressure to support applications such as VoIP, video-on-demand, and online gaming.

- **Resource constraints**—Network managers are being expected to do more with less; the number of network devices to be managed is increasing dramatically, and budgets may be flat, or even going in the opposite direction. In multi-vendor environments, with multiple separate network management tools, the ratio of devices to network administrators is nowhere near as high as it could be with a unified management system.

In order to deal with these challenges, network operators would be wise to consider two complimentary strategies:

1. Invest in a unified, single-pane-of-glass network management solution that provides visibility across entire networks, enabling complete management of resources, services and users. HP Intelligent Management Center (IMC) can provide this.

2. Automate as much of the management of the network as possible. This is where HP Network Automation comes in. HP NA automates the complete operational lifecycle of network devices from provisioning to policy-based change management, compliance, and security administration.

Many networks are heterogeneous in nature, and to provide maximum value, HP NA supports a set of network devices from over 70 vendors—including virtual devices—providing comprehensive network change and configuration management coverage for an extensive range of devices.

HP NA can be combined with HP Network Node Manager i (NNMi) software to deliver an integrated solution that unifies network fault, availability, and performance with change, configuration, compliance, and automated diagnostics.

Let us now look at the functionality of HP NA using the four pillars of **Discover and Track**, **Change and Configure**, **Audit and Enforce**, and **Maintain and Support** (see Figure 7-12.

Note

If you feel that you have had a flash of déjà vu, and that you have seen these four pillars before, you are not entirely incorrect. In Chapter 6, we saw the four pillars of HP Server Automation, which shares the same origins as HP NA (and HP Operations Orchestration for that matter).

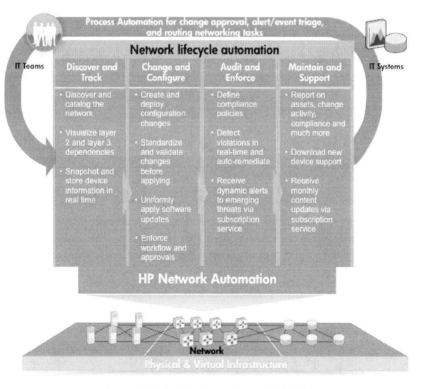

Figure 7-12. The four pillars of HP NA

Discover and Track

There is a saying that goes along the lines of "if it cannot be measured, it cannot be managed", and in a networking environment, this can be translated into "if you do not know what devices are on your network, cannot manage them". HP NA automates the discovery of network devices, and this eliminates the need for network administrators to spend their time performing manual discovery.

Many network administrators may be comfortable with using a CLI, and while this is a useful skill, the ability to quickly generate layer 2 and layer 3 graphical representations of the network can help to quickly identify devices that are inactive or out of compliance. This capability also eliminates the laborious process of manually creating network diagrams. Layer 2 network maps can identify the hosts connected to specific switches or interfaces by MAC address.

The current state of the network, including topology and virtual LAN (vLAN) information can be captured in a snapshot. Taking a snapshot means that the configuration data can be stored, checked, and backed up. In the event that a network device fails, the device configuration snapshot can be used to rapidly prepare a replacement device for use.

Change and Configure

Rather than network administrators having to manually apply configuration changes to each individual device, they can deploy network-wide configuration changes quickly, reliably, and systematically. If a configuration error causes a network problem, they can easily and quickly repair the configuration and bring the network device(s) back into service.

Network configuration changes can be automatically validated against policies to proactively avoid misconfigurations and noncompliant changes. If a particular change is found to be out of compliance, HP NA alerts the administrator to make appropriate corrections before applying the change.

Automated software synchronization and image management makes it possible to create a software repository, and to synchronize all device software images across the entire network. Image management can automatically identify, download, and install the recommended software image for network devices.

Complex change management approval processes with flexible rules can be created and enforced in real time. Changes—including changes made by a direct command line interface (CLI) session—can be blocked until they have been cleared by the approval process. Multiple tasks can be combined into a project workflow to determine whether the system should proceed to the next step.

Audit And Enforce

HP NA can take device configuration snapshots whenever changes are detected, and this can feed into the compliance checking and auto-remediation function of HP NA. The HP NA policy engine can check to see whether the configuration meets corporate or external standards. Policies could define the strength of device passwords, whether appropriate ACLs have been defined, or the policy could be more complex and define settings for each individual interface.

Devices that violate standards and are found to be non-compliant can be remediated (brought back into compliance) automatically.

The HP Live Network website at http://www.hp.com/go/livenetwork provides access to the Security & Compliance Service for Network Automation. This is a subscription service that delivers security vulnerability policies and up-to-date compliance policies that can help with identifying networking issues. With these detailed policies, security and compliance issues can be rectified quickly, and without expending a lot of resources.

Maintain and Support

The HP Business Service Automation (BSA) Essentials reporting package is included with HP NA, and this makes it possible to create customized network compliance reports for ITIL, SOX, HIPAA, PCI DSS, amongst others.

Drivers for new devices can be downloaded from the HP Live Network, which provides access to free Network Automation content provided by HP. This includes drivers, command scripts, policies and other Network Automation content.

The HP live network also provides access to paid-for content via a subscription service.

HP NA Deployment Topology

HP NA topology is very similar to the topology of HP SA deployments. HP NA supports Single Core, Multi-Master and Satellite deployments just like HP SA, and can be used to implement highly-available and disaster-tolerant network management solutions for geographically-dispersed networks.

In summary, HP Network Automation helps large enterprises and service providers to reduce costs by automating time-consuming manual change, configuration, and compliance tasks. Network security can be enhanced by using the integrated security alert service to help with recognizing and remediating security vulnerabilities before they affect the network. Network stability and uptime can be optimized by preventing the inconsistencies and misconfigurations that are at the root of many network problems. Large enterprises and service providers running a public cloud need to mitigate the risk of downtime, and HP NA can play a major role in minimizing the time and effort needed to perform major upgrades or fixes to network devices in this environment.

HP CSA Installation and Configuration

Finally, let us look at some of the configuration steps in setting up a CSA environment. Figure 7-13 shows an example of the CSA configuration process.

 Note
The installation and configuration process may change with new versions of the CSA product.

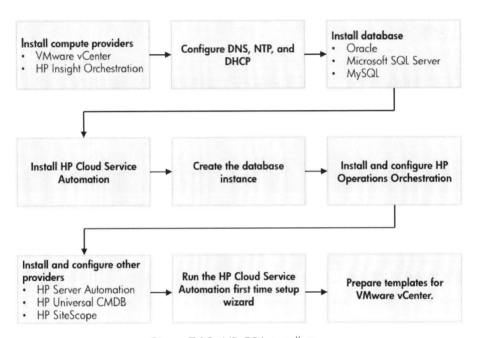

Figure 7-13. HP CSA installation

The installation needs to be planned properly as some choices have to be made regarding which providers and database will be used as well as what type of security/user authentication should be used.

1. Install Compute Providers. These are used to provision infrastructure for HP Cloud Service Automation:

   ■ VMware

   ■ HP Matrix infrastructure orchestration (included with Matrix OE)

2. Configure DNS, NTP and DHCP on the CSA server.

   ■ Each of the HP Cloud Service Automation solution products communicate with each other using DNS name and address resolution.

   ■ All HP CSA servers should be configured to synchronize with a Network Time Protocol (NTP) source that is continuously available.

- A working DHCP server is needed to dynamically assign IP addresses to new VMs provisioned by HP CSA.

3. Select and install resource management database. This database is used by HP CSA for resource management; other providers may also have database requirements:

   - Oracle

   - Microsoft SQL Server

   - MySQL

4. Install HP CSA

   - HP recommends that HP CSA is installed on the same server as HP Operations Orchestration

5. Create the database instance

   - The CSA installation includes scripts that can be used to create the database instance for one of the supported database management systems.

6. If an existing OO installation does not exist, install and configure HP OO. Otherwise, patch and update existing OO installation as appropriate.

   - Install HP Operations Orchestration Central and Studio

   - Install Patch and Content Installer Updates

7. Install and configure additional providers (for monitoring, configuration management, and application deployment):

   - HP SiteScope for monitoring

   - HP Universal CMDB for configuration management

   - HP Application Deployment Manager for application deployment

8. Run the HP CSA First Time Setup Wizard

   - The First Time Setup Wizard completes configuration of the database connection and HP Operations Orchestration settings.

9. Prepare templates for VMware vCenter

   - HP CSA creates virtual machines from virtual machine templates. A template that includes HP Server Automation Agent software must be installed to allow applications (such as Apache and MySQL) to be deployed to the image.

There are several additional optional configuration steps that are highly recommended:

- Configure SSL security for Service Request Catalog and the Provider Console

- Configure LDAP authentication for Service Request Catalog

- Configure LDAP authentication for the Provider Console

For information about the supported components and versions, see the *HP Cloud Service Automation—Solution and Software Support Matrix.*

HP CloudSystem Enterprise Product Mapping

Now that we have described the individual components of the CloudSystem Enterprise solution, let us finish this chapter by seeing which products are responsible for providing the functions in the Demand, Delivery and Supply layers of the HP Cloud Functional Reference Architecture, and in the Design/deploy, Provision, Use, and Assure phases of the cloud services lifecycle. Figure 7-14 shows a high-level overview of the product mapping, and Figure 7-15 shows a more detailed view.

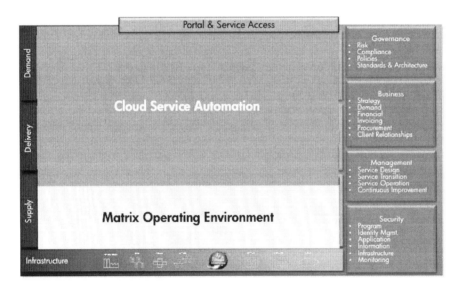

Figure 7-14. HP CloudSystem Enterprise product mapping overview

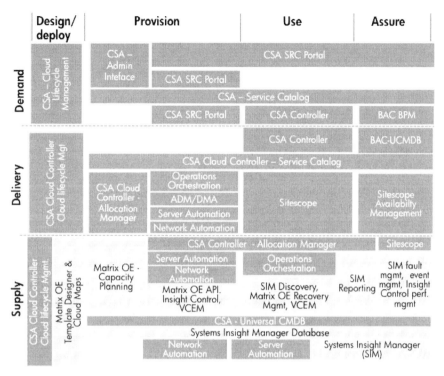

Figure 7-15. HP CloudSystem Enterprise product mapping detail

---

 Note

The features in light grey are provided by Matrix OE and the features in dark grey are provided by HP CSA.

Test Preparation Questions and Answers

The following questions will help you measure your understanding of the material presented in this chapter. Read all the choices carefully, as there may be more than one correct answer. Choose all correct answers for each question.

Questions

1. What distinguishes the HP CloudSystem Enterprise from the CloudSystem Matrix?

    a. It utilizes the Matrix OE.

    b. It includes Database and Middleware Automation software.

    c. It is designed for service providers.

    d. It is based on HP Blade technology.

2. Which product is a required component of Cloud Service Automation?

    a. HP SiteScope

    b. HP Server Automation

    c. HP Operations Orchestration

    d. HP infrastructure orchestration

3. What is the purpose of HP CSA lifecycle integrations?

    a. To call upon the services of external providers

    b. To provide multi-site failover

    c. To streamline application development

    d. To assist with the design of Service Templates

4. What is HP Operations Orchestration?

    a. An installation tool for VMs

    b. A process automation solution

    c. An infrastructure monitoring tool

    d. A studio of troubleshooting tools

5. How does Server Automation Enterprise Edition build upon the functionality of the Starter Edition?

    a. It allows management of an unlimited number of servers.

    b. It gives customers the ability to provision the infrastructure.

    c. It provides agentless monitors.

    d. It includes Matrix OE.

6. What is Network Automation designed to accomplish?

    a. It allows proactive avoidance of misconfigurations.

    b. It gives customers the ability to back up their data.

    c. It provisions applications automatically.

    d. It installs Matrix OE.

7. How does Network Automation reduce administration costs?

    a. It improves administrator training using network-based lessons.

    b. It improves user response times by providing Auto Port Trunking

    c. It deploys network-wide configuration changes quickly and reliably

    d. It enables business applications to be failed over to a DR site.

8. What is the first task in setting up a CSA environment?

    a. run the HP CSA first time setup wizard

    b. install and configure HP OO

    c. install compute providers

    d. run a baseline infrastructure provisioning report

Answers

1. ☑ **B.** Database and Middleware Automation software is included with the HP Cloudsystem Enterprise.
   ☒ **A** is incorrect, because all CloudSystems use Matrix OE. **C** is incorrect, because this is the HP CloudSystem Service provider. **D** is incorrect, because all CloudSystems are based on HP Blade technology.

2. ☑ **C.** HP Operations Orchestration is a required component of Cloud Service Automation.
   ☒ **A** is incorrect, because it is an integrated solution. **B** is incorrect, because it is an integrated solution. **D** is incorrect, because it is an integrated solution.

3. ☑ **A.** HP CSA Lifecycle Integrations provide a mechanism for calling upon the services of external providers.
   ☒ **B** is incorrect, because Lifecycle Integrations do not provide multi-site failover. **C** is incorrect, because Lifecycle Integrations do not streamline application development. **D** is incorrect, because CSA is not targeted at application development.

4. ☑ **B.** HP Operations Orchestration is a process automation solution.
   ☒ **A** is incorrect, because OO is not just a VM installation tool. **C** is incorrect, because OO is not a monitoring tool. **D** is incorrect, because Lifecycle Integrations do not assist with the design of Service Templates.

5. ☑ **A.** The Server Automation Enterprise Edition builds upon the functionality of the Starter Edition by allowing management of an unlimited number of servers.
   ☒ **B** is incorrect, because this applies to the Starter Edition. **C** is incorrect, because this is in the Starter Edition. **D** is incorrect, because Matrix OE is included in all CloudSystem solutions.

6. ☑ **A.** Network Automation allows proactive avoidance of misconfigurations.
   ☒ **B** is incorrect, because HP NA is not used for data backup. **C** is incorrect, because HP NA does not provision applications automatically. **D** is incorrect, because HP NA is concerned with device management; it does not install Matrix OE.

7. ☑ **C.** Network Automation reduces administration costs by deploying network-wide configuration changes quickly and reliably.
   ☒ **A** is incorrect, because training is not a function of HP NA. **B** is incorrect, because user response times not a primary objective. **D** is incorrect, because DR for business applications is not a feature of HP NA.

8. ☑ **C.** The first task in setting up a CSA environment is to install compute providers.
   ☒ **A** is incorrect, because this is step 8. **B** is incorrect, because this is step 6. **D** is incorrect, because this is not one of the installation and configuration steps.

8 HP CloudSystem Service Provider

EXAM OBJECTIVES

✓ Define HP CloudSystem Service Provider.

✓ Describe HP Aggregation Platform for SaaS (AP4SaaS) concepts and components.

ASSUMED KNOWLEDGE

You should be in possession of the HP APC - Converged Infrastructure Solutions (2010) certification.

INTRODUCTION

We have seen that HP CloudSystem is available in three configurations: CloudSystem Matrix, CloudSystem Enterprise and CloudSystem Service Provider and that each of the offerings is based on a single unified architecture combining hardware, software and services.

In this chapter, we will look in detail at HP CloudSystem Service Provider and, in particular, at the HP Aggregation Platform for SaaS (AP4SaaS) software components that are an integral part of the solution.

Before we look in detail at the components of CloudSystem Service Provider, it will be worthwhile to describe the business challenges that service providers face, and that will help us to understand the value proposition for CloudSystem Service Provider.

Service Provider Business Challenges

Service providers face the same primary challenge as all commercial enterprises; namely, to increase profitability. There are only two ways to achieve this; the first is to increase revenue and the second is to decrease costs (or a combination of both). Revenue can be increased by attracting new customers, selling a wider range of products to existing customers, or selling higher-margin products to both new and existing customers. The first option, attracting new customers, will be a priority for all service providers, leading to a great deal of competitive pressure. For hosting providers, managed service providers (MSPs), and communications service providers (CSPs), this means competing against public cloud suppliers like Amazon, Google, and Microsoft. The second and third options involve being able to quickly and cost-effectively bring new products and services to market. Bringing new products and services to market can be very costly, so service providers need to find a way to do so at low-cost, whilst maintaining a high-quality customer experience.

Many businesses already understand the value of using Software as a Service (SaaS) offerings, and seem to be keen to take advantage of the pay-per-use nature of these services to help them to decrease capital expenditure, and to remove the need for managing in-house application provisioning and licensing. This is good for the customers (SMBs and enterprise businesses), but how does the service provider benefit? Figure 8-1 illustrates the situation where many business customers purchase SaaS offerings directly from a SaaS provider, with the service provider having no insight into what is happening. Services purchased in this way are often referred to as *over-the-top*, meaning that the service provider does not know what is going on. The service provider may generate revenue by providing the *pipe (*communication channels*)*, but will be missing out on other revenue-generating opportunities. In some cases, the entire provider-customer relationship bypasses the service provider.

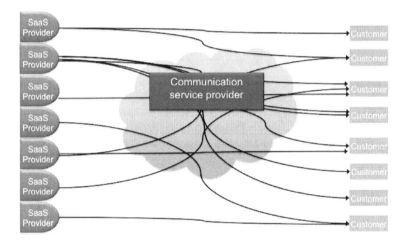

Figure 8-1. Customers buying services directly from SaaS providers

CloudSystem Service Provider has been designed to help service providers overcome these challenges by giving them a valuable role that can increase their market share and enhance profitability. It does this by enabling them to become providers of cloud services to business customers—not only services they can deliver themselves, but also bundles of services that may be sourced (aggregated) from multiple third-party suppliers. Service aggregation—the process of providing access to services from multiple suppliers via a customer portal—is central to the operation of CloudSystem Service Provider, and is realized by the included HP Aggregation Platform for SaaS (AP4SaaS) software (see Figure 8-2). In short, CloudSystem Service Provider includes everything that service providers need to quickly roll out new and differentiating cloud services and make them available to their customers. By becoming a recognized provider of SaaS bundles, the service provider can steer business customers away from using their favorite search engine to locate SaaS providers, and in the process can drive new revenue streams and improve profitability.

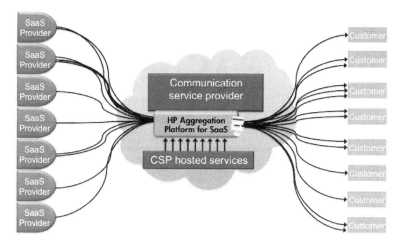

Figure 8-2. Aggregating SaaS services with AP4SaaS

The communications market is very competitive, and service providers need to be able to bring services to market quickly if they are to gain competitive advantage. A key part of reducing time to market (TTM) is managing the lifecycle of SaaS providers. This lifecycle starts with capturing information relating to the SaaS provider's organization and services (referred to as *on-boarding* or *service ingestion*) and deciding whether to do business with them, through to enabling a particular SaaS provider's service to be offered for sale via the service provider's portal, through to the eventual deletion of the SaaS provider's service from the system. AP4SaaS includes an administration portal that simplifies that management of SaaS providers and of the services they offer, leading to accelerated TTM and optimization of new revenue-generating opportunities.

Following the on-boarding and enabling of SaaS provider services, customer service plans are created that enable business customers to subscribe to the services via the AP4SaaS marketplace portal. In addition, contracts with the providers of the SaaS services are created at this time.

When SaaS Services are successfully integrated with AP4SaaS, they can be used to create commercial *products* and *bundles* that can be sold to customers. Products include one or more SaaS services, service plans, prices, and presentation information for those service plans that will be displayed on the SaaS Marketplace Portal. This ability to create service bundles by combining (aggregating) services from multiple providers gives the service provider the ability to create attractive offerings that provide value to business customers.

One other benefit to the service provider is that they can become a one-stop-shop for businesses looking for SaaS offerings. Rather than using a general search engine to search for SaaS services, business customers can visit the service provider's marketplace portal and select the service they need. The business customer does not need to concern themselves with dealing with the individual providers of the SaaS services; they simply order (and pay for) the service from the service provider.

CloudSystem Service Provider Components

CloudSystem Service Provider is built by using the major components of CloudSystem Enterprise, to which additional software and services are added. The main difference between the CloudSystem Enterprise and CloudSystem Service Provider platforms is the *core platform*. CloudSystem Service Provider builds on the CloudSystem Enterprise solution by adding Aggregation Platform for SaaS and moving Network Automation from extensions to core. In addition, the Hybrid Delivery Strategy Service has been removed.

We will continue our discussion of CloudSystem Service Provider by looking at the HP Aggregation for SaaS software.

HP Aggregation Platform for Software as a Service (SaaS)

In order for communications service providers (CSPs) to provide cloud services to business customers, they need a mechanism for centralizing and automating IaaS, PaaS, and SaaS service delivery.

HP AP4SaaS is the foundation for the HP Cloud Services Enablement for CSPs (HP CSE for CSPs) program, and streamlines operations for both service providers and their business customers by automating key processes. These processes include provisioning, activation, administration, mediation, charging, revenue settlement and service assurance.

To enable integration with billing systems, AP4SaaS includes HP Internet Usage Manager (IUM); a mediation solution that provides comprehensive usage collection and processing for voice, data, content and multimedia services and is in use today around the world by leading service providers.

AP4SaaS enables the delivery of Anything as a Service. At the time of writing, AP4SaaS supports four main classes of services out of the box, with more services to be added in the future. The four main classes of services are:

- Infrastructure as a Service (IaaS)

- Communications as a Service (CaaS)

- Device Management as a Service (DMaaS)

- Business Applications as a Service (BAaaS)

 Note

In Chapter 1, we defined three generalized cloud delivery models as IaaS, PaaS, and SaaS.

CaaS, DMaaS and BAaaS can be considered to be more specialized delivery models, and for the purposes of our discussion in this chapter, specific to the HP Cloud Services Enablement for CSPs (HP CSE for CSPs) program.

Infrastructure as a Service (IaaS)

Telecommunications providers (telcos) are looking for new ways to generate revenue. They see network traffic increasing, but not necessarily their revenues. They understand that businesses have two major concerns with cloud: security and performance. Businesses need to be sure that their data is secure and that the service will always be available. Most businesses already have a relationship with one or more telcos, and may consider that the telcos can be trusted and therefore are ideally placed to meet their need for security and availability.

The challenge for the telcos is to deploy private cloud for internal use, and at the same time use cloud technology to generate new revenue streams by offering their IT resources on a pay-as-you-go basis to their customers. The customers can consume these resources without having to invest in their own IT systems; For example, they simply order a VM and storage from the telco's website and begin to use it within minutes. And because the telco operates a pay-as-you-go service, the customer only pays for what they use. Examples of well-known companies who offer this kind of service include Amazon and Google.

Communications as a Service (CaaS)

AP4SaaS enables telcos to offer a one-stop shop to their customers for communications services such as automated voice services, messaging, and collaboration. Communications service providers (CSPs) can offer their business customers a pay-as-you-go way of accessing communications services without the customers having to invest heavily in infrastructure. Customers get access to state-of-the-art communications services that can help them create competitive advantage and increase their revenue streams.

The CSPs can offer their own, as well as third-party solutions. Examples of services available at the time of writing include:

- **Messaging:** Based on Exchange 2010, and including e-mail, calendar, contact management, integrated voicemail and e-mail archiving

- **Collaboration**

  - Business users are provided with a variety of Microsoft SharePoint 2010 productivity and business process management tools such as team rooms, business forms, content management, and business information analysis.

  - HP Virtual Room for Web conferencing, online collaboration, and instant messaging tools

  - HP Audio Conference that can be combined with HP Virtual Room to give voice and video conferencing capability

- **Business Voice Services:** Based on HP's network interactive voice response (IVR) system, including *auto attendant* for automatic inbound call routing, *virtual office receptionist* speech recognition-based call routing system, *automatic call distribution* for incoming call queuing and routing based on agent availability, and *call recorder* for recording inbound and outbound calls.

Device Management as a Service (DMaaS)

Employees of SMBs and enterprise businesses are making more and more use of smartphones and other mobile devices, which means that business applications and sensitive data are being stored on those devices. This sensitive data needs to be secured, and the mobile devices need to be managed effectively to make sure that the businesses are able to get the most from their investment. Device Management as a Service is a way for telcos to drive new revenue streams by offering device management services to business customers.

DMaaS services include:

- **HP Mobile Device Management**: Can be used to automatically back up device content, to enforce IT security policies, and to distribute, update, manage, and de-provision enterprise applications on mobile devices.

- **Mobile data backup**: Provides address book functionality that automatically synchronizes all contact information, and secure over-the-air transfer of contacts, calendar entries, notes, SMS, MMS, photos, videos, ringtones, and bookmarks.

- **PC data backup**: Provides automatic backup of servers, computers, and mobile phones.

Business Applications as a Service (BAaaS)

Many businesses could benefit from using business applications such as enterprise resource planning (ERP), customer relationship management (CRM), and human resources (HR), but may feel that the cost of purchasing, installing, and managing the applications is prohibitive. AP4SaaS enables CSPs to aggregate services from third-party SaaS providers and offer them for purchase to business customers via a marketplace portal. In doing so, **the CSP becomes the single point of contact for the consumption of business application services**.

AP4SaaS Marketplace Portal

AP4SaaS provides a marketplace portal that the CSP's customers (the SMBs and enterprise businesses, remember?) can use to browse for and to purchase services. The portal, which is highly customizable (to reflect the image and branding of the CSP), is shown in Figure 8-3.

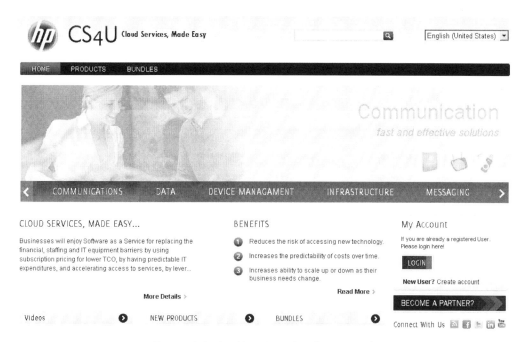

Figure 8-3. AP4SaaS marketplace portal

Browsing through the voice products category shows several services available for order: For example, Virtual Receptionist, Automated Call Distribution, and Auto Attendant (see Figure 8-4). The price of each service is displayed, and the customer would simply select the service they require, put it in their shopping basket, and provide payment details—an experience that will be familiar to anyone who has ever purchased anything from a website.

The customer is not aware of the origin of the service delivery (and really should not care); it may be delivered directly from the CSP's datacenter, or it may be a service that has been sourced from a business partner of the CSP.

Figure 8-4. Marketplace portal showing voice products

In summary, the HP AP4SaaS software in the CloudSystem Service Provider solution enables communications service providers to increase their revenue streams by offering services— delivered internally, *and* aggregated from external suppliers—to business customers. In doing so the CSPs can differentiate themselves from their competitors by offering an online store for purchasing pre-defined service bundles with enhanced security, availability, performance, and delivery at a reasonable, predictable cost.

HP CloudSystem Service Provider Product Mapping

Now that we have described the individual components of the CloudSystem Service Provider solution, let us finish this chapter by seeing which products are responsible for providing the functions in the Demand, Delivery and Supply layers, and in the Design/deploy, Provision, Use, and Assure phases. Figure 8-5 shows a high-level overview of the product mapping, and Figure 8-6 shows a more detailed view.

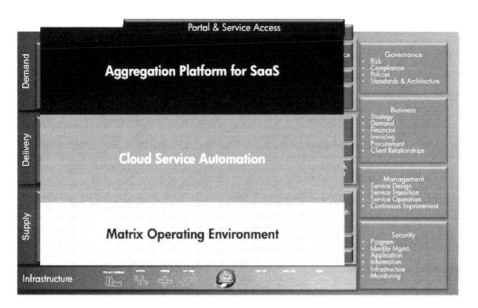

Figure 8-5. HP CloudSystem Service Provider product mapping overview

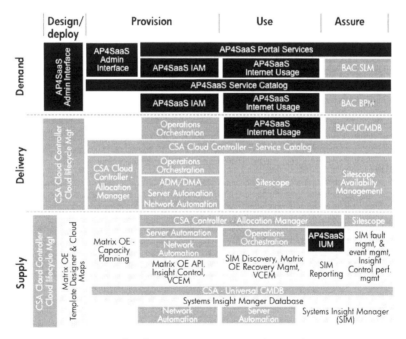

Figure 8-6. HP CloudSystem Service Provider product mapping

 Note

The features in light grey are provided by Matrix OE, the features in mid grey are provided by HP CSA, and the features in dark grey are provided by AP4SaaS.

Test Preparation Questions and Answers

The following questions will help you measure your understanding of the material presented in this chapter. Read all the choices carefully, as there may be more than one correct answer. Choose all correct answers for each question.

Questions

1. What is the central purpose of HP CloudSystem Service Provider?

    a. an easily serviceable infrastructure

    b. service aggregation

    c. private cloud

    d. blade technology infrastructure

2. Which main class of service differentiates HP CloudSystem Service Provider from CloudSystem Matrix?

    a. Training as a Service

    b. Infrastructure as a Service

    c. Communications as a Service

    d. Finance as a Service

3. Which is a primary component of CloudSystem Service Provider only?

    a. BladeSystem infrastructure

    b. Matrix OE

    c. Network Automation

    d. Serviceguard

4. What is included in AP4SaaS?

    a. Internet Usage Manager

    b. Operations Orchestration

    c. Systems Insight Manager

    d. capacity planning

Answers

1. ☑ **B.** The central purpose of HP CloudSystem Service Provider is service aggregation.
   ☒ **A** is incorrect, because HP CloudSystem Service Provider may be based on an easily serviceable infrastructure, but that is not its main purpose. **C** is incorrect, because CloudSystem Matrix is ideal for private cloud. **D** is incorrect, because all CloudSystems are based on HP Blade technology.

2. ☑ **C.** The HP CloudSystem Service Provider supports Communications as a Service.
   ☒ **A** is incorrect, because it is not a current offering. **B** is incorrect, because it is an offering of other CloudSystems. **D** is incorrect, because it is not a current offering.

3. ☑ **C.** The CloudSystem Service Provider includes Network Automation.
   ☒ **A** is incorrect, because it is true of all CloudSystems. **B** is incorrect, because it is true of all CloudSystems. **D** is incorrect, because ServiceGuard is optional, not standard.

4. ☑ **A.** AP4SaaS includes Internet Usage Manager.
   ☒ **B** is incorrect, because OO is part of CSA. **C** is incorrect, because it is included in Matrix OE. **D** is incorrect, because it is part of Matrix OE.

9 Sizing and Configuration

EXAM OBJECTIVES

✓ Identify guiding principles required to propose an appropriate solution based on customer needs.

✓ Describe sizing and configuration guidelines.

ASSUMED KNOWLEDGE

You should be in possession of the HP APC - Converged Infrastructure Solutions (2010) certification.

INTRODUCTION

We have been looking at the building blocks of the HP CloudSystem solutions, and we have seen that we have a solution for everything from simple, homogenous IaaS, all the way through to very complex, heterogeneous, multi-tier PaaS and SaaS requirements. In this chapter we will discuss the criteria for evaluating customer needs and choosing the CloudSystem offering that most closely meets those needs. We will then go on to describe guidelines for the sizing and configuration of the solution.

Evaluating customer needs

Solution selection criteria are multi-dimensional, and are dependent on the customer situation and business needs. In order to select the most appropriate solution, questions will need to be asked (and answered) in several important areas:

- **Scalability**: Does the customer have a global presence or multiple data centers?

- **Heterogeneity**: Does the customer have a preference for third-party or non-BladeSystem HP hardware?

- **Time to implement**: Does the customer need their cloud services to be up and running in a very short timeframe?

- **Green field or existing infrastructure**: Is the customer willing to purchase new hardware, or do they have existing infrastructure that they want to reuse?

- **Only build on private cloud or use hybrid resources**: Does the customer have a need for using both private and public cloud services?

- **Key cloud characteristic**: Does the customer need IaaS, PaaS, SaaS, a service catalog, bursting, monitoring, billing, etc?

- **Workload characteristics**: Understanding the nature of the workloads can give an early pointer to the components that should be present in the solution. For example, if the customer wishes to deploy a simple LAMP stack, HP ProLiant Blades may be sufficient. However, if the customer wishes to deploy a highly scalable mission-critical environment, HP Integrity Blades running HP-UX would be indicated. Once we know about the workloads, we can look for an associated HP Cloud Map to see what infrastructure components are included.

HP has identified three primary *use cases*, and these can be used as a basis for selecting the most appropriate CloudSystem solution for a particular customer situation (see Figure 9-1).

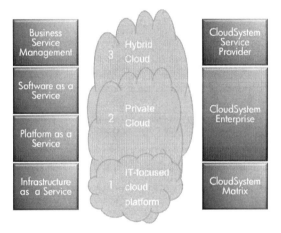

Figure 9-1. Three Primary Use Cases

The three primary use cases are based on where the customer is now and where they would like to be in the future. They are positioned as follows:

1. **IT-focused IaaS**: Designed for use within the IT department. Provides basic IaaS capabilities and allows the provisioning of the environment for specific applications (for example, through HP Cloud Maps). Built around CloudSystem Matrix, this would be a good place to start if the customer is interested in starting to use cloud within the IT department (for example, in a test and development or production pilot environment) to gain experience.

2. **Private cloud with PaaS or SaaS**: Designed for customers wanting to implement a business user-focused private cloud in a homogeneous or a heterogeneous environment. Built around CloudSystem Enterprise, this would be a good place to start if the customer wants to start the implementation of a private cloud and offer PaaS or SaaS services with advanced application-to-infrastructure lifecycle management to business users. The key focus here is on the management of the entire application stack.

3. **Hybrid cloud with business service management**: Designed for service provider customers who are ready for a complete XaaS (IaaS/PaaS/SaaS) cloud journey in a heterogeneous production environment. CloudSystem Service Provider would be a good place to start if the customer wants to include sophisticated integration with service management solutions (BSM, OMi, Tivoli, etc.), billing, external services, and services aggregated from multiple external service providers (with the associated onboarding/service ingestion, offer creation, and bundling) in the service catalog.

The use cases presented here are based on the assumption that the customer is interested in building their own cloud environment. They are examples of some of the available use cases—we could have included additional use cases that are aligned with the CloudSystem solutions.

For those customers who do not want to build, own, and manage their own dedicated private cloud, HP Enterprise Cloud Services–Compute offers a pre-built, asset-free, enterprise-grade cloud computing service.

Let us now look closer at the positioning and characteristics of each use case.

Use Case One: IT-Focused IaaS

There are several customer needs and characteristics that may make use case one a good place to start. These include:

- Customer is doing an initial project to understand what the cloud is all about and to prove that an internal, private cloud provides business benefit.

- Customer is just looking for the provisioning of infrastructure (IaaS) in a homogeneous environment with pre-defined operating systems. They will typically start with pre-defined VM images in an image library, and will provide a compact selection of VM sizes (for example, extra small, small, medium, large, and extra large).

- Typical use cases are test and development, and infrastructure standardization and automation, mainly for use within the IT department. They can start in a non-production environment (test and development) and grow into production.

- Beyond infrastructure provisioning, the customer may want to deploy simple applications and perform patch management.

- Low cost and rapid time to implement is an important factor.

For the customer requiring an IT-focused cloud platform delivering IaaS, the ideal starting point is HP CloudSystem Matrix. This on-premise cloud solution provides infrastructure as a service for IT organizations as well as basic application deployment and monitoring. This offering enables businesses to provision infrastructure and applications in minutes, not months.

Use Case Two: Private Cloud with PaaS or SaaS

There are several customer needs and characteristics that would make use case two a good place to start. These include:

- Customer needs to deliver comprehensive, multi-tier application services to the business users.

- Customer is looking at a broader IT transformation into a shared services center or internal private cloud, and is wanting a richer service catalog (IaaS, PaaS, SaaS) and a more enhanced user portal experience with cost transparency or chargeback.

- Customer is looking to a hybrid delivery model, including legacy applications, private/public cloud, and a broad range of cloud services.

- Customer is looking at bursting internal cloud to external providers.

- Customer wants to leverage current investments in infrastructure and enterprise service management and integrate them into an enterprise cloud model.

- Customer is interested in using a broader range of multi-vendor storage, servers, and networking.

For the customer requiring a private cloud with PaaS or SaaS, the ideal starting point is HP CloudSystem Enterprise. This is the best solution for anyone looking to deploy the full range of service models (IaaS, PaaS, and SaaS) and deliver them directly to line-of-business users. This offering provides a single view of all services—whether they are from on-premise clouds, public clouds, or traditional IT—and it includes advanced application-to-infrastructure lifecycle management.

Use Case Three: Hybrid Cloud with Business Service Management

There are several customer needs and characteristics that would make use case three a good place to start. These include:

- Customer is a large enterprise or service provider.

- Customer wants to complement service offerings with services sourced from public clouds in a way that is transparent to the user.

- Customer wants to aggregate services from several external suppliers.

- Customer wants integrated billing. In other words, there should be only one bill for services sourced from several external suppliers, rather than separate bills from each external supplier.

- Customer wants integrated service level and user experience management.

For the customer requiring hybrid cloud with business service management, the ideal starting point is HP CloudSystem Service Provider. CloudSystem Service Provider builds on the CloudSystem Enterprise offering and enables service providers to drive new revenue growth by enabling them to provide a public cloud IaaS and SaaS, including aggregation and management of those services.

Sizing and Configuration

The HP CloudSystem sizing and configuration process can be divided into three main phases:

- **Discovery**: This phase focuses on understanding the customer needs for number and types of workload, number and types of instances (a single instance could comprise several VMs, networks, and storage tiers), number of physical and virtual servers, and amount of memory and storage required.

- **Design**: This phase focuses on the selection of CPUs and blades, calculation of the number of VMs per blade, the number of blades, the number of enclosures, the choice of storage systems, system specifications such as IP and SAN bandwidth, and power and cooling requirements.

- **Build**: This phase is where the bill of materials (BOM) is built. The BOM should include all software, hardware, and services required by the solution.

Figure 9-2 illustrates the process of discovering the customer needs, selecting servers, and building a bill of materials. The figure is an example of the process that is generally followed, and it should be noted that there could be many more products that would need to be added to the configuration (based on customer needs).

It may be necessary to go through the design phase several times, as we may be designing to a price, rather than designing for perfection.

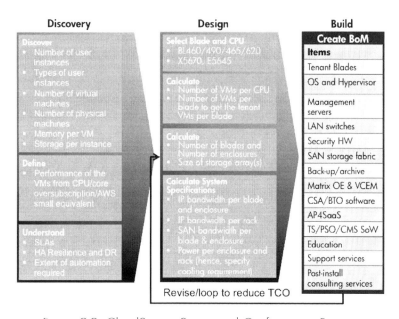

Figure 9-2. CloudSystem Sizing and Configuration Process

Note
The term *physical machine* in Figure 9-2 relates to a physical server that will run an application workload, not a virtual machine (VM) host system.

Discovery Phase

The first stage of the *discovery* phase focuses on finding out the number and types of user instances, the number of virtual machines and physical nodes, how much memory the virtual machines (VMs) should have, and how much storage is needed per instance.

The second stage of the discovery phase focuses on defining the performance of the VMs. This involves mapping the VM to some kind of physical machine—which may be a fraction of a standard server. Amazon has defined what they call a *standard compute unit* based on a particular Xeon processor/clock speed, and we can use this definition as a standard reference point for a VM.

This definition can be used to calculate how many VMs can be placed on each core, and from each core, how many VMs can be placed on each processor, and from each processor, how many VMs can be placed on each blade. Alternatively, the customer may have already decided upon the over-provisioning ratio, and they will define how many VMs they would like per core.

So, either the customer tells us how many VMs they would like on each core, or we calculate the number using the Amazon Web Services (AWS) EC2 *standard compute unit*, where one EC2 Compute Unit provides the equivalent CPU capacity of a 1.0-1.2 GHz 2007 AMD Opteron or 2007 Intel Xeon processor. It is very important to get this right, as it will have a direct impact on the cost of the solution. For example, doubling the number of VMs per physical server results in needing half the number of servers, which results in a reduction in hardware costs.

The final stage of the discovery phase then aims to build an understanding of the requirements for high availability and disaster recovery. We also need to understand the level of automation the customer requires. This will be dependent on the skill of the users. As an example, imagine that the customer is implementing a private cloud based on CloudSystem Matrix, and the users accessing the service via the portal are reasonably sophisticated. These users can be given a great deal of control over their decisions, with fewer functions requiring automation. Contrast this with a customer implementing a public cloud solution, where the end-user is not at all sophisticated, and needs to be presented with a very simple, completely automated experience.

Once we have gathered all of the data in the discovery process, we can move into the design phase.

Design Phase

Certain blades and CPUs are recommended because they have been used over and over again, and we are confident that their power and performance characteristics will translate into a good solution. The example blade and CPU choices shown in Figure 9-3 are chosen according to the need for AMD or Intel processors and for power and speed. As new CPUs and blades are introduced, the choices will of course change to include the new models. We can then use Passmark analysis (to be discussed shortly) to calculate the number of blades that are needed to meet the VM requirements. Once we have calculated the number of blades, we can determine the number of enclosures.

The choice of the storage array(s) will be dependent upon the required capacity, availability, and need for features such as thin-provisioning and virtual domains (which allow for secure isolation of application data on a consolidated multi-tenant storage system). For guidance, we can refer to the *small*, *medium*, and *large* example base CloudSystem configurations that we saw in Chapter 4:

- **Small**: 1 c7000, 8 servers (bl46xG7 blades), with optional **P6300 EVA** storage (27.9TB raw)

- **Medium**: 1 c7000, 16 servers (bl46xG7 blades), with optional **HP 3PAR F200** storage (51.8TB raw)

- **Large**: 4 c7000s, 64 servers (bl46xG7 blades), with optional **HP 3PAR F400** storage (145.4TB raw)

We then need to calculate the system specifications. We need to think about the amount of network bandwidth per blade and per enclosure. Failing to do this can result in network bottlenecks. We also need to think about the SAN bandwidth per blade and the power per enclosure. These systems can be very dense and it is possible for us to load an enclosure from top to bottom and consume in the region of 25KW. We need to check that the data center has the capability to supply the required amount of power and cooling.

VM Design Guidelines

Our goal is to design VMs that have no bottlenecks and that will adequately meet the needs of the users. To assist in the sizing process we can use an equivalent of the Amazon EC2 VM instance. All Amazon EC2 instances are priced based on hourly usage and instance type. Each instance type consists of a certain number of EC2 Compute Units (ECU) and a set RAM size. The EC2 *Standard Instances*—well suited for most applications—are:

- **Small:** 1 EC2 Compute Unit (1 virtual core with 1 EC2 Compute Unit), 1.7 GB memory, 160 GB instance storage

- **Large:** 4 EC2 Compute Units (2 virtual cores with 2 EC2 Compute Units each), 7.5 GB memory, 850 GB instance storage

- **Extra large:** 8 EC2 Compute Units (4 virtual cores with 2 EC2 Compute Units each), 15 GB memory, 1,690 GB instance storage

One Amazon EC2 compute unit (ECU) provides the equivalent CPU capacity of a 1.0–1.2 GHz 2007 AMD Opteron or 2007 Intel Xeon processor, and is roughly equivalent to a *PassMark CPU* score of 400. We can calculate the EC2 equivalent of a particular processor by taking the Passmark CPU score and dividing it by 400. As an example, the Passmark score for the 2.93GHz Intel Xeon X5670 is 8,795. Divide this by 400 to get a score of 21 ECU. This means that the Xeon X5670 processor in our example should be able to host approximately 21 small, five large or two extra-large EC2-equivalent VMs.

Note
CPU Passmark scores are available at http://www.cpubenchmark.net/cpu_list.php.

The cpubenchmark website may show data for *Dual CPU* or *Quad CPU* systems (the term CPU being synonymous with the term processor—a package containing one or more cores). In order to calculate the ECU per processor, take the Passmark CPU Mark and, for a Dual CPU system, divide by two to get the Passmark score per processor. Divide this number by 400 to find the ECU-equivalent score for a single processor. For example, the cpubenchmark website shows the *[Dual CPU] AMD Opteron 6174* as having a Passmark score of 15,498. As it is a dual-CPU (processor) system, divide by two to find the Passmark score for one processor of 7749. Divide this number by 400 to find the ECU-equivalent for the processor, which is 19.3725. Round down to find the nearest integer of 19.

The recommended network bandwidth for each VM, according to Gartner, should be at least 100Mb/s for IP traffic and 200Mb/s for SAN traffic. (NOTE: iSCSI is all IP traffic, so it becomes 300Mb/s for IP traffic.)

100Mb/s for IP traffic is considered by some to be not enough, but it is generally good enough as a starting point. In a highly-virtualized environment a very large amount of IP traffic will be coming from the system, which can result in a large number of cables emerging from a single enclosure. In this scenario, we may need to specify a switch such as the HP 5900 or HP 125xx to provide TOR functions.

The hypervisor vendors recommend that each VM should be configured with at least 3–4GB user memory plus RAM for the OS (500MB for Linux, 1GB for Windows). Additional memory may be required to satisfy the needs of the application(s) being hosted on the VM, but caution should be exercised when specifying memory, as RAM is relatively expensive and adding too much can be very costly.

Another consideration when specifying RAM is the DIMM density. High-density DIMMs, such as 16GB and 32GB, are relative expensive when compared with lower-density ones such as 2GB and 4GB. The current and future requirements for RAM need to be assessed, and the most cost-effective DIMMs selected.

Microsoft recommends that we take account of the overhead required by Hyper-V virtualization technology by configuring an additional 10–25% of hardware resources. More details can be found at http://msdn.microsoft.com/en-us/library/cc768529%28BTS.10%29.aspx.

VMware say that ESX VM overhead memory depends on the number of virtual CPUs, the configured memory for the guest operating system, and on whether a 32-bit or 64-bit guest operating system is being used.

A table listing the overhead for each case can be found at http://pubs.vmware.com/vi301/resmgmt/wwhelp/wwhimpl/common/html/wwhelp.htm?context=resmgmt&file=vc_advanced_mgmt.11.18.html.

Server Guidelines

Figure 9-3 shows the number of CPUs, cores per CPU, cores per blade, etc., for a selection of HP Blades. As previously noted, these choices will change as new CPUs, DIMM densities, and blades are introduced. It is for this reason that we should focus on the principle, rather than on the model numbers.

Servers											
Blade Option	CPU Type	Slots in enclosure	Speed (GHz)	ECU per processor	Number of proc.	Cores per proc.	Cores per blade	Max Memory (GB)	Max VM per Blade	Memory per VM (GB)	Max VM per enclosure
BL460c G7 General Virtualization	X5650	0.5	2.66	19	2	6	12	192	38	5.0	608
BL685c General Virtualization	6174	1	2.2	19	4	12	48	512	76	6.7	608
BL460c G7 Dedicated and 4-core Virtualization	E5640	0.5	2.66	13	2	4	8	192	26	7.4	416

Some applications cannot use more than 4 cores | More VMs to recover if blade fails | Above minimum requirement

Figure 9-3. Selection of HP Blades

Several checks should be made:

1. How many CPU cores can the application make use of? Certain applications cannot use more than four cores, so there is no point in configuring a VM with more than four cores, as the rest will be wasted.

2. How many VMs are going to be hosted on a single blade? If a blade fails, we have to take account of the recovery process. The BL685 in our example can host up to 76 VMs, and in the event of a blade failure, it is possible that the recovery process would be too slow. In certain environments, it is possible that the business could cope with slow recovery from failure, whereas in other environments, rapid recovery may be a requirement.

3. Is the blade capable of supporting the required amount of memory? Divide the maximum memory supported by the blade by the maximum VM per blade to reach the *Memory per VM*, and make sure that it meets the RAM requirements for the VMs.

General principles that apply to the sizing process include:

- Use HP Blades in c7000 enclosures to get lower power consumption than rack-mounted servers.

- Use Virtual Connect/FlexFabric to reduce ownership costs and number of cables.

- Use one or two standard blades with options limited to memory and disk wherever possible. Ideally, local storage would be replaced by SAN storage.

- Use memory DIMMs configuration rules to get best performance.

Service Level Agreements

Service level agreements (SLAs) provide a common understanding about services, priorities, responsibilities, guarantees, warranties and penalties.

SLAs that customers expect from their private cloud may be very different from those that are offered by traditional public cloud providers. Several factors need to be determined and agreed upon with the customer:

- What performance levels are expected? We need to consider CPU, memory, networking, and storage performance.

- What availability is expected and how will it be calculated?

- Are there any legal compliance requirements?

- How will the systems and data be secured?

- What are the data retention policies? We need to consider the location of the data and the legal implications of storing data in a different jurisdiction. When data are deleted (either accidentally or on purpose), are they really deleted, or can they be recovered?

The key concept to think about is whether we design for perfection or for price. With an unlimited budget, we can come close to perfection, but how many customers will be prepared to pay the price? We could seek to modify the SLA to allow us to deploy less equipment and, therefore, reduce the price.

High Availability (HA)

In order to design a solution that meets customers' need for service availability, we must agree with the customer on their definition of availability. Several questions need to be answered:

- When is a system defined to be not available?

- What does available mean? Server running? Applications running?

- How long does the system have to be down before it is classed as unavailable? For certain customers, a certain amount of downtime may be acceptable, and this is often referred to as the *not counted window*. Only outages longer than the not counted window get counted. For other customers, the concept of the not counted window will not apply; if the system is down and it was not planned, it is considered down.

If a system can be down for five minutes without causing the customer problems, this gives us the opportunity to restart the system within the not counted window, leaving the availability at 100%.

For example, if server recovery time is four minutes and the not counted window is five minutes, then zero unavailable time gets accrued. System recovery within the not counted window is shown in Figure 9-4.

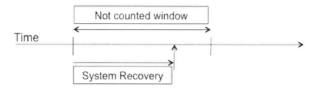

Figure 9-4. System Recovery Within the *Not Counted* Window

If the system recovery time is longer than the not counted window, the system is deemed to be unavailable, and this will be added to the unavailable time. This is shown in Figure 9-5.

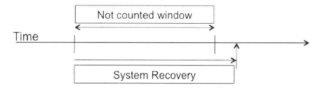

Figure 9-5. System Recovery Outside of the *Not Counted* Window

Amazon approaches the availability of AWS services by calculating an *annual uptime percentage*. This is calculated by taking the percentage of five-minute periods (our not counted window) during the service year in which Amazon EC2 was in the state of *Region Unavailable* and subtracting this number from 100%.

HA Design

When designing a system for high-availability, the major objective is to avoid single points of failure (SPOFs).

Several elements should be considered when designing CloudSystem solutions:

- The C7000 chassis supports six power supplies (three pairs). The appropriate number of supplies should be configured with resilience in mind.

- Server blades are typically connected to more than one redundant Virtual Connect module.

- Virtual Connect Enterprise Manager provides automated profile failover for blades.

- Hypervisors should be clustered (for example, using vSphere clustering).

- Make sure that a backup solution for tenants and management systems is included. A combination of D2D and tape may be appropriate.

HA and Disaster Recovery (DR) for the Management Systems

So far, we have been discussing the guidelines for the servers that host the application workloads (otherwise known as the tenant array). We now need to consider the servers on which the management software will run.

If the CMS or other management systems (those systems running CSA, Server Automation, SiteScope, etc.) should fail, the tenant array will continue to run. The failure should of course be rectified as soon as possible, but workloads running on the systems managed by the CMS and the other management systems will not be adversely affected.

For CloudSystem Matrix, a pair of rack-mount servers for the Central Management System (CMS) is recommended. These CMS servers run SIM, Insight Control, Matrix OE, and VCEM. As previously stated, CSA for Matrix (Server Automation and SiteScope) can consume a lot of resources and it is recommended that blades (BL460c or similar with 96GB RAM) within the C7000 are used to host Server Automation and SiteScope.

For CloudSystem Enterprise and Service Provider, an HP Blade enclosure is recommended to run the cloud software (CSA and AP4SaaS). A pair of rack-mount servers for the CMS running SIM, Insight Control, Matrix OE, and VCEM is still recommended, as it is important to get the CMS up and running before the rest of the system is configured.

The CMS should be protected with a standby system that can be brought online in the event of a CMS failure. If we lose contact with the CSA software, we have a problem, but our tenants are still running. In this situation, the CMS should still be running, and can be used to find out why the system running the CSA software has gone down. Without the CSA software, we lose the ability to provision new services and to de-provision existing ones.

The management software (CSA, AP4SaaS, etc.) running on the management systems needs to be protected, and each piece of software has its own rules defined by the business unit owning the software.

 Warning
Running VCEM on a blade running under the control of Virtual Connect should be avoided. VCEM manages the LAN and SAN connections, and in the event that the blade fails, it may prove difficult to establish a remote connection to the system.

Service Continuity

As a general guideline, the priority for system protection is:

1. Tenant systems

2. CMS (running SIM, Insight Control, Matrix OE, VCEM)

3. Remaining management systems

Additional Design Considerations

- Protected VMs are allocated from pools with clustered resources. Virtual server failure may trigger the motion of the VM within the same virtual cluster.

- Physical servers rely on classic clustering such as:

    - Windows Cluster, as of Windows Enterprise Edition

    - HP ServiceGuard

    - Linux RedHat HA Add-on

- Management server failure does not prevent users' workloads that are currently running from continuing to run. There may be a negative impact on the monitoring of the resources and its automated flex up/down capability coupled with the inability to manage the services until the impacted management features resume.

Having completed these steps, we will be in a position to create the bill of materials (BoM).

Build Phase

The BOM can either be created manually, or, for HP employees and registered HP partners, with a tool such as HP SalesBUILDER for Windows (SBW).

Once the BOM has been completed, the cost of ownership should be checked and a decision made whether to go back and change some of the numbers to bring the cost down. For example, the mix between physical and virtual servers could be adjusted. The customer might not have specified the mix, and this is the time to fine-tune it to optimize the cost.

Another way to optimize the cost of the solution is by increasing the resilience of the system and specifying a reduced level of support. For example, adding several spare blades to the configuration may mean that, rather than requiring a 24 x 7 level of support, a next-day fix is sufficient. In the event of a blade failure, one of the spare blades can take over from the failed blade, resulting in minimal business impact and reduced total cost of ownership (TCO). A three-year Care Pack at the appropriate level is recommended, as this is lower in cost than a one-year Care Pack followed by two year's worth of support contract.

 Note
SBW can be accessed via the HP Smart Portal:

Europe, Middle East and Africa: http://www.hp.com/eur/smartportal

Canada and U.S.: http://www.hp.com/go/partnerportal:

Asia Pacific: http://www.hp.com/partners/ap

Care Pack information can be found at HP Care Pack Central, which can be accessed via the Care Pack Central link on http://www.hp.com/go/carepack

---

Test Preparation Questions and Answers

The following questions will help you measure your understanding of the material presented in this chapter. Read all the choices carefully, as there may be more than one correct answer. Choose all correct answers for each question.

Questions

1. Which customer need would indicate a hybrid cloud with business service management?

    a. Customer wants to leverage existing infrastructure.

    b. Customer is doing initial project to assess the cloud.

    c. Customer wants to aggregate services from several external suppliers.

    d. Low cost and rapid time to implement is critical.

2. Which customer need would indicate an IT focused IaaS?

    a. Customer needs to provision infrastructure in a homogeneous environment with pre-defined operating systems.

    b. Customer needs to deliver complete application services to business users.

    c. Customer desires integrated service level and user experience management.

    d. Customer wants integrated service usage and billing.

3. Which general principal applies to the sizing process?

    a. Configure system based on rules for latency domains.

    b. Calculate minimum number of users.

    c. Incorporate existing IT infrastructure.

    d. Use HP Blades in a C7000 enclosure.

4. Which is the most bandwidth-critical area in a cloud environment?

    a. analog signal

    b. network

    c. processor

    d. backup

Answers

1. ☑ **C.** There are several customer needs and characteristics that would make use case three, hybrid cloud with business service management, a good place to start. One of them is that a customer wants to aggregate services from several external suppliers.

   ☒ **A** is incorrect, because this applies to use case two, private cloud with PaaS or SaaS. **B** is incorrect, because this applies to use case one, IT-focused IaaS. **D** is incorrect, because this is use case one.

2. ☑ **A.** There are several customer needs and characteristics that may make use case one, IT-focused IaaS, a good place to start. One of them is that a customer is just looking for the provisioning of infrastructure in a homogeneous environment with pre-defined operating systems.

   ☒ **B** is incorrect, because this is case two, private cloud with PaaS or SaaS. **C** is incorrect, because use case three, hybrid cloud with business service management, applies. **D** is incorrect, because this is use case three .

3. ☑ **D.** Use HP Blades in c7000 enclosures to get lower power consumption than rack based servers.

   ☒ **A** is incorrect, because latency domains do not apply to CloudSystem. **B** is incorrect, because minimum number of users is not a basic criterion. **C** is incorrect, because use of existing IT infrastructure is not a general principle of the sizing process.

4. ☑ **B.** Cloud solutions are very network-intensive, and it is vital that enough network bandwidth is available.

   ☒ **A** is incorrect, because analog signal bandwidth is not of primary concern in cloud environments. **C** is incorrect, because processor bandwidth is not of primary concern in cloud environments. **D** is incorrect, because backup may consume network resources, but it is a subset of network-consuming activities.

10 HP Cloud Service

EXAM OBJECTIVES

✓ Define HP consulting and support services for cloud computing.

✓ Define HP Enterprise Services for cloud computing.

✓ Describe HP partner programs.

ASSUMED KNOWLEDGE

You should be in possession of the HP APC - Converged Infrastructure Solutions (2010) certification.

INTRODUCTION

In this chapter, we will be looking at HP services for cloud computing. The term *services* can have several meanings; the first is associated with consulting and support services, which include activities such as discovery workshops, strategy development, solution design, implementation, and solution support. These services are delivered by HP Technology Services, HP Enterprise Services, and HP Partners, and involve one or more consultants engaging with the customer for a period of several hours, days, or weeks.

The second meaning is associated with the kind of services that enable a user to consume virtual infrastructure and access online storage capacity on-demand (think back to Chapter 1 and the example of deploying an Amazon Machine Image). HP Enterprise Cloud Services-Compute (ECS-Compute) and HP Cloud Services are programs that fall into this second category.

The chapter concludes with taking a look at the programs that HP has put in place to assist business partners with their cloud computing initiatives.

HP Technology Services for Cloud Computing

Services are an integral element of an HP CloudSystem solution. HP Technology Services provide consulting and implementation services to ensure customers have the right cloud strategies in place, plot a pragmatic path to the cloud, and integrate HP CloudSystem solutions seamlessly into existing customer environments.

HP has a rich portfolio of services for cloud computing that can help customers on their journey to the cloud. The services are designed to address people, process, and technology transformation challenges, and aim to smooth the process of deploying an initial foundation solution, and maybe ultimately moving all the way to a hybrid cloud compute environment based on HP CloudSystem.

The services are arranged into four categories: *Plan*, *Implement*, *Operate*, and *Secure* (see Figure 10-1). Before we look at each service in detail, let us look at customer adoption stages for HP cloud services.

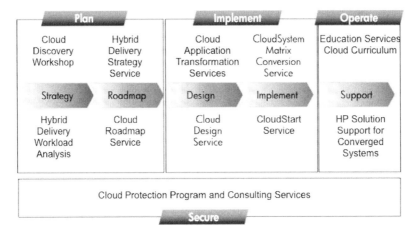

Figure 10-1. HP Technology Services For Cloud Computing

Cloud Services Customer Adoption Stages

Customers may be in different stages of cloud adoption, and it is for this reason that not every customer will need all of the available services; the appropriate services should be selected based on customer needs. Also, it is not necessary to go through each HP cloud service sequentially; it is possible to jump between different stages, as the customer's needs dictate.

Customers who are evaluating whether cloud computing is right for their business needs will have many questions that will need to be answered. These include:

- Are we ready for cloud computing?

- What should we be doing in terms of evaluating and planning?

- How cost-effective is cloud computing?

- What steps should we take and when?

- What is the business case for cloud computing?

The services in the *Plan* category will be of great value to these customers.

For those customers who have already decided to implement cloud-based solutions, the services in the *Implement*, *Operate*, and *Secure* categories will be of great value.

Figure 10-2 provides a guide for the selection of cloud services, based on the customer's business needs.

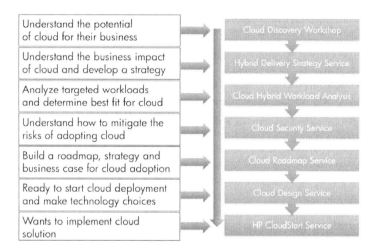

Figure 10-2. Cloud Services Customer Adoption Stages

Most customers will benefit from the Cloud Discovery Workshop, Cloud Hybrid Workload Analysis, Cloud Roadmap, Cloud Design and CloudStart services. The remainder of the services can be included as dictated by the customer's business needs.

Plan

HP Cloud Discovery Workshop

Getting the most out of cloud computing is not a simple exercise. Many CIOs are still unsure about the best way to begin their cloud journey and about the return on investment (ROI), total cost of ownership (TCO), and risks that may be associated with a transition to the cloud. They will be asking questions such as:

- Will cloud services cost less than similar services from internal sources?

- Will our business be able to roll out new services faster than the competition?

- Will these services be secure enough to protect business and customer data?

- Will the IT organization have sufficient governance and control to meet service levels?

- Will the organization be able to comply with policies, regulations, and audits?

The HP Cloud Discovery Workshop is between one-half and one day in duration, and can help CIOs answer these questions by covering cloud topics such as:

- **Setting the scene**: Providing a discussion around business and technology needs, an overview of cloud computing trends, and answers to common questions.

- **Cloud concepts and architecture**: Defining cloud consumer and provider roles, service strategy, concepts, and architecture, while outlining various cloud sourcing models and types of cloud computing.

- **Cloud transformation journey**: Identifying cloud-related strategic opportunities and priorities, as well as critical success factors for making the most of cloud computing.

- **Cloud service portfolio**: Developing and defining the service portfolio and structure.

- **Cloud economics and financials**: Delivering business value and ROI, financing, and aligning with business priorities.

- **Cloud infrastructure and facilities**: Building the cloud infrastructure by converging servers, storage, software, and networks and optimizing facilities.

- **Cloud security and availability**: Understanding multi-tenant security and risk to be able to design highly available and secure cloud services—spanning regulatory compliance, data confidentiality, cross-system authentication, authorization, and contracting.

- **Cloud service management**: Managing end-to-end services using Information Technology Infrastructure Library (ITIL) best practices, and automation software, and adapting these best practices for cloud computing.

- **Application and information**: Understanding different workloads, user and developer needs, and application and information services that can be *cloud enabled*.

- **Governance and organization**: Determining staffing models, change management, service governance, and training

- **Cloud roadmap**: Defining the tactical plan for the next 30 to 60 days and beyond.

HP Hybrid Delivery Workload Analysis

This service is between four to eight weeks in duration, and analyzes workloads to determine the optimum method for service delivery. The three methods are cloud services, hosted/managed services, and internal service.

Workload characterization includes two major activities:

1. It analyzes the workload inherent characteristics (usage pattern, CPU, memory, I/O, and behavior) using patented HP agent-less tools, and then looks at four service hosting attributes for that workload.

    -   **Operational** requirements such as functionality, ability to customize or time to service

    -   **Financial** hosting costs such as capital and operational cost models, transfer in/out costs, migration in/out costs, cost of downtime

    -   **Technical** service requirements including security assessment and SLAs: availability, continuity, and regulatory

    -   **Organizational** impact including control/transparency, change/upgrade policies, governance, etc.

    This provides a clear picture (or *fingerprint*) of how the workload behaves and what its hosting requirements would be.

2. The fingerprint is then compared against the three sourcing models (cloud services, hosted/managed services, internal service) and scored. The scores can then be used to determine which of the three sourcing models is most appropriate for the workload.

HP Hybrid Delivery Strategy Service

The Hybrid Delivery Strategy Service is a one- to two-day engagement with an HP consultant who helps customers to understand the selection criteria, integration, and optimized usage of the various IT operating models, including cloud computing.

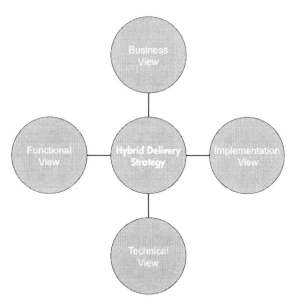

Figure 10-3. HP Hybrid Delivery Workload Analysis

The discussion focuses on four primary business-of-IT topic areas (see Figure 10-3):

- **Business view**: IT industry developments, IT business management, and integration with other disciplines in the company.

- **Functional view**: Pros and cons of different operating models and value chain models.

- **Technical view**: Various operating model components (finance, operational, governance models, infrastructure, and systems).

- **Implementation view**: Implementation scenarios and choices, including greenfield, transformational, evolutionary, and people.

This activity helps the customer to define the program, projects, priorities, required effort, and main activities that are needed in order to move to a hybrid delivery model. It also creates a high level overview of the optimal mix of operating models specific to needs of a particular organization.

 Note

The Hybrid Delivery Strategy Service addresses all service delivery models, of which cloud is one. This differs from the Cloud Discovery Workshop in that the latter is a deep dive into one type of delivery model—cloud.

The two workshops are not competitive or mutually exclusive. Indeed, the Hybrid Delivery Strategy Service can run in front, side-by-side, or even after a Cloud Discovery Workshop. It gives the customer a different perspective that they can use to decide what suits them best, depending on their business needs.

The Strategy Service is for organizations looking to understand what hybrid delivery is and how it would be defined and implemented for them. It does not deal with characterizing workloads of specific services.

The Hybrid Delivery Workload Analysis service is *downstream* from the Strategy Service and is for organizations already in a hybrid delivery environment. It examines individual services to determine the optimal delivery approach for each.

HP Cloud Roadmap Service

The HP Cloud Roadmap Service helps to build a structured roadmap and understanding of the program, projects, and main activities to transform an IT organization from any current state into a balanced cloud computing organization, aligned with the needs of the business. The service is a consulting engagement between HP experts and the customer's IT team, with a duration of between four and 12 weeks, depending upon the size and complexity of the organization.

The service is separated into three modules:

- **Module I: Future state definition**: The aim of this module is to develop a high level architecture of the future operating model, to match the cloud strategy.

- **Module II: Program plan development**: This module deals with current state analyses, gap analyses, and program planning across service management, technical architecture, culture, staff, governance, and other domains.

- **Module III: Business case development**: This module focuses on the business and ROI case, and includes ROI analysis, cash flow analysis, payback period, and alternative scenarios.

The service helps to identify opportunities for business and IT to benefit from the cloud, and to develop a high level architecture of the future operating model to match the cloud strategy. Current state analyses, gap analyses, and program planning are used to provide recommendations for the ideal service strategy, governance, and program model for incorporating cloud capabilities. The last module focuses on developing a business case and providing a practical, step-by-step roadmap of projects for cloud adoption.

Implement

Cloud Application Transformation Services

Cloud Application Transformation Services is a service provided primarily by HP Enterprise Services (ES). The ES Infrastructure Modernization consulting team works with customers' CIOs or IT directors and conducts a *cloud suitability* assessment of customers' applications, and develops a transition plan for the customers' portfolio of applications. Following the development of the transition plan, the ES Applications Modernization team has the responsibility for the re-architecture and/or re-platform implementation work on the applications. The main aim of this program is to help customers reduce their own applications and infrastructure footprint and to reduce capital expenditure.

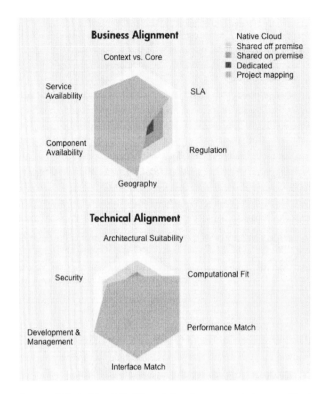

Figure 10-4. The HP Cloud Applications Advisory Tool

The HP Cloud Applications Advisory Tool is used to analyze applications for cloud suitability based on a number of business and technical alignment aspects (see Figure 10-4). The HP team provides a set of recommendations based upon the findings.

HP Cloud Design Service

HP Cloud Design Service provides a comprehensive, scalable cloud infrastructure design based on the HP Cloud Functional Reference Architecture. It is for enterprise customers who are ready to start cloud implementations, make technology choices, set standards, and do detailed planning, and who have cloud budget, support, vision, and a roadmap in place. The design service is a six to eight week engagement, and uses the Reference Architecture as a guideline to create a personalized design for a particular customer.

The Reference Architecture covers everything needed to get an end-to-end cloud service up and running. The Reference Architecture provides a common framework for all cloud engagements, and accommodates different technologies, software stacks and cloud service requirements. As we saw in Chapter 3, the Reference Architecture defines functional blocks that can be mapped to software components from HP and third-party vendors. Every functional component to build a cloud service is listed, and this ensures that no component is overlooked. It also helps to identify overlaps between multiple technologies and vendors.

The deliverables of the design service include:

- **Cloud portfolio architectural analysis**: This includes an analysis of strategic technical road-maps, business functional requirements, and application technical requirements, and a validation of design standards

- **Detailed design development**: This includes the development of a detailed infrastructure design including hardware, OS, storage, network, software, hypervisor, application servers, back-up and recovery design, recommendations for management tools, and bill of materials for implementation

- **Implementation plan**: This includes the design and deployment of organizational processes and procedures, migration plans, cost estimates, and a support plan.

HP CloudSystem Matrix Conversion Services

One of the most commonly asked questions about HP CloudSystem is if it is for greenfield environments only. The answer is no. For existing HP customers, there is a straightforward upgrade path from either a BladeSystem environment or a VirtualSystem environment. In addition, HP can build clouds by deploying CSA software on non-HP hardware, if required.

These services, performed by HP Services experts, enable customers to leverage their investment in HP BladeSystem and to move to a complete, fully supported HP CloudSystem Matrix environment (see Figure 10-5).

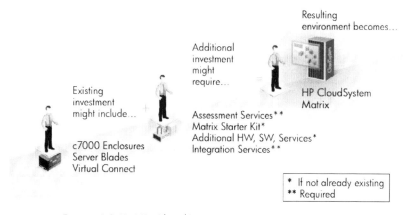

Figure 10-5. HP CloudSystem Matrix Conversion Services

There are three key steps to achieving a full conversion:

Step 1. Initial assessment: HP experts assess the inventory and report on the existing HP BladeSystem equipment—that is, the equipment that will be converted to HP CloudSystem Matrix.

Step 2. Site-specific preparation: This step will vary greatly depending on the equipment to be converted. This may include the purchase and installation of additional required hardware and software in preparation for the conversion to CloudSystem Matrix. This might include some of the following: redundant Virtual Connect and Matrix Operating Environment licenses and associated hardware and software support. The HP CloudSystem Matrix Conversion Services require the purchase or pre-existence of at least one Matrix enclosure.

Step 3. Conversion to HP CloudSystem Matrix: HP experts perform the conversion. The result of this step is a complete, fully supported HP CloudSystem Matrix environment.

HP CloudStart

HP CloudStart is the quickest way for customers to get started delivering infrastructure as a service (IaaS) from a private cloud with HP CloudSystem. CloudStart is a fixed scope, pre-integrated private cloud solution delivered by HP Cloud Consulting Services that can get customers up and running with private cloud in as little as 30 days following installation of the system. HP consultants work with the customer and give them coaching on how to use and get the best out of their investment. The service provides a real-life, hands-on experience, and can get the first production loads running on the system in just four weeks.

Built on HP CloudSystem Matrix, the HP CloudStart Solution simplifies and speeds up private cloud deployments. Consisting of hardware, software, and services, and delivering up to four compute services (Windows and Linux), the service enables businesses to deliver pay-per-use services reliably and securely from a common portal, while offering the ability to scale and deploy new services automatically.

After a CloudStart implementation, customers can add other elements of HP CloudSystem to create more advanced hybrid cloud solutions.

In the four weeks following the installation and start up of HP CloudSystem Matrix, HP organizes workshops to define cloud computing needs and capabilities, implement, and customize the solution. Some of the specific activities that the HP CloudStart offers, as a part of the first cloud compute service, include:

- A series of workshops to shape and define the best HP CloudSystem configuration and customization option
- Up to four compute services that can be created out of any combination of:
  - Two operating systems: Linux and Windows
  - Two size compute choices from S, M, L, XL, and XXL

- Physical or virtual choices

- One hypervisor: Hyper-V or VMware vSphere

- Service definition, pricing, and specification for the four compute services selected

- Services that are ready for business consumption, with full automation, design, implementation, and testing of the selected compute services, including:

  - Customization of HP CloudSystem Matrix

  - Storage set-up—link in up to two storage tiers

  - Backup Integration—link in up to two backup policies

  - Security policy review and planning

  - Basic integration with operations

Operate

Education Services Cloud Curriculum

HP Education Services has expanded its curriculum to support the growing interest in, and adoption, of cloud computing solutions. In addition to training in the areas of HP Converged Infrastructure, HP Insight software (HP SIM, Insight Foundation, Insight Control, Matrix OE, VCEM, etc.), HP Storage, HP Networking, security, and IT Service Management, cloud-specific training courses are also available. These courses include:

- **HP Education Cloud Simulation**: This one-day simulation uses a game in which teams compete to gain a better understanding of cloud dependencies, challenges, and benefits. The HP cloud maturity model is used to help students understand the impact and business benefits of cloud. Students leave the course with a better understanding of how to implement and manage cloud projects and deal with cloud dependencies.

- **Cloud Foundation**: This one-day course provides students with a firm understanding of cloud computing and how it relates to their business. Course topics include public versus private cloud, the cloud sourcing model, enabling technologies, cloud management, and service level management.

- **Architecting HP CloudSystem Solutions**: This two-day course teaches students how to identify, describe, position, and specify the correct HP CloudSystem solution based on customer needs, and prepares new candidates for the HP ASE—Cloud Architect v1 certification.

- **HP CloudSystem Matrix Infrastructure Administration**: This three-day course focuses on the skills required to manage and run an HP CloudSystem Matrix solution, and includes topics covering dynamic infrastructure provisioning, continuous consolidation and energy-aware planning, and infrastructure repair and recovery.

More information on the HP Education Services cloud curriculum can be found at http://www.hp.com/education/sections/cloud.

HP Solution Support for Converged Systems

Integrated solutions require integrated and seamless support. Having a single point of accountability is a major reason for customers to want to work with a single vendor for all their cloud needs.

HP Solution Support is consistent across all HP Converged Systems—VirtualSystem, CloudSystem and AppSystems—and provides a single point of accountability for the total solution, including hardware, software, and networking in the customer's virtualized environment, giving them a simplified support experience (see Figure 10-6). Customers benefit from proactive problem prevention, accurate problem diagnosis, and rapid problem resolution. HP support specialists resolve the problem—including complex, multivendor problems—and collaborate with internal experts to resolve issues, so customers can focus on their business.

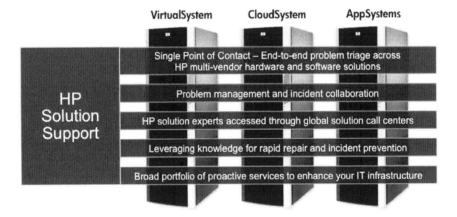

Figure 10-6. HP Solution Support

Secure

HP Cloud Protection Program and Consulting Services

There are risks inherent with cloud computing, and mitigating these risks is a top priority for customers and for HP.

The HP Cloud Protection Program can help to mitigate common threats defined by Cloud Security Alliance (CSA), while addressing process, compliance, and operational security needs in an enterprise hybrid cloud environment.

The HP Cloud Protection Program includes:

- **HP Cloud Protection Consulting Services**: These services address people, technologies, processes, and policies to ensure that they are prepared and protected against the risks associated with cloud computing. The services include:

  - **HP Cloud Protection Workshop**: This workshop provides in-depth discussion and high-level recommendations on cloud security strategy, while leveraging cloud security best practices.

  - **HP Cloud Protection Roadmap:** This service provides risk and compliance gap analysis, and highlights the changes that may be needed with existing security policies in order to guide cloud design activities.

  - **HP Cloud Protection Design:** This service leverages the HP Cloud Protection Reference Architecture to provide a comprehensive design and implementation plan that defines policy, procedure, process, people, and proof components of cloud security.

  - **HP Cloud Protection Implementation:** This service enables additional security during cloud implementations, through virtualization protection and software verification. It leverages ITIL-based cloud management principles and provides security controls based on best practices and industry standards.

  - **HP Cloud Protection Foundation Service:** This service provides hardening of HP CloudSystem solutions at the virtualization level, along with hypervisor-specific configuration hardening.

- **HP Cloud Protection Center of Excellence**: This is a physical lab environment where unified testing and integration of HP and partner products are managed. Collaboration with HP Software, HP Labs, VMware, and other third-party products provide tested virtualization and cloud service-level protection.

- **HP Cloud Protection Reference Architecture**: As previously stated, there are many risks associated with cloud computing. In order to mitigate the risks inherent in hybrid environments, it is vital that all security aspects are considered and accounted for. The HP Cloud Protection Reference Architecture covers cloud security from several perspectives, including business, functional, technical, and implementation, and ensures that proper security controls are defined across all dimensions.

 Note
See http://www.cloudsecurityalliance.org for more information on common security threats.

HP Enterprise Services For Cloud Computing

We will now discuss the services that enable a user to deploy virtual infrastructure and access online storage capacity on-demand. At the time of writing, there are two such services: HP Enterprise Cloud Services–Compute and HP Cloud Services.

HP Enterprise Cloud Services—Compute (ECS-Compute)

HP Enterprise Cloud Services–Compute (ECS-Compute) is a service that delivers cloud computing services for core business applications and processes in a flexible, scalable, and automated environment on HP-owned and managed hardware. The ECS-Compute service represents a cloud-based managed services offering, which offers self-service users access to the resources of a *virtual private* cloud, with high levels of performance, availability, and strict security and privacy policies (see Figure 10-7).

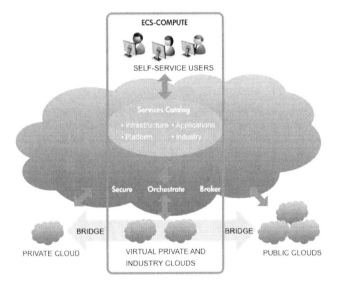

Figure 10-7. HP ECS-C

Bundles of server, storage, network, and security are consumed as a service, and the users pay only for the resources that they reserve. The service can scale rapidly—up to a customer-defined limit—to meet the changing needs of the business.

Workloads are securely hosted on physical or virtual servers in HP next-generation data centers, and HP assists with the selection of the best HP data center to meet the needs of the business while maintaining compliance with industry and/or government regulations.

There are currently two ECS-Compute offerings from HP—HP-Managed Server and Client-Managed Server. With HP-Managed Server, HP manages the hardware and the operating system; with Client-Managed Server, HP manages the hardware and the customer is responsible for managing the operating system. Windows, SUSE Linux Enterprise Server, and Red Hat Enterprise Linux servers are available in small, medium, large, and extra large sizes.

Figure 10-8 illustrates the levels of standardization and time to provision of outsourcing, ECS-Compute, and public cloud solutions. ECS-Compute leverages the strengths of both outsourcing and public cloud; namely, strong SLA guarantees, high levels of security, relatively short contract terms, and both single- and multi-tenancy.

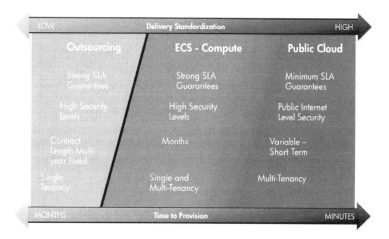

Figure 10-8. HP ECS-Compute Compared to Outsourcing and Public Cloud

HP Cloud Services

HP Cloud Services (in private beta at the time of writing) is designed to provide business-grade, open source-based, developer-focused public cloud infrastructure. Built on HP software and hardware located in HP data centers, and leveraging OpenStack Nova technology, the initial offerings include HP Cloud Compute and HP Cloud Object Storage.

Note
For more information on Openstack Nova, visit http://nova.openstack.org

HP Cloud Compute

HP Cloud Compute provides access to a web-based interface, a CLI, and an API that can be used to deploy publicly accessible virtual machines on-demand.

The HP Cloud Compute service uses the terms *flavor* (or *size*), *image*, and *server*.

- **Flavor** refers to a combination of CPU, memory, and disk space, with choices including:

  - Extra small—1vCPU, 1GB RAM, and 40GB disk space

  - Small—2 vCPU, 2GB RAM, and 80 GB disk space

  - Medium—2vCPU, 4GB RAM, and 160 GB disk space

  - Large—4 vCPU, 8GB RAM, and 320 GB disk space

- **Image** refers to a collection of files used as a base installation (typically, an operating system), including:

  - Ubuntu Oneiric 11.10 Server 64-bit

  - Ubuntu Natty 11.04 Server 64-bit

  - Ubuntu Maverick 10.10 Server 64-bit

  - Ubuntu Lucid 10.04 64-bit

  - CentOS 5.6 Server 64-bit

- **Server** refers to an instance created by combining a *flavor* with an *image*.

When creating a server, the user is given the option of configuring a *Security Group*, which can be used to define firewall rules, and to configure an SSH *key pair*, which can be used to securely access the server. In addition, the user is able to select whether they would like a public IP address with which to access the server.

The service is ideal for many general-purpose data center needs. One common use case is for web farms (servers handling web traffic) that may need to scale up owing to peaks in demand at certain times of the day. Rather than the customer needing to provide extra capacity in their own data center, the web service can be scaled-up using the HP-hosted resources of HP Cloud Compute.

HP Cloud Object Storage

HP Cloud Object Storage leverages OpenStack Object Storage to provide a means for storing and retrieving objects on a pay-per-use basis from publicly accessible physical machines that are configured as highly redundant clusters in HP data centers.

Note
For more information on OpenStack Object Storage, visit http://openstack.org/projects/storage

The HP Cloud Object Storage service uses the terms *object* and *container*.

- **Object** refers to the thing being stored (typically, one or more files). An unlimited number of objects can be stored.

- **Container** refers to a compartment in which objects are stored. Containers are *private* at the time of creation, and can be made *public* and accessible to anyone, if required.

The service is ideal for many redundant storage needs. Common use cases include archival of data, where files are moved from the customer's data center to an HP data center; file sharing, where files are allocated a public URL that enables them to be shared by people anywhere in the world; and for storing website images, which could be useful in the event that local network bandwidth needs to be conserved.

 Note
For more information on HP Cloud Services, visit http://www.hpcloud.com

HP Cloud Assure

HP Cloud Assure is a service that is delivered via HP Software-as-a-Service and has been designed to address three primary concerns that customers have when assessing cloud computing; namely, security, availability, and performance. HP Cloud Assure is a turnkey service that requires no installation of software or agents on the servers or networks where the applications reside, and provides access to experts who perform security scans, deploy availability monitoring, and execute performance tests using HP SaaS cloud services and software. The software used includes HP Application Security Center, HP Business Availability Center, and HP Performance Center.

HP Cloud Assure for security enables the scanning of web applications, middleware, operating systems, and the network. In addition, it is able to perform penetration testing to uncover potential application vulnerabilities. It also protects cloud applications—being provided or being consumed—against unauthorized data access.

HP Cloud Assure for availability provides visibility of service uptime and performance, and enables the isolation of potential issues with end-user experience. It aids the isolation of application performance problems, and can be used to perform trend analysis for business analytics and to predict and prevent failures.

Cloud Assure for performance measures a service provider's capability to deliver the necessary connectivity and bandwidth to meet the needs of the end-users. It offers a complete application performance testing service to make sure cloud providers meet end-user bandwidth and connectivity requirements, and that the cloud applications scale to support peak usage. It also provides IT and business managers information relating to end-user experience.

HP Partner Programs

HP AllianceONE Partner Program

HP AllianceONE is a program for ISV/IHV/OEM/SIs and development partners that brings together several existing HP partner programs under the Converged Infrastructure umbrella hosted on the AllianceONE program portal.

The program is aligned to deliver Converged Infrastructure (CI) value to HP partners by providing technical, go-to-market (GTM), and collaboration benefits. CI is based on open standards and, thus, HP is enabling all partners to take advantage of the superior power and cooling advantages, orchestrated and automated deployment capabilities, and agility with shared services enabled by HP Converged Infrastructure.

The HP AllianceONE website is at http://www.hp.com/go/allianceone

---

 Note

The Developer & Solution Partner Program (DSPP) portal name will migrate to the AllianceONE program portal over time.

HP CloudAgile Program

The HP CloudAgile program is intended to cover a broad range of service providers who acquire HP products and services to support solutions hosted for end customers. Service providers (SPs) may include telcos/operators, hosting providers, cloud service providers, ISVs and SIs that want to expand into cloud services, Value Added Resellers that want to deliver IT as a service, and managed service providers. This program is positioned under the AllianceONE partner program.

CloudAgile provides service providers with unprecedented opportunities to accelerate and extend their market reach. The program enables participants to deliver services faster, engage with more customers, and improve financial flexibility.

CloudAgile encompasses technology across the HP Enterprise Business portfolio, including servers, storage, networking, software, and services. CloudAgile is intended to cover a broad range of service providers who acquire HP products and services to support solutions hosted for end customers.

CloudAgile Benefits	Premier Invitation only	Select Leading providers	Business Emerging providers
MULTIPLY SALES REACH			
HP and channel "compensation neutral" co-selling	√	√	
Targeted account engagement	√		
Partner business manager	Dedicated	√	Program support
CAPTURE NEW MARKETS			
Offer certified services (cloud hosting, bursting, etc)	√	√	
SaaS offerings with HP IT Performance Suite	√	√	
HP promotion of partner service offering	Premium	√	√
ACCELERATE DELIVERY			
Innovative financing models to mitigate risk	√	√	√
Flexible HP Software licensing for qualified partners	√	√	
Demo/solution development access	Onsite and virtual	Onsite and virtual	Virtual
Joint marketing	√	√	
AllianceONE program support	√	√	√

Figure 10-9. HP CloudAgile Benefits

CloudAgile has three tiers (see Figure 10-9):

■ **Premier** partners are by invitation only, and will have extensive dedicated resources available.

■ **Select** partners are other leading providers around the world, and will have a rich set of offerings available.

■ **Business** partners who do not meet the criteria for the other two categories will still be able to access program elements through self-service options.

The program has three key benefits:

1. **Multiply sales reach**: HP provides a program that allows *compensation neutral* co-selling with HP and partners. This means that HP encourages the HP sales reps to drive business to HP CloudAgile partners while still compensating the HP reps in such a way that they remain in a neutral position between an end customer buying something directly from HP or buying something from a certified partner. For certain partners, HP will even engage in joint account targeting and planning that will help really drive business to the top service provider partners.

2. **Capture new market opportunities**: HP is offering programs that allow SPs to enter new markets such as private cloud hosting and cloudbursting services enabled by the HP CloudSystem platform. CloudAgile partners will be able to become certified HP CloudSystem hosters, delivering private clouds to enterprise customers while ensuring client service levels are sustained.

3. **Accelerate cloud service delivery**: HP is delivering a set of go-to-market tools including financing and training. Partners can leverage free resources through the HP AllianceONE Partner Program, including the Cloud Operating Environment (CLOE) and access to loaner HP CloudSystem equipment to support proofs of concept.
   The CLOE service provides members with highly automated, secure, self-service access to virtual machines. These VMs can be used to test, port, debug, verify, and tune applications on multiple platforms and configurations.

Partners can also leverage HP Software solutions for SaaS offerings. HP will support them with flexible licensing that allows them to pay as they grow. HP is also working on other ways to promote partner cloud service offerings to HP customers, such as inclusion of bursting partners in the Matrix service catalog.

Finally, there is a comprehensive set of financing, demo, and marketing tools available. Innovative financing models through HP Financial Services helps SPs refocus capital on innovation for growth and risk mitigation.

The HP CloudAgile Program website is at http://www.hp.com/go/allianceone

HP Cloud Solutions Lab

The HP Cloud Solutions Lab is dedicated to the joint development of HP CloudSystem offerings. AllianceONE partners will have the opportunity to earn the new Cloud Ready Insignia from HP. The Cloud Ready insignia differentiates partner offerings through rigorous testing and validation conducted by HP.

The HP Cloud Solutions Lab was established to build complete, fully tested cloud solutions. The lab is staffed with dedicated engineers whose expertise spans many aspects of the complete cloud architecture: applications, automation, converged infrastructure, security, Cloud Maps, and more. As a factory-based R&D organization for cloud solutions and Cloud Maps, the HP Cloud Solutions Lab provides development, customization, and integration to accelerate how HP designs, builds, tests, and delivers complete end-to-end cloud solutions.

The Cloud Solutions Labs are R&D and engineering focused, and as such they are not involved in customer facing opportunities, demonstrations, or PoCs (proof of concepts).

More information can be found on the AllianceONE website at http://www.hp.com/go/allianceone.

Test Preparation Questions and Answers

The following questions will help you measure your understanding of the material presented in this chapter. Read all the choices carefully, as there may be more than one correct answer. Choose all correct answers for each question.

Questions

1. Which service would you recommend to help a customer understand the potential of cloud computing for their business?

   a. HP Cloud Roadmap Services

   b. HP CloudStart Service

   c. HP Cloud Discovery Workshop

   d. HP Cloud Hybrid Workload Analysis

2. Which HP training course teaches the ability to identify, describe, position, and specify the correct HP CloudSystem solution?

   a. Cloud Foundation

   b. HP CloudSystems Matrix Infrastructure Administration

   c. HP Education Cloud Simulation

   d. Architecting HP CloudSystem Solutions

3. Which cloud service addresses the concerns of security, availability, and performance?

   a. HP Alliance One Partner Program

   b. HP Cloud Assure

   c. HP Mission Critical Support

   d. HP Enterprise Services

4. Which compute services does HP CloudStart deliver?

   a. Windows and HPUX 11iV3

   b. Linux and Windows

   c. Linux and HPUX 11iV3

   d. OpenVMS and Linux

5. Which HP CloudAgile benefit is available to emerging providers?

    a. Innovative financing models

    b. Joint marketing

    c. Targeted account engagement

    d. SaaS offerings with HP IT Performance Suite

6. What does the HP Cloud Solutions Lab offer?

    a. Proof of Concept testing

    b. Customer demonstration of Cloud Services

    c. Implementation assistance for CloudSystem Matrix

    d. Joint development of CloudSystem offerings

Answers

1. ☑ **C.** The HP Cloud Discovery Workshop helps customers understand areas such as cloud-related strategic opportunities and priorities, as well as critical success factors for making the most of cloud computing.
   ☒ **A** is incorrect, because it is aimed at building a structured roadmap. **B** is incorrect because it is concerned with implementing the service. **D** is incorrect, because it covers the optimum method for delivery.

2. ☑ **D.** This two-day course teaches students how to identify, describe, position, and specify the correct HP CloudSystem solution, based on customer needs.
   ☒ **A** is incorrect, because it covers the basics of cloud. **B** is incorrect, because it is an introduction to the cloud. **C** is incorrect, because it is concerned with management of the solution.

3. ☑ **B.** HP Cloud Assure addresses three primary concerns that customers have when assessing cloud computing; security, availability, and performance.
   ☒ **A** is incorrect, because it is an HP partner program. **C** is incorrect because it is a support option. **D** is incorrect, because it is an HP organization.

4. ☑ **B.** HP CloudStart activities include the creation of Linux and Windows compute services.
   ☒ **A** is incorrect, because HPUX is not an option. **C** is incorrect, because HPUX is not an option. **D** is incorrect, because OpenVMS is not an option.

5. ☑ **A.** HP Financial Services offers innovative financing models to emerging (Business), Select, and Premier partners.
   ☒ **B** is incorrect, because it is available to Premier and Select partners only. **C** is incorrect, because this is for Premier partners only. **D** is incorrect, because it is available to Premier and Select partners only.

6. ☑ **D.** The HP Cloud Solutions Lab is dedicated to the joint development of HP CloudSystem offerings.
   ☒ **A** is incorrect, because training is not a function. **B** is incorrect, because the lab does not offer customer demonstrations. **C** is incorrect, because the lab does not provide implementation assistance for HP CloudSystem.

11 HP Cloud Resources

EXAM OBJECTIVES

✓ Explain how to access and use the HP Solution Demo Portal.

✓ List and describe additional HP CloudSystem resources.

ASSUMED KNOWLEDGE

You should be in possession of the HP APC - Converged Infrastructure Solutions (2010) certification.

INTRODUCTION

In this chapter, we will look at several resources that will help us to not only enhance our knowledge of HP cloud solutions, but also to help our customers to understand what HP is doing in the cloud arena, and how the HP cloud solutions can benefit their businesses.

Let us begin by looking at the HP Solution Demo Portal.

HP Solution Demo Portal

The HP Solution Demo Portal provides a central location for demonstrations, webinars, and supporting collateral that showcases how HP technologies lead, innovate, and transform enterprise business. Live and pre-recorded demos of HP hardware, software, services, and partnerships are available, and these demos can be used to show customers how HP can help solve their business and IT problems. The Solution Demo Portal is available at http://www.hp.com/go/SolutionDemoPortal.

First, we will demonstrate how to use the Solution Demo Portal interface, and than we will describe all of the demos available at the time of writing.

There are six main *booth categories* that comprise the first level of the portal (see Figure 12-1):

- Converged Infrastructure
- HP CloudSystem

- Software

- Services

- Business Technology Solutions

- Partners

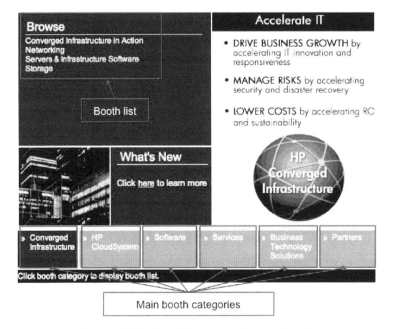

Figure 11-1. The HP Solution Demo Portal

Choosing the booth category of interest, and then selecting a booth from the booth list will display all available pre-recorded and live demonstrations as well as supporting collateral for that particular topic. In order to schedule a live demo, it will be necessary to contact an HP sales representative. We will focus on the pre-recorded demos in this chapter.

As an example, clicking on the **HP CloudSystem** booth category will cause the HP CloudSystem booth list to be displayed, as shown at the top-left of Figure 11-2. Selecting **HP CloudSystem Matrix: Private Cloud IaaS Solution** displays the booth entries for this solution (bottom right of Figure 11-2).

 Note

The HP CloudSystem demos are also available at http://www.hp.com/go/CloudSystem-Demos.

Figure 11-2. HP CloudSystem Matrix Booth

Selecting the booth entry for **Automation** will display all of the available demos for that topic. Hovering over the entries in the left-hand pane will display a description of that demo in the right-hand pane. Clicking a demo in the left-hand pane will cause a **Play** and **Send It** control to appear at the bottom of the right-hand pane, as shown in Figure 11-3.

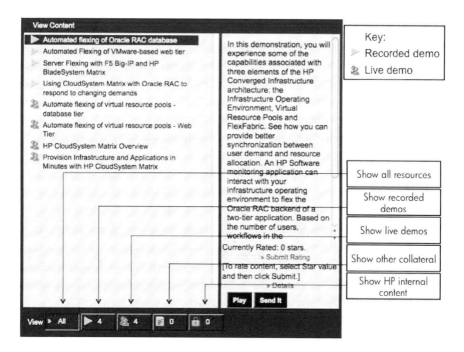

Figure 11-3. Automation Demos

We now have the option of selecting:

- **Play**: if we want to play the video immediately.
- **Send It**: if we want to send a link to the demo via email.

The buttons at the bottom left of the screen can be used to filter the items that are shown in the left-hand pane, so if only the recorded demos are of interest, simply select the button with the green triangle to filter out all other content. The *other collateral* content, when present, may include .doc, .wmv, .ppt, .pdf, and .html documents.

Note

Some of the demo files on the Solution Demo Portal need to be completely downloaded onto your local system before they will play. You may see a blank page while the file is downloading.

Demos available at the time of writing are listed in Table 11-1.

Table 11-1. Solution Demo Portal CloudSystem Demos

BOOTH: HP CLOUDSTART: Deploy a Private Cloud in 30 days		
Booth Entry	**Demo**	**Description**
Getting Started	Cloud Discovery Workshop	Describes the Cloud Discovery Workshop experience.
Getting Started	HP CloudStart	Discusses how Carnegie Mellon University got their private cloud up and running within 30 days.

BOOTH: HP CloudSystem ENTERPRISE: Hybrid Cloud PaaS Solution		
Booth Entry	**Demo**	**Description**
CloudSystem Enterprise Introduction	HP CloudSystem Enterprise Introduction	High-level introduction to CloudSystem Enterprise
Automation	Automated flexing of Oracle RAC database	Shows the use of Business Availability Center and Sitescope to automatically add a node to a RAC (based on number of RAC users) using an OO flow within IO.
Automation	Automated flexing of VMware-based web tier	Companion to *Automated flexing of Oracle RAC database* video.
Automation	Using HP CloudSystem Matrix with Oracle RAC to respond to changing demands	Shows the use of the Cloud Map for Oracle RAC. Also shows OO flows being used to manually deactivate a RAC node.

Booth Entry	Demo	Description
Provisioning	HP CloudSystem Enterprise Overview - Requesting a Service	Shows how CloudSystem Enterprise uses CloudSystem Matrix as a compute provider.
Provisioning	Creating a Service	Shows how easy it is to create and publish a service using HP CloudSystem Enterprise.
Provisioning	HP CloudSystem Matrix Provisioning applications with HP Server Automation	Shows IO Designer being used to build a solution. Also shows Server Automation installing Oracle Weblogic Server into a VMware VM running Windows.
Provisioning	Modifying a Service	Shows how to modify a service using CloudSystem Enterprise.
Provisioning	Ordering a Service	Shows how to order a service using CloudSystem Enterprise.
Provisioning	Using HP CloudSystem Enterprise to provision a WordPress application	Shows provisioning of a LAMP infrastructure and a Wordpress application with CloudSystem Enterprise.
Infrastructure Lifecycle Management	Identifying the right recommendations for hardware consolidation	Shows the use of Capacity Advisor to plan the consolidation of legacy physical servers onto VMware VMs.
Infrastructure Lifecycle Management	Manage data center power consumption needs	Shows Insight Control power management and power capping.
Infrastructure Lifecycle Management	Optimize network bandwidth with HP Virtual Connect Flex-10	Shows the use of VCEM to modify Flex-10 profiles (and change Flex NIC speed from 4 to 8Gb/sec)
Solutions	Deploy a 4node Oracle RAC database utilizing HP Cloud Maps for RAC	Shows the use of Cloud Maps to create a template for deploying RAC onto bare metal blades (with Virtual Connect).
Solutions	Creating a Service - HP Cloud Service Automation	Shows how to create and publish a service using CSA.
Solutions	Modifying a Service - HP Cloud Service Automation	Shows how to modify a service using CSA.
Solutions	Ordering a Service - HP Cloud Service Automation	Shows how to order a service using CSA.
Monitoring	HP CloudSystem Enterprise - Monitoring a Service	Shows a service request with associated SLA and integration with CMDB.

BOOTH: HP CloudSystem MATRIX: Private Cloud IaaS Solution

Booth Entry	Demo	Description
CloudSystem Matrix Introduction	HP CloudSystem Matrix Introduction	Very high-level introduction to CloudSystem Matrix.
Provisioning	HP CloudSystem with Public Cloud Bursting for Hybrid Service Provisioning	Demonstrates HP CloudSystem bursting to public cloud.
Provisioning	INFRASTRUCTURE: Designing and provisioning IT infrastructure services	Shows creation of service catalog template and subsequent ordering of VMware VM. Also shows the use of an OO workflow to *check software compliance on resume*. Also shows the approval request being sent to Service Manager using an OO flow (the standard *send email* flow has been modified to use Service Manager), and when the approval has been granted in SM another OO flow tells IO that the request was approved.
Provisioning	INFRASTRUCTURE: HP CloudSystem Matrix Provisioning applications with HP Server Automation	This demo is available in another booth and has already been described.
Provisioning	INFRASTRUCTURE: HP Storage Provisioning Manager with Matrix OE (via Insight Dynamics)	Shows the use of SPM to create a storage catalog and then use the catalog entries during service provisioning. Also shows the use of tags and Bronze, Silver, and Gold service groups.
Provisioning	INFRASTRUCTURE: Matrix OE: Provisioning HP-UX Infrastructure	Shows how Matrix OE simplifies HP-UX infrastructure provisioning.
Provisioning	INFRASTRUCTURE: Provision Infrastructure and Applications in Minutes with HP CloudSystem Matrix	Shows IO templates being used to order a service. Also shows Server Automation installing LAMP. Then uses included OO flows to instruct SiteScope Server to enable/disable agentless monitors.
Provisioning	SERVICE CATALOGS: Accelerate the creation of a service catalog for Microsoft Exchange	Shows the use of HP MS Exchange sizer output xml file to create a 5000-user IO template by importing the file into IO Designer.

Booth Entry	Demo	Description
Provisioning	SERVICE CATALOGS: Establishing a Service Catalog for Microsoft Exchange	This demo is available in another booth and has already been described.
Automation	Automated flexing of Oracle RAC database	This demo is available in another booth and has already been described.
Automation	Automated Flexing of VMware-based web tier	This demo is available in another booth and has already been described.
Automation	Flexing IT Service with Microsoft Hyper-V and HP CloudSystem Matrix	Shows MS System Center Virtual Machine Manager being used to move VMs from one host to another.
Automation	Server Flexing with F5 Big-IP and HP BladeSystem Matrix	Shows servers being moved between two different services whose workloads peak at different times. Uses an OO flow to gracefully deactivate nodes from an Exchange cluster.
Automation	Using HP CloudSystem Matrix with Oracle RAC to respond to changing demands	This demo is available in another booth and has already been described.
Monitoring	HP CloudSystem Matrix	Shows template design and publishing to catalog. Shows VM OS and Oracle Weblogic being deployed using Server Automation.
Monitoring	Identifying the right recommendations for hardware consolidation	This demo is available in another booth and has already been described.
Monitoring	INFRASTRUCTURE: HP Storage Provisioning Manager with Matrix OE (via Insight Dynamics)	This demo is available in another booth and has already been described.
Infrastructure lifecycle management	Anticipating power requirements for your business needs	Shows Insight Power Manager to measure power consumption of thermal data ESX hosts. Also shows capping power consumption of C3000 enclosure.
Infrastructure lifecycle management	Controlling and managing server maintenance costs	Shows Insight Remote Support Advanced being used to find systems that are out of warranty and using Server Migration P2V to move their workloads to VMs.

Booth Entry	Demo	Description
Infrastructure lifecycle management	Enable Converged Infrastructure and business services mapping in uCMDB	Shows uCMDB and SIM integration being used to gather advanced configuration information, including dependencies between different layers of application services. Also shows simulating failures of certain servers and the resulting effect on the application services.
Infrastructure lifecycle management	Energy Aware Planning (ProLiant)	Shows the use of Matrix's real-time capacity planning capabilities to quickly and easily consolidate workloads in an energy-efficient manner.
Infrastructure lifecycle management	Identifying the right recommendations for hardware consolidation	This demo is available in another booth and has already been described.
Infrastructure lifecycle management	Manage data center power consumption needs	Shows the use of Insight Power Management to discover power consumption and thermal mapping of BladeSystem enclosures. Also shows C7000 enclosure power capping.
Infrastructure lifecycle management	Optimize network bandwidth with HP Virtual Connect Flex-10	Shows online changes to Flex-10 network bandwidth allocations.
Solutions	CLOUD MAPS: Deploy a 4node Oracle RAC database utilizing HP Cloud Maps for RAC	Shows how to use an HP Cloud Map to deploy a 4node Oracle RAC database.
Solutions	CLOUD MAPS: HP Cloud Map with CloudSystem Matrix for VMware vCloud Director	Shows IO being used to add nodes to a VMware cluster.
New Technology Update	Cloud Bursting with HP CloudSystem Matrix – Demo	Demonstrates populating the service catalog from downloadable Cloud Maps. Shows administrator and user portals. Also shows selection of OS, Hypervisor, DB and bursting provider.
New Technology Update	Cloud Bursting with HP CloudSystem Matrix – Overview	Introduces the concept of bursting.

BOOTH: HP CloudSystem SERVICE PROVIDER: Complete platform for providing cloud services

Booth Entry	Demo	Description
CloudSystem Service Provider Introduction	HP CloudSystem Service Provider Introduction	High-level overview of Cloud-System Service Provider.
Billing	Rogers Communications and HP IUM	Discusses the use of HP Internet Usage Manager.

BOOTH: HP SOFTWARE: Cloud Management Software solutions

Booth Entry	Demo	Description
HP Cloud Service Automation (CSA)	Creating a Service - HP Cloud Service Automation	Shows how to create and publish a service using HP Cloud Service Automation.
HP Cloud Service Automation (CSA)	HP Cloud Service Automation - Monitoring a Service	Shows how to use CSA to request a service with an SLA and how the CMDB is integrated.
HP Cloud Service Automation (CSA)	Modifying a Service - HP Cloud Service Automation	Shows how to modify a service using HP Cloud Service Automation.
HP Cloud Service Automation (CSA)	Ordering a Service - HP Cloud Service Automation	Shows how to order a service using HP Cloud Service Automation.
HP Matrix Operating Environment (OE)	INFRASTRUCTURE: HP Storage Provisioning Manager with Matrix OE	This demo is available in another booth and has already been described.
HP Matrix Operating Environment (OE)	INFRASTRUCTURE: Matrix OE: Provisioning HP-UX Infrastructure	This demo is available in another booth and has already been described.
HP Matrix Operating Environment (OE)	Matrix OE: Continuous Consolidation (Microsoft Hyper-V)	Shows the use of the HP Matrix Operating Environment's real-time capacity planning with Microsoft Hyper-V.
HP Matrix Operating Environment (OE)	Matrix OE: Continuous Consolidation (VMware ESX)	Shows the use of logical server management and capacity planning capabilities to make ongoing improvements in resource utilization.
HP Matrix Operating Environment (OE)	Matrix OE: Converged Infrastructure Overview	Shows how matrix OE can dynamically adjust IT resources

Booth Entry	Demo	Description
HP Matrix Operating Environment (OE)	Matrix OE: Disaster Recovery-ready using HP Recovery Management	Shows how Matrix OE Recovery Management can provide DR protection.
HP Matrix Operating Environment (OE)	Matrix OE: Everyday High Availability (ProLiant)	Shows Matrix OE moving workloads to improve uptime.
HP Matrix Operating Environment (OE)	Matrix OE: Provisioning Integrity Virtual Machines infrastructure	Shows template-based provisioning for Integrity VM.
HP Matrix Operating Environment (OE)	Matrix OE: Use a converged infrastructure solution to deliver shared services	Shows Matrix OE logical server management, capacity planning and infrastructure orchestration.
HP Matrix Operating Environment (OE)	Optimize Power with Matrix OE (using Microsoft Virtual Server)	Shows how consolidation can optimize power utilization with Microsoft virtual machines.
HP Matrix Operating Environment (OE)	Optimize Power with Matrix OE (using VMware ESX)	Shows how consolidation can optimize power utilization with VMware virtual machines.
HP Matrix Operating Environment (OE)	Provision an ESX host with HP Matrix OE infrastructure orchestration	Shows rapid provisioning of VMware ESX hosts.

Other Cloud Resources

- http://www.hp.com/go/CloudSystem is the main HP external website for HP CloudSystem. It contains details of the CloudSystem offerings along with links to videos, white papers, and customer case studies.

- http://www.hp.com/go/CloudSystemDemos is a quick route to the *Deliver Iaas: cloudsystem matrix* page within the Solution Demo Portal.

- http://www.hp.com/go/MatrixDemos is an alternative route to the *Converged Infrastructure > Servers & Infrastructure Software > HP CloudSystem Matrix > Datacenter Use Cases > Use Cases* page within the Solution Demo Portal.

- http://www.hp.com/go/cloudmaps is the home of HP Cloud Maps and can be used to view and download Cloud Maps for leading business applications.

- Visit the HP Cloud blog at http://www.hp.com/go/scalingthecloud to see what is new.

- Sign up for the HP Cloud Services private beta at http://www.hpcloud.com, so you can test, experience, and provide input on HP's two initial cloud services: HP Cloud Compute and HP Cloud Object Storage.

- http://www.hp.com/hpinfo/hptv.html is the HP Videos website. It contains videos and podcasts on Enterprise Business, alliances, customers/solutions, events, imaging and printing, industries, networking, servers, storage, and technical/real story.

- The CloudSystem Matrix QuickSpecs give detailed technical information on HP CloudSystem Matrix and can be accessed at http://www.hp.com/go/quickspecs. **HP Product Bulletin is also available from this site.**

- The HP Enterprise Business Community at http://h30499.www3.hp.com/hpeb is a place to meet other users, share thoughts and best practices, find solutions to technical challenges, or talk to the experts.

  The EB Community home page contains an *HP Communities* section, which includes a link to the HP Enterprise Business Blogs. The blogs cover topics such as *Enterprise Software*, *Inside the Datacenter*, *Networking*, *Servers*, *Services*, and *Storage*. Searching for *cloud* will produce results that include links to cloud-related articles, white papers, and webinars.

- The HP Developer Resource Center for CloudSystem addresses common developer questions to make it easier to adopt cloud computing with HP CloudSystem. It is at:

http://h21007.www2.hp.com/portal/site/dspp/menuitem.863c3e4cbcdc3f3515b49c108973a801/?ciid=b12ca027e0d61310VgnVCM100000a360ea10RCRD

- Matrix OE release notes, user guides, etc. can be found at: http://www.hp.com/go/matrixoe/docs

- Insight Control documentation can be found at http://www.hp.com/go/insightcontrol

- The HP Partner Portal can be found at:

    - http://www.hp.com/eur/smartportal for Europe, Middle East and Africa

    - http://www.hp.com/go/partnerportal for Canada and U.S.

    - http://www.hp.com/partners/ap for Asia Pacific

- The main HP Converged Infrastructure website is at http://www.hp.com/go/ci

- The National Institute of Standards and Technology website is at http://www.nist.gov

- The Microsoft cloud portal is at http://www.microsoft.com/en-us/server-cloud/private-cloud/default.aspx

- The VMware cloud portal is at http://www.vmware.com/solutions/cloud-computing/index.html

Test Preparation Questions and Answers

The following questions will help you measure your understanding of the material presented in this chapter. Read all the choices carefully, as there may be more than one correct answer. Choose all correct answers for each question.

Questions

1. What is the primary objective of the HP Solution Demo Portal?

   a. Proof of concept testing for HP CloudSystems

   b. A central point for demonstrations and further collateral

   c. Product briefs

   d. Detailed pricing and quotations for solutions

2. Which booth discusses the use of the HP Internet Usage Manager?

   a. Cloud Management Software Solutions

   b. HP CloudSystem Matrix

   c. HP CloudSystem Service Provider

   d. Business Technology Solutions

3. Which resource will quickly give information on delivering IaaS?

   a. HP Alliance One Partner Program

   b. http://www.hp.com/go/CloudSystemDemos

   c. http://h30499.www3.hp.com/hpeb

   d. HP Enterprise Videos website

4. Which resource gives detailed technical information on HP CloudSystem Matrix?

   a. CloudSystem QuickSpecs

   b. http://www.hp.com/go/cloudmaps

   c. http://hp.feedroom.com

   d. The HP CloudStart booth

Answers

1. ☑ **B.** The HP Solution Demo Portal provides a central location for demonstrations, webinars, and supporting collateral that showcase HP technologies.

   ☒ **A** is incorrect, because proof of concept testing is not part of this resource. **C** is incorrect, because product briefs are not a primary part of this resource. **D** is incorrect, because detailed pricing requires consultation with HP or partner sales staff.

2. ☑ **C.** The HP CloudSystem Service Provider booth discusses the use of HP Internet Usage Manager.

   ☒ **A** is incorrect, because this booth does not include IUM. **B** is incorrect, because this booth is concerned with the private cloud IaaS solution. **D** is incorrect, because this booth is not primarily a CloudSystem resource.

3. ☑ **B.** http://www.hp.com/go/CloudSystemDemos is a quick route to the *Deliver Iaas: cloudsystem matrix* page within the Solution Demo Portal.

   ☒ **A** is incorrect, because it is aimed at partners. **C** is incorrect, because it is concerned with meeting other users. **D** is incorrect, because it contains videos and podcasts about enterprise business.

4. ☑ **A.** The CloudSystem Matrix QuickSpecs give detailed technical information on HP CloudSystem Matrix and can be accessed at http://www.hp.com/go/quickspecs.

   ☒ **B** is incorrect, because it is concerned with HP Cloud Maps. **C** is incorrect, because it contains videos and podcasts about enterprise business. **D** is incorrect, because it describes the Cloud Discovery Workshop experience.

12 Sample Test

INTRODUCTION

The *HP ASE - Cloud Architect V1* certification validates your ability to specify and architect a spectrum of cloud services. These include private, public, and hybrid cloud, and IaaS, PaaS, and SaaS.

The intent of this book is to set expectations about the context of the exam and to help candidates prepare for it. Recommended training to prepare for this exam can be found at the HP ExpertOne website (http://www.hp.com/go/ExpertOne), as well as in books like this one. It is important to note that although training is recommended for exam preparation, successful completion of the training alone does not guarantee that you will pass the exam. In addition to training, exam items are based on knowledge gained from on-the-job experience and application, as well as other supplemental reference material that may be specified in this guide.

MINIMUM QUALIFICATIONS

In order to achieve the *HP ASE - Cloud Architect V1* certification, you must hold the *APC – Converged Infrastructure Solutions [2010]* certification. In the future, the *ATP – Converged Infrastructure Solutions Architect, v1* will also fill this prerequisite.

The candidate should have a thorough understanding of HP Converged Infrastructure and its components, including HP servers, storage, networking, power and cooling, software, security, and services.

CANDIDATE PROFILE

The HP ASE - Cloud Architect V1 certification is ideal for solution architects and technical presales professionals who need to recognize cloud opportunities and apply the right solutions to the right environments.

Typical candidates often hold one of the following job roles or certifications:

- IT architect/enterprise architect
- Principal technology consultant
- HP ExpertONE certified professional with infrastructure design experience

EXAM DETAILS

The following are details about the exam:

- **Exam ID:** HP0-D14

- **Number of items**: 62

- **Item types**: multiple choice (single-response), multiple choice (multiple-response), drag-and-drop

- **Exam time**: 105 minutes

- **Passing score**: 68%

- **Reference material**: No online or hard copy reference material will be allowed at the testing site.

HP0-D14 Testing Objectives

14%—Identify fundamental architectures, products, and solutions for HP CloudSystems

- Identify storage components

- Identify power and cooling components

- Identify server components

- Identify management software

- Identify cloud fundamentals, terms, and processes

34%—Identify HP CloudSystem offerings

- List and describe HP CloudSystem and HP VirtualSystem offerings and deployment models

- Identify how HP CloudSystem supports HP's Converged Infrastructure

- Describe the business benefits of HP Cloud Service Automation

- Describe the HP Cloud Functional Reference and mapping to HP CloudSystem offerings

- Describe the use and content of HP CloudSystem portals

16%—Plan and design an HP CloudSystem solution

- Develop an HP CloudSystem solution or an upgrade of an existing solution

- Plan and design an HP CloudSystem solution

36%—Describe HP CloudSystem implementations

- List and describe functionalities of Orchestration solutions

Test Preparation Questions and Answers

The following questions will help you measure your understanding of the material presented in this book. Read all of the choices carefully, as there may be more than one correct answer. Choose all correct answers for each question.

Questions

1. Match the service model to the virtual machine state.

   a. Infrastructure as a Service (IaaS)

   b. Platform as a Service (PaaS)

   c. Software as a Service (Saas)

   1. The virtual machine includes software development tools

   2. The virtual machine runs an operating system

   3. The virtual machine includes full applications

2. Which statement describes the term orchestration?

   a. The process of making services available via a network

   b. The execution of a pre-defined workflow used in the process of provisioning and managing infrastructure

   c. The process of collecting server, storage, network, and application availability and performance data across physical and virtual infrastructure

   d. The process of providing access to services from resource pools (such as traditional IT, private, and public cloud)

3. Which statement describes the term brokering?

   a. The process of making services available via a network

   b. The execution of a pre-defined workflow used in the process of provisioning and managing infrastructure

   c. The process of collecting server, storage, network, and application availability and performance data across physical and virtual infrastructure

   d. Providing access to a choice of services from resource pools such as traditional IT, private, and public cloud

4.   What are key attributes in cloud computing? (Select two.)

   a.   Metered by use

   b.   Overall charged

   c.   Service-based

   d.   Client-server based

   e.   Thin provisioned

5.   Match the type of delivery to the cloud model.

   a.   Public cloud   1.   On-premise

   b.   Virtual private cloud   2.   Off-premise

   c.   Private cloud

6.   Match the description of the key initiative to the HP solution that will assist customers on the journey to the Instant-On Enterprise.

   a.   Application transformation   1.   Right method, right time, right cost

   b.   Converged infrastructure   2.   Break silos

   c.   Hybrid delivery   3.   Architect solution for change

   d.   Enterprise security   4.   Protect assets without constricting flow

7.   Which description is correct regarding the requirement for orchestration in the HP Converged Infrastructure?

   a.   Fault-tolerant, mission-critical technologies and high-availability policies are utilized to provide the appropriate level of availability for each business application.

   b.   The infrastructure to support new business applications is provisioned using automated workflows, creating an application-aligned infrastructure that can be scaled up or down according to the needs of each application.

   c.   HP Converged Infrastructure is built on standard, common architectures and integrates with the most commonly used hypervisors, operating systems, and applications.

   d.   This approach enables the use, and re-use, of common components throughout the data center—from x86 to NonStop systems—and provides the ability to combine existing and new technologies, and to scale capacity over time.

8. Order the steps of the HP cloud management lifecycle. (1 to 4)

   a. Automate the provisioning and monitoring

   b. Manage service lifecycle

   c. Publish the service templates

   d. Design service templates

9. Match the correct term to the description of cloud service lifecycle management.

   a. Use   1. This area is concerned with monitoring the service

   b. Deploy   2. This area is concerned with the process of making products/services available

   c. Assure   3. This area takes care of the things that need to happen while the service is being employed

   d. Provision   4. This area begins when a user chooses a service and ends when that service is made available for use

10. Which layer of the HP Cloud Functional Reference Architecture interfaces directly with the infrastructure services?

    a. Supply

    b. Service

    c. Delivery

    d. Demand

11. What is the function of the demand layer in the HP Cloud Functional Reference Architecture?

    a. It deploys and configures the service instance.

    b. It provides access to the self-service portals.

    c. It manages all of the infrastructure services for the HP CloudSystem.

    d. It provides infrastructure elements for service delivery.

12. What is the function of the delivery layer in the HP Cloud Functional Reference Architecture?

    a. It deploys and configures the service instance.

    b. It provides access to the self-service portals.

    c. It manages all of the infrastructure services for the HP CloudSystem.

    d. It provides infrastructure elements for service delivery.

13. Label the layers of the HP Cloud Functional Reference Architecture.

    a. Supply layer

    b. Demand layer

    c. Delivery layer

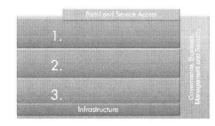

14. Which term describes the service designer portal in an HP CloudSystem solution?

    a. This is where the service architect designs the services and their associated infrastructure elements.

    b. This provides authorized users with access to predefined service definitions contained in the service catalog.

    c. This is used for monitoring the services, events, and processes.

    d. This is used by IT staff to manage resources such as servers, storage, and networks.

15. Which term describes the self-service portal in an HP CloudSystem Matrix solution?

    a. This is where the service architect designs the services and their associated infrastructure elements.

    b. This provides authorized users with access to predefined service definitions contained in the service catalog.

    c. This is used for modifying the pre-built standard OO workflows.

    d. This is used by IT staff to manage resources such as servers, storage, and networks.

16. What are functionalities of the HP Cloud Functional Reference Architecture delivery layer? (Select two.)

    a. Resource management

    b. User access

    c. Order management

    d. Request processing

    e. Service usage

17. What are functionalities of the HP Cloud Functional Reference Architecture demand layer? (Select two.)

    a. Resource management

    b. User access

    c. Order management

    d. Request processing

    e. Service usage

18. What is the functionality of the HP Cloud Functional Reference Architecture supply layer?

    a. Resource management

    b. User access

    c. Order management

    d. Request processing

    e. Service usage

19. Order the activities of provisioning a service in an HP CloudSystem solution from step 1 to step 7.

    a. Service composition   1.

    b. Service usage   2.

    c. Request a service   3.

    d. Resource provisioning   4.

    e. Order initiation   5.

    f. Service configuration and activation   6.

    g. Service deprovisioning   7.

20. HP Aggregation Platform for SaaS is included in which HP CloudSystem offering?

    a. HP Virtual System

    b. HP CloudSystem Matrix

    c. HP CloudSystem Service Provider

    d. HP CloudSystem Enterprise

21. Which HP storage system is recommended when using the HP CloudSystem Matrix Starter Kit?

    a. HP Lefthand P4500

    b. HP Enterprise Virtual Array

    c. HP 3PAR F200 Storage System

    d. HP P2000 G3 MSA

22. Which statement is true regarding HP Cloud Maps?

    a. They are a building block for the creation of a service catalog.

    b. They are a guideline for OS configuration and server activation.

    c. They are the hardware configurations for an HP CloudSystem solution.

    d. They are rules for bursting in an HP CloudSystem Service Provider.

23. Which core platform component differentiates HP CloudSystem Enterprise from HP CloudSystem Matrix?

    a. HP Matrix Operating Environment

    b. HP Storage Essentials

    c. HP Database and Middleware Automation

    d. HP AP4SaaS

24. When CSA initiates a lifecycle action, it can call upon the resources of which providers? (Select two.)

    a. Compute

    b. Availability

    c. Infrastructure

    d. System

    e. Runtime Configuration Management

25. What monitoring provider does HP CSA use?

    a. HP Matrix Infrastructure Orchestration

    b. HP Application Deployment Manager

    c. HP Universal Configuration Management Database

    d. HP SiteScope

26. Which core platform components differentiate HP CloudSystem Service Provider from HP CloudSystem Enterprise? (Select two.)

    a. HP Network Automation

    b. HP Database and Middleware Automation

    c. HP Cloud Consulting and Implementation

    d. HP Cloud Service Automation

    e. HP Aggregation Platform for SaaS

27. When using HP Intelligent Resilient Framework (IRF), what is a benefit of rapid recovery and network re-convergence in the event of a network failure?

    a. Reduced cost of planned maintenance

    b. Reduced risk of application unavailability

    c. Disaster-tolerant networking solutions protect the business against the risk of network downtime

    d. All network bandwidth that has been purchased is available

28. Which HP software products are included in HP CSA for Matrix? (Select two.)

    a. HP Fortify

    b. HP Tipping Point

    c. HP Server Automation

    d. HP SiteScope

    e. HP Infrastructure Orchestration

29. Match the HP product to the appropriate task in an HP CloudSystem solution.

    a. Monitor applications   1. HP Matrix Operating Environment

    b. Create infrastructure services   2. HP CSA for Matrix

    c. Provision applications

30. Which statement is true regarding HP Server Automation?

    a. Starter Edition is used in HP CloudSystem Matrix and HP Cloud System Enterprise.

    b. Enterprise Edition is used in HP CloudSystem Service Provider only.

    c. Starter Edition is used in HP CloudSystem Enterprise only.

    d. Enterprise Edition is used in HP CloudSystem Enterprise and HP CloudSystem Service Provider.

31. What are the main topologies used in an HP Server Automation environment? (Select three.)

    a.   Dual core

    b.   Single core

    c.   Multimaster mesh

    d.   Branch

    e.   Satellite

    f.   Subordinated

32. When designing an HP CloudSystem Enterprise Solution, which component is included in Server Automation Enterprise Edition?

    a.   HP Hybrid Delivery Workload Analyzer

    b.   HP Database and Middleware Automation Software

    c.   HP Operations Orchestration

    d.   HP Cloud Service Automation Portal Server

33. HP SiteScope falls under which CSA provider category?

a.   Monitoring

    a.   Application

    b.   Compute

    c.   Runtime Configuration Management

34. HP Matrix Operating Environment falls under which CSA provider category?

    a.   Monitoring

    b.   Application

    c.   Compute

    d.   Runtime Configuration Management

35. Which statement is correct regarding HP Cloud Service automation software? (Select two.)

    a.   It provides orchestrated deployment of Service Level Agreement (SLA) workflows.

    b.   It provides monitoring and management and automates service workflows to HP service systems.

    c.   It provides management of HP Converged Infrastructure compute resources and their resource pools.

    d.   It provides orchestrated deployment of compute resources.

    e.   It provides orchestrated deployment of complex multi-tier applications.

36. Match the HP CSA Foundation components with the correct layer and place.

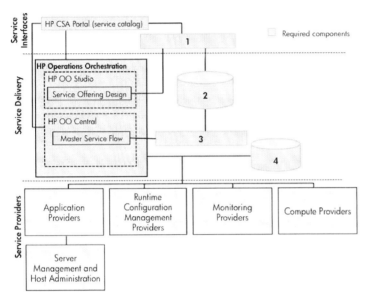

a. HP OO flows   1.
b. HP CSA Database   2.
c. HP CSA Provider console   3.
d. HP CSA Controller   4.

37. Which components work together to automate the service delivery process? (Select two.)

   a. HP CSA Database
   b. HP CSA Controller
   c. HP OO Studio
   d. HP OO Central
   e. HP CSA Provider console

38. Which component is used by the Service Designer to design service offerings, which are then made available to the Service Publisher?

   a. HP OO Studio
   b. HP OO Central
   c. HP CSA Provider Console
   d. HP CSA Controller
   e. HP CSA Portal

39. Which statement is correct regarding HP CSA users and portals?

    a. A single person can be responsible for only one user role and one portal.

    b. A single person can be responsible for more than one user role and portal.

    c. A single person can be responsible for only one user role, but more than one portal.

    d. A single person can be responsible for more than one user role, but only one portal.

40. In the management cycle of an HP CSA solution, what does the HP CSA Administrator do?

    a. Uses the HP OO Studio to design and manage services

    b. Manages and maintains computer providers or data centers

    c. Manages access and permissions as well as system settings

    d. Selects flows to publish as a service

41. Which phase of the sizing and configuration process is involved in the selection of CPUs and blades?

    a. Build

    b. Design

    c. Discovery

    d. Configure

42. Which statement is correct when talking about the discovery phase of sizing an HP CloudSystem solution?

    a. Calculation of the number of VMs per blade is included in this phase.

    b. A bill-of-materials, which includes all required software, hardware, and services, is created.

    c. The choice of storage systems and their configuration is made.

    d. Customer needs for number and types of workload and VMs are reviewed.

43. What is the recommended network bandwidth for each VM in an HP CloudSystem solution?

    a. At least 1Gb/s for IP traffic

    b. At least 800 Mb/s for SAN traffic

    c. At least 2Gb/s for SAN traffic

    d. At least 100 Mb/s for IP traffic

44. Which statement is correct when designing the RAM configuration of the server blades in an HP CloudSystem solution?

    a. The current and future requirements for RAM need to be assessed, and the most cost-effective DIMMs selected.

    b. High-Density DIMMs should be configured to offer best performance to the virtual machines running on the physical server blade.

    c. Lower-Density DIMMs should be configured to offer best price and lower Total-Cost-of-Ownership for the solution.

    d. A mixture of High-Density and Lower-Density DIMMs should be configured to guarantee best performance.

45. What are general principles that apply to the sizing process of an HP CloudSystem solution? (Select two.)

    a. Use one or two standard blades with options limited to memory and disk wherever possible.

    b. Use High-Density memory DIMMs and apply configuration rules to get best performance.

    c. Use Virtual Connect and HP BladeSystem SAN switches to offer LAN and SAN connectivity.

    d. Use HP Blades in c7000 enclosures to get lower power consumption than rack-mounted servers.

    e. Use HP storage systems to minimize unplanned downtime in case of data center failure.

46. Which highly available CMS solution is recommended for an HP CloudSystem Matrix Solution?

    a. A dedicated c3000 enclosure

    b. A pair of rack-mount servers

    c. A BL460c G7 blade

    d. A BL460c G7 Windows cluster

47. The Passmark CPU score for the *[Dual CPU] AMD Opteron 6174* is reported by the cpubenchmark website to be 15,498. What is the ECU-equivalent score for a single processor?

    a. 8

    b. 19

    c. 38

    d. 76

48. Which statement is true regarding availability of the Central Management System (CMS)?

    a. The CMS should be protected with VMware Fault Tolerance to achieve availability.

    b. The CMS should be protected with an image to recover from failure.

    c. The CMS should be protected with a ServiceGuard cluster system.

    d. The CMS should be protected with a standby system.

49. Which service should be offered to a customer who needs support in the implementation phase of a cloud project? (Select two.)

    a. Cloud System Matrix Conversion Service

    b. Cloud Roadmap Service

    c. Cloud Discovery Workshop

    d. SmartCloud Services

    e. Cloud Start Service

50. Which service should be offered to a customer who needs support in the planning phase of a project? (Select two.)

    a. Cloud System Matrix Conversion Service

    b. Cloud Roadmap Service

    c. Cloud Discovery Workshop

    d. Model Agile Cloud Services

    e. Cloud Start Service

Answers

1. ☑ **A-2, B-1,C-3.** Infrastructure as a Service (IaaS) = The virtual machine runs an operating system, Platform as a Service (PaaS) = The virtual machine includes software development tools,Software as a Service (Saas) = The virtual machine includes full applications. *For more information, see Chapter 1.*

2. ☑ **B.** Orchestration refers to the execution of a pre-defined workflow used in the process of provisioning and managing infrastructure. *For more information, see Chapter 1.*
   ☒ **A** is incorrect; this is a description of hosting. **C** is incorrect; this describes monitoring. **D** is incorrect; this describes brokering.

3. ☑ **D.** Brokering refers to providing access to a choice of services from resource pools such as traditional IT, private, and public cloud. *For more information, see Chapter 1.*
   ☒ **A** is incorrect; this is a description of hosting. **B** is incorrect; this describes orchestration. **C** is incorrect; this describes monitoring.

4. ☑ **A and C.** Cloud computing should be metered by use and be service-based. *For more information, see Chapter 2.*
   ☒ **B** is incorrect; this is not a key attribute of cloud computing. **D** is incorrect; cloud computing is not client-server based. **E** is incorrect; thin-provisioned storage is highly desirable in a cloud environment, but it is not essential.

5. ☑ **A-2.** Public Cloud = Off-premise. Amazon, Google, RackSpace, etc., house their infrastructure in their own data centers, not in our customers' data centers. **B-2.** Virtual Private Cloud = Off-premise. An example of Virtual Private Cloud is HP ECS-Compute, where the infrastructure is housed in HP data centers. **C-1.** Private Cloud = On-premise. Private Cloud solutions are normally hosted in the customer's own data center. *For more information, see Chapter 2.*

6. ☑ **A-3, B-2, C-1, D-4.** Application Transformation = Architect solution for change, Converged Infrastructure = Break silos, Hybrid Delivery = Right method, right time, right cost, Enterprise Security = Protect assets without constricting flow. *For more information, see Chapter 2.*

7. ☑ **B.** The infrastructure to support new business applications is provisioned using automated workflows. *For more information, see Chapter 2.*
   ☒ **A** is incorrect; this describes *resilience.* **C** is incorrect; this describes *open.* **D** is incorrect; this describes *modular..*

8. ☑ **A-3, B-4, C-2, D-1.** Step 1 is design service templates. Step 2 is publish the service templates. Step 3 is automate the provisioning and monitoring. Step 4 is manage service lifecycle. *For more information, see Chapter 3.*

9. ☑ **A-3, B-2, C-1, D-4.**
Use = This area takes care of the things that need to happen while the service is being employed. Deploy = This area is concerned with the process of making products/ services available. Assure = This area is concerned with monitoring the service. Provision = This area begins when a user chooses a service and ends when that service is made available for use. *For more information, see Chapter 3.*

10. ☑ **A.** The supply layer interfaces directly with the infrastructure services. *For more information, see Chapter 3.*
☒ **B** is incorrect; there is no such layer. **C** and **D** are incorrect; these layers do not interface directly with the infrastructure services.

11. ☑ **B.** The demand layer provides access to the self-service portals. *For more information, see Chapter 3.*
☒ **A** is incorrect; the delivery layer does this. **C** is incorrect; the supply layer does this. **D** is incorrect; this is provided by the infrastructure.

12. ☑ **A.** The delivery layer deploys and configures the service instance. *For more information, see Chapter 3.*
☒ **B** is incorrect; the demand layer does this. **C** is incorrect; the supply layer does this. **D** is incorrect; this is provided by the infrastructure.

13. ☑ **A-3, B-1, C-2.**

For more information, see Chapter 3.

14. ☑ **A.** The service designer portal is where the service architect designs services and their associated infrastructure elements. *For more information, see Chapter 3.*
☒ **B** is incorrect; this describes the user self-service portal. **C** is incorrect; this describes the service manager portal. **D** is incorrect; this describes the IT administrator portal.

15. ☑ **B.** The self-service portal provides authorized users with access to predefined service definitions contained in the service catalog. *For more information, see Chapter 3.*
☒ **A** is incorrect; this describes the service designer portal. **C** is incorrect; this describes OO Studio. **D** is incorrect; this describes the IT Operations Console.

16. ☑ **D** and **E.** Request Processing and Service Usage are functionalities of the delivery layer. *For more information, see Chapter 3.*
☒ **A** is incorrect; the supply layer does this. **B** is incorrect; the demand layer does this. **C** is incorrect; the demand layer does this.

17. ☑ **B and C.** User Access and Order Management are functionalities of the demand layer. *For more information, see Chapter 3.*
    ☒ **A** is incorrect; the supply layer does this. **D and E** are incorrect; the delivery layer does this.

18. ☑ **A.** Resource Management is functionality of the supply layer. *For more information, see Chapter 3.*
    ☒ **B and C** are incorrect; the demand layer does this. **D and E** are incorrect; the delivery layer does this.

19. ☑ **A-3, B-6, C-1, D-4, E-2, F-5, G-7.** *For more information, see Chapter 3.*

    1. Request a service
    2. Order initiation
    3. Service composition
    4. Resource provisioning
    5. Service configuration and activation
    6. Service usage
    7. Service deprovisioning

20. ☑ **C.** HP Aggregation for SaaS is included with HP CloudSystem Service Provider. *For more information, see Chapters 2 and 4.*
    ☒ **A, B and D** are incorrect; these offerings do not include AP4SaaS.

21. ☑ **B.** The HP Enterprise Virtual Array is recommended when using the HP CloudSystem Matrix Starter Kit. *For more information, see Chapter 4.*
    ☒ **A, C and D** are incorrect; these storage systems are not recommended when using the HP CloudSystem Matrix Starter Kit.

22. ☑ **A.** HP Cloud Maps are building blocks for the creation of a service catalog. *For more information, see Chapter 4.*
    ☒ **B** is incorrect; HP Cloud Maps are not concerned with OS configuration and server activation. **C** is incorrect; HP Cloud Maps include templates for hardware and software configuration, workflows, and scripts. **D** is incorrect; HP Cloud Maps do not include rules for bursting in HP CloudSystem Service Provider..

23. ☑ **C.** HP Database and Middleware Automation is included with CloudSystem Enterprise, but not with HP CloudSystem Matrix. *For more information, see Chapter 4.*
    ☒ **A** is incorrect; HP Matrix OE is present in all HP CloudSystem offerings. **B** is incorrect; HP Storage Essentials is not a core component of any HP CloudSystem offering. **D** is incorrect; HP AP4SaaS is a core component of HP CloudSystem Service Provider.

24. ☑ **A and E.** Compute and Runtime Configuration Management are two of the providers that CSA can call upon. *For more information, see Chapter 7.*
    ☒ **B, C and D** are incorrect; there are no such providers.

25. ☑ **D.** HP CSA uses HP SiteScope as a monitoring provider. *For more information, see Chapter 7.*
    ☒ **A** is incorrect; HP Matrix Infrastructure Orchestration is a compute provider. **B** is incorrect; HP Application Deployment Manager is an application provider. **C** is incorrect; HP SiteScope is a monitoring provider.

26. ☑ **A and E.** HP Network Automation and HP Aggregation Platform for SaaS are core platform components of HP CloudSystem Service Provider but not HP CloudSystem Enterprise. *For more information, see Chapter 4.*
    ☒ **B, C, and D** are incorrect; these core components are common to both offerings.

27. ☑ **B.** Reduced risk of application unavailability is a benefit of IRF's rapid recovery and network re-convergence. *For more information, see Chapter 5.*
    ☒ **A, C and D** are incorrect; these are not benefits of rapid recovery and network re-convergence in the event of a network failure.

28. ☑ **C and D.** HP Server Automation and HP SiteScope are included in HP CSA for Matrix. *For more information, see Chapter 6.*
    ☒ **A, B and E** are incorrect; they are not included in HP CSA for Matrix.

29. ☑ **A-2, B-1, C-2.** Monitor applications = HP CSA for Matrix. Create infrastructure services = HP Matrix Operating Environment. Provision applications = HP CSA for Matrix. *For more information, see Chapter 6.*

30. ☑ **D.** HP Server Automation Enterprise Edition is used in HP CloudSystem Enterprise and HP CloudSystem Service Provider. *For more information, see Chapters 6 and 7.*
    ☒ **A** is incorrect; HP Cloud System Enterprise uses HA SA Enterprise Edition. **B** is incorrect; SA Enterprise Edition is used in HP CloudSystem Enterprise and HP CloudSystem Service Provider. **C** is incorrect; SA Starter Edition is used in HP CloudSystem Matrix.

31. ☑ **B, C and E**. Single Core, Multimaster Mesh, and Satellite are the main topologies used in an HP Server Automation environment.
    ☒ **A, D and F** are incorrect; they are not HP Server Automation topologies.

32. ☑ **B.** HP Database and Middleware Automation Software is included in Server Automation Enterprise Edition. *For more information, see Chapter 7.*
    ☒ **A, C, and D** are incorrect; these are not included in Server Automation Enterprise Edition.

33. ☑ **A.** HP SiteScope is a monitoring provider. *For more information, see Chapter 7.*
    ☒ **B** is incorrect; HP ADM is an application provider. **C** is incorrect; VMware vCenter and HP Matrix infrastructure orchestration are compute providers. **D** is incorrect; HP uCMDB is a Runtime Configuration Management provider.

34. ☑ **C.** HP Matrix Operating Environment is a compute provider. *For more information, see Chapter 7.*

☒ **A** is incorrect; the monitoring category includes HP SiteScope. **B** is incorrect; the application category includes HP ADM. **D** is incorrect; the Runtime Configuration Management category includes HP uCMDB.

35. ☑ **D and E.** HP Cloud Service automation software provides orchestrated deployment of compute resources and orchestrated deployment of complex multi-tier applications.

☒ **A, B, and C** are incorrect; HP Cloud Service automation software is not designed to perform these actions. *For more information, see Chapter 7.*

36. ☑ **A-4, B-2, C-1, D-3.** *For more information, see Chapter 7.*

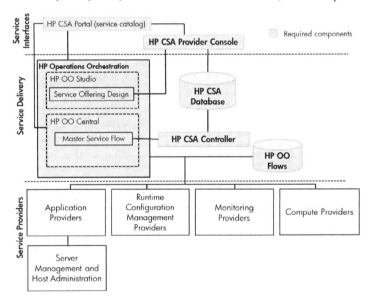

37. ☑ **B and D.** HP CSA Controller and HP OO Central work together to automate the service delivery process. *For more information, see Chapter 7.*

☒ **A** is incorrect; the HP CSA database stores information regarding service instances and their lifecycle states. **C** is incorrect; HP OO Studio is used by the Service Designer to design service offerings. **E** is incorrect; the **HP CSA Provider Console** is used by the *Service Publisher* to populate the Service Request Catalog.

38. ☑ **A.** HP OO Studio is used by the Service Designer to design service offerings. *For more information, see Chapter 7.*

☒ **B** is incorrect; when an end-user subscribes to a service, the request is sent to HP OO Central, which determines whether the service instance should be created, modified, or terminated. **C** is incorrect; the Service Publisher uses the **HP CSA Provider Console** to make service offerings available for end-users to order. **D** is incorrect; the HP CSA Controller, along with OO Central, drives the service lifecycle actions to launch task-specific flows. **E** is incorrect; the **HP CSA portal** provides a simple graphical interface that enables *end-users* to subscribe to service offerings.

39. ☑ **B.** A single person can be responsible for more than one CSA user role and portal. *For more information, see Chapter 7.*

   ☒ **A, C, and D** are incorrect; a single person can be responsible for more than one user role and portal.

40. ☑ **C.** The HP CSA Administrator manages access and permissions as well as system settings. *For more information, see Chapter 7.*

   ☒ **A** is incorrect; **HP OO Studio** is used by the Service Designer to design service offerings. **B** is incorrect; management and maintenance of computer providers or data centers is not part of the role of the HP CSA Administrator. **D** is incorrect; the Service Publisher is responsible for selecting flows to publish.

41. ☑ **B.** CPUs and blades are selected in the design phase. *For more information, see Chapter 9.*

   ☒ **A** is incorrect; the build phase is where the BoM is created. **C** is incorrect; the discovery phase is where the number and types of user instances, number of virtual machines, memory per VM, etc., are determined. **D** is incorrect; there is no configure phase.

42. ☑ **D.** Customer needs for number and types of workload and VMs are reviewed in the discovery phase. *For more information, see Chapter 9.*

   ☒ **A and C** are incorrect; this is performed in the design phase. **B** is incorrect; the BoM is created in the build phase.

43. ☑ **D.** The recommended network bandwidth for each VM in an HP CloudSystem solution is at least 100 Mb/s for IP traffic. *For more information, see Chapter 9.*

   ☒ **A, B, and C** are incorrect; the recommended network bandwidth is at least 100 Mb/s for IP traffic.

44. ☑ **A.** The current and future requirements for RAM need to be assessed, and the most cost-effective DIMMs selected. *For more information, see Chapter 9.*

   ☒ **B** is incorrect; this could raise the cost unnecessarily. **C** is incorrect; using low-density DIMMs could consume all available DIMM slots and leave no room for expansion. **D** is incorrect; mixing DIMMs of different densities is unlikely to give the best performance.

45. ☑ **A and D.** Use one or two standard blades with options limited to memory and disk wherever possible, and use HP Blades in c7000 enclosures to get lower power consumption than in rack-mounted servers. *For more information, see Chapter 9.*

   ☒ **B** is incorrect; the use of high-density DIMMs could raise the cost unnecessarily. **C** is incorrect; Virtual Connect and FlexFabric are recommended to reduce ownership costs and number of cables. **E** is incorrect; use of HP storage systems will not necessarily minimize unplanned downtime in case of data center failure, unless disaster tolerance has been included in the design of the solution.

46. ☑ **B.** A pair of rack-mount servers is recommended for a highly available CMS for an HP CloudSystem Matrix Solution. *For more information, see Chapter 9.*

    ☒ **A, C and D** are incorrect; a pair of rack-mount servers is recommended for an HP CloudSystem Matrix Solution.

47. ☑ **B.** For a Dual CPU system, divide the Passmark score by two to get the Passmark score per processor. Divide this number by 400 to find the ECU-equivalent score for a single processor. 15,498 / 2 = 7749. 7749 / 400 = 19 (rounded down). *For more information, see Chapter 9.*

    ☒ **A, C, and D** are incorrect; the per processor ECU-equivalent score is calculated as above.

48. ☑ **D.** The CMS should be protected with a standby system. *For more information, see Chapter 9.*

    ☒ **A, B, and C** are incorrect; the CMS should be protected with a standby system.

49. ☑ **A and E.** Cloud System Matrix Conversion Service and Cloud Start Service may be appropriate in the implementation phase of a cloud project. *For more information, see Chapter 10.*

    ☒ **B and C** are incorrect; these services are more appropriate for the planning phase of a project. **D** is incorrect; this is not an HP service offering.

50. ☑ **B and C.** Cloud Roadmap Service and Cloud Discovery Workshop may be appropriate in the planning phase of a project. *For more information, see Chapter 10.*

    ☒ **A and E** are incorrect; these are more appropriate for the implementation phase. D is incorrect; this is not an HP service offering.

A Cloud Competitive Landscape

EXAM OBJECTIVES

There should be no competitive questions in the exam. The objectives of this appendix are to:

✓ Identify the cloud competitive landscape.

✓ Explain the strengths of HP cloud solutions.

INTRODUCTION

There are several companies competing for market share in the cloud arena. In this appendix we will discuss the cloud competitive landscape; including the products and solutions offered by key competitors of HP. It will not be possible to provide an exhaustive picture of all of the competitor's offerings; rather, we will give an overview based on publicly available information. In addition, we will limit our discussion to companies who provide one or more hardware or software solutions that help customers to deploy their own cloud solutions. We will also highlight the strengths of HP cloud solutions.

 Note
This information was correct at the time of writing. It is likely that competitive offerings will change over time

Cloud Competitive Landscape

When we look at the cloud competitive landscape, the first thing to notice is that there is a mix of infrastructure vendors, such as IBM, Cisco, VCE Company (VMware, Cisco, EMC), Oracle, and NetApp. There are also traditional software vendors, such as CA Technologies and BMC Software.

Let us take a look at all of these vendors' cloud products and solutions to see what they have to offer.

IBM

IBM's vision for cloud computing is called IBM SmartCloud, and comprises three main elements:

- **IBM SmartCloud Foundation**: A set of technologies, including application development and deployment, cloud infrastructure, cloud provisioning, cloud management, cloud integration, and cloud security, that form the basis for building and deploying private and hybrid clouds.

- **IBM SmartCloud Services**: Infrastructure (IaaS) and platform (PaaS) capabilities delivered as a service. IaaS solutions include IBM SmartCloud Enterprise and Enterprise+. PaaS solutions include IBM SmartCloud Application Services. Also included is IBM SmartCloud managed backup services.

- **IBM SmartCloud Solutions**: Software as a service (SaaS) business solutions.

Let us now take a closer look at each element.

IBM SmartCloud Foundation

As previously mentioned, IBM SmartCloud foundation comprises a set of technologies that are essential for effective cloud computing. These technologies include:

- **Application development and deployment**: IBM Workload Deployer is a hardware appliance that can be used to deploy and manage applications in a private cloud. It provides access to virtual images of IBM middleware and can reduce setup time for WebSphere environments. It provides support for WebSphere Application Server Hypervisor Edition on ESX, Power and System z.

- **Cloud infrastructure**: The journey to an IBM cloud begins with building a virtualization foundation using:

  - **IBM Power**: PowerVM provides a secure and scalable server virtualization environment for AIX, IBM i, and Linux environments on IBM POWER processor-based systems. IBM also offers POWER-based blades for the BladeCenter.

  - **System x/BladeCenter**: System x and BladeCenter are scalable x86 platforms that support the choice of hypervisors from Microsoft, VMware, Red Hat, and SUSE.

  - **IBM BladeCenter Foundation for Cloud**: Combines a choice of IBM, Cisco or Brocade networking, IBM BladeCenter H chassis, IBM Blade servers HS22, HS22V, HX5 and HX5+MAX5, and IBM Systems Director 6.2 into an integrated virtualization platform with converged networking, virtualized servers, storage, and management.

  - **System z (mainframe)**: Virtualization on System z enables the sharing of processor, memory, network, I/O, and cryptographic features, and enables the consolidation of multiple systems and software stacks onto a single platform.

  - **IBM Systems Director VMControl**: VMControl simplifies the management of virtual environments across multiple virtualization technologies and hardware platforms. The combination of IBM Systems Director and VMControl can reduce the total cost of ownership of virtualized environments—servers, storage and networks—by decreasing management costs, increasing asset utilization, and linking infrastructure performance to business goals. Features include creation, management, and relocation of virtual machines, and deploying of virtual images.

- **Storage Virtualization solutions**: These solutions include:

    - **IBM SAN Volume Controller**: Centralized management for storage infrastructure.

    - **IBM Scale Out Network Attached Storage (SONAS)**.

    - **IBM Storwize V7000**: A virtualized storage system designed to consolidate block and file workloads into a single storage system.

    - **IBM System Storage DS8800**: A flagship high-performance, high-capacity IBM storage system.

    - **IBM System Storage N series**: An integrated storage solution supporting Fibre Channel, iSCSI, and NAS protocols.

    - **IBM System Storage TS7650G ProtecTIER Deduplication Gateway**: A data deduplication solution for improved backup and disaster recovery operations.

    - **IBM Tivoli Storage Productivity Center**: A suite of storage infrastructure management tools that centralize, simplify, automate, and optimize tasks associated with storage systems, storage networks, replication services, and capacity management.

    - **IBM XIV Storage System**: A high-end, distributed, highly parallel disk storage system.

The IBM cloud journey continues with private cloud offerings, called *entry cloud* solutions:

- **IBM Starter Kit for Cloud x86 Edition**: An entry-level private cloud software offering that allows users of IBM BladeCenter Foundation for Cloud virtualization platform and select IBM System x and BladeCenter servers to request and provision an environment quickly through a web-based interface.

- **IBM Starter Kit for Cloud Power Edition**: Starter Kit for Cloud is a solution that builds upon IBM PowerVM virtualization and IBM Systems Director VMControl. It enables rapid scalability by allowing additional servers or blades to be added to the cloud infrastructure. It also includes basic workload metering to support a pay-per-use business model.

- **IBM zEnterprise Starter Edition for Cloud**: An entry-level cloud offering for deploying an IaaS Cloud delivery model for Linux on System z environments. It enables the provisioning of Linux on System z images under z/VM using Tivoli Provisioning Manager.

- **IBM SmartCloud Provisioning**: An entry-level IaaS platform that allows companies to get cloud-enabled within a few hours. It prevents service outages by automatically working around hardware failures and supporting in-place adding, removing, and upgrading of physical servers.

The IBM cloud journey continues with deploying advanced cloud functionality—including full lifecycle management, automated provisioning, and metering using:

- **IBM CloudBurst on System x**: A pre-integrated service delivery infrastructure that incorporates a self-service portal, service catalog, and automated workflows for accelerated deployment of private cloud. This solution is built on the IBM System x platform, brings the advantages of the latest IBM BladeCenter, and enables management of both physical and virtual workloads using a single interface to servers, storage, and networking resources.

- **IBM CloudBurst on Power Systems**: This solution is similar to IBM CloudBurst on System x, except this one uses IBM Power systems.

- **Tivoli Service Automation Manager**: Enables users to request, deploy, monitor, and manage the lifecycle of cloud computing services. It is included in IBM CloudBurst and integrates with IBM WebSphere CloudBurst to speed the delivery of WebSphere-based services. Support is offered for Linux operating systems.

- **IBM Service Delivery Manager**: A pre-integrated software stack, deployed as a set of virtual images that automate IT service deployment, monitoring, and cost management. It includes a self-service portal, automated provisioning and de-provisioning of resources, real-time monitoring of physical and virtual resources, usage and accounting chargeback capabilities, and prepackaged automation templates and workflows for common resource types.

- **Cloud provisioning**: IBM SmartCloud Provisioning provides businesses with an infrastructure- as-a-service (IaaS) cloud, reducing costs and providing a highly scalable, rapid deployment environment for running applications and reacting to dynamic changes in user resource demands. It is an entry-level platform that allows companies to get cloud-enabled within a few hours.

- **Cloud management**: IBM Cloud Service Delivery and Management solutions provide visibility, control, and automation across private, public, and hybrid cloud environments.

- **Cloud integration**: WebSphere Cast Iron Cloud Integration enables businesses to make connections between public clouds, private clouds, and on-premise applications. This solution provides integration with Salesforce.com, Oracle CRM, SAP, and Oracle ERP, and is available as a self-contained physical appliance, a virtual appliance, and a complete multi-tenant cloud service.

- **Cloud security**: The IBM blueprint for building and deploying secure software includes IBM Secure Engineering Framework, providing security best practices for developing products and applications; IBM Enhanced Security, enabling secure access in cloud, SOA, complex portal and web application environments; and Secure Information Access, enabling access to the security expertise IBM offers on current and emerging cyber-security issues via the IBM Institute for Advanced Security.

IBM SmartCloud Services

IBM SmartCloud Services are platform (PaaS) and infrastructure (IaaS) capabilities delivered as-a-service. Services include:

- **IBM SmartCloud Application Services**: IBM's platform as a service offering, this solution enables the development, deployment, management, and integration of PaaS applications in the cloud.

- **IBM SmartCloud Enterprise and Enterprise+**: IBM's infrastructure as a service offerings, these solutions are designed to provide rapid and secure access to enterprise-class virtual server IaaS environments. IBM SmartCloud Enterprise+ provides hosted, managed, private cloud infrastructure services.

- **IBM SmartCloud managed backup services**: These solutions include Fastprotect online, providing cost-effective cloud backup for PCs; remote data protection for PCs, delivering professionally managed, cloud-based data backup and protection services for PCs; and remote data protection for servers, an automated, scalable, cloud-based backup and recovery solution for data that is distributed on servers, desktops, and laptops in various geographic locations.

IBM SmartCloud Solutions

IBM SmartCloud solutions are a suite of cloud-based software as a service (SaaS) capabilities. The solution categories include:

- **Collaboration and social business**: IBM SmartCloud for Social Business (formerly known as LotusLive) enables simplified purchase and access to business-grade file sharing, communities, web meetings, instant messaging, mail, and calendar functionality.

- **Business process management**: IBM Blueworks Live (formerly known as BPM Blueprint) is a browser-based, collaborative, business process management solution.

- **Web analytics and enterprise marketing**: The IBM Coremetrics Digital Marketing Optimization Suite uses customer profiles, web analytics, and digital marketing execution to turn site visitors into repeat customers by delivering a compelling experience throughout each customer's digital lifecycle.

- **Business analytics and optimization**: The IBM business analytics and optimization (BAO) strategic intellectual property insight platform (SIIP) uses advanced analytics and natural language capabilities to enable businesses to gain useful knowledge from chemical and biological data stored in patent databases and scientific journals. The insight gained can be used for strategic decision-making.

- **Smarter cities**: IBM Intelligent Operations Center for Cloud is a SaaS solution that allows cities of all sizes to integrate information across city operations to help improve the delivery of city services.

More information on IBM's cloud offerings is available at http://www.ibm.com/cloud.

Cisco

Cicso's primary cloud solution is called CloudVerse. It is a unified cloud platform that comprises four main elements:

- **Cisco Cloud Applications and Services**: A range of cloud-based business applications and services delivered by Cisco partners and service providers.

- **Cisco Unified Data Center**: An architecture for supporting multiple cloud and virtualization strategies.

- **Cisco Cloud Intelligent Network**: Provides interconnect capabilities within and between data centers. Integrates with the Unified Data Center to provide an end-to-end platform for cloud delivery.

- **Cisco Cloud Enablement Services**: A portfolio of professional and technical services delivered by Cisco and partners. Services are offered for cloud strategy, cloud planning and design, cloud implementation, and cloud optimization.

Let us now take a closer look at each element.

Cisco Cloud Applications and Services

Cisco Cloud Applications and Services are focused on delivering application services to any device, in any location, at any time, while optimizing performance, security, and reliability.

The portfolio includes:

- **Hosted services**: These include Cisco Hosted Collaboration Solution (HCS), which enables Cisco partners to provide a range of Cisco collaboration applications *as-a-service* to their customers. The supported applications include Cisco Unified Communications Manager, Cisco Unity Connection, Cisco Unified Presence, Cisco Unified Mobility for Nokia, iPhone, and Google Android clients, Cisco WebEx Meeting Center, and Cisco Unified Enterprise Attendant Console. Also included is Cisco TelePresence Callway, which is a subscription-based telepresence service for small to medium-sized business. By purchasing Cisco TelePresence endpoints and subscribing to the Callway-hosted service, customers can make unlimited calls to Cisco TelePresence endpoints as well as to any standards-based video product that can make Internet calls.

- **Cisco's Collaboration Cloud portfolio**: This portfolio includes a set of applications and services that enables users to access communications, telepresence, customer contact, meetings, and instant messaging services from Cisco and Cisco partners.

- **Cisco Videoscape**: This enables service providers to combine content from TV, online, and on-demand sources with social media, communications, and mobility to create a unified video experience for customers.

- **Cisco Cloud Security solutions**: These solutions provide web and email security and include Cisco ScanSafe Cloud Web Security, which analyzes web requests for malicious or inappropriate content, and Cisco IronPort Cloud Email Security, which provides protection from malware such as spam and viruses.

■ **Third-party cloud services and applications**: These include a large range of third-party cloud services and applications that have been pretested with CloudVerse.

Cisco Unified Data Center

Cisco Unified Data Center is an architecture for supporting multiple cloud and virtualization strategies. It has three main components:

■ **Cisco Unified Fabric**: Based on the Cisco Nexus family of switches and providing high-speed connectivity with security and high-availability.

■ **Cisco Unified Computing**: The Cisco Unified Computing System (Cisco UCS) integrates Cisco x86 servers (Cisco UCS B-Series Blade Servers and Cisco UCS C-Series Rack-Mount Servers), network, and I/O resources into one system and uses model-based service templates to automate server configuration processes. It also provides a single, programmable management interface that can scale to hundreds of blades and thousands of virtual machines. When combined with the Cisco Unified Fabric framework, Cisco UCS gives IT managers a wire-once platform for providing elastic and agile pools of virtualized resources. Through open APIs, Cisco UCS provides flexibility in platform choice and network integration and migration.

■ **Cisco Unified Management**: This provides a self-service, open management platform for integrating data center resources such as computing, applications, network services, security, storage, and cloud computing.

Cisco Cloud Intelligent Network

Cisco Cloud Intelligent Network is focused on reliable, secure, and predictable delivery of cloud services. It provides connections within and between data centers, and integrates with the Cisco Unified Data Center to provide an end-to-end delivery platform for cloud services.

The Cisco Cloud Intelligent Network strategy encompasses three areas:

Cisco Cloud Customer Connect: This enables the secure delivery of services from the source to the end-user, and includes business-oriented policy controls and context-aware security capabilities that help to maintain appropriate levels of QoS.

Cisco Cloud-to-Cloud Connect: This enables data center networks to be extended across data centers and clouds.

Cisco Network Management and Automation: This includes a large range of products that are designed to help customers optimize and automate management of their networks. Management categories, with each category containing one or more management solutions, include Collaboration and Unified Communications Management, Configuration and Change Management, Connected Energy Network Management and Automation, Data Center

Management and Automation, Network Analysis Module (NAM) Products, Optical Management, Performance Management, Policy Management for Prime, Routing and Switching Management, Security and Identity Management, Video, Cable and Content Delivery Management, and Wireless Management.

Cisco Cloud Enablement Services

Cisco Cloud Enablement Services are delivered by Cisco and their partners and include:

- **Cloud Enablement Services for Building IaaS Clouds**: This provides customized strategy, planning and design, implementation, and optimization based on a customer's targeted private cloud offering. Services include Cloud Strategy Service, Cloud Planning and Design Service, Cloud Implementation Service, and Cloud Optimization Service.

- **Cloud Enablement Services for Adopting Clouds**: This service helps customers to adopt a public cloud model based on their current environment and business goals.

More information on Cisco's cloud offerings is available at http://www.cisco.com/go/cloud.

Virtual Computing Equipment Company (VCE)

Virtual Computing Environment Company (VCE) is an alliance between Cisco, EMC, and VMware. Its major offering, the VCE Vblock Infrastructure Platform, offers pre-integrated infrastructure bundles delivered by the VCE Company (formerly Acadia). The core focus of this offering is Infrastructure as a Service using VMware virtual resources. VCE recently announced a strategic alliance with BMC Software that will combine the solutions of both companies to address the growing market demand for converged infrastructures in cloud computing projects.

Designed to work with almost any application, Vblock Infrastructure Platforms have been tested and validated to work with many major applications, including Microsoft Exchange, Microsoft SharePoint, Oracle RAC, SAP, and VMware View.

Vblock Infrastructure Platforms are scaled for customer technical and business requirements and include the following elements:

- Virtualization by VMware vSphere and VMware vCenter Server

- Networking by Cisco (including Nexus 5548, MDS 9148, MDS 9506, and MDS 9513)

- Computing by Cisco Unified Computing System (UCS), (including B200-M2, B230-M1, B250-M2, B440-M1, and B200-M2 blade option)

- Storage by EMC (including EMC VNX 7500, VNX 5700, VNX 5500, VNX 5300, and EMC Symmetrix VMAX)

- Management by EMC Ionix Unified Infrastructure Manager (UIM). UIM is included in every Vblock Infrastructure Platform to manage the configuration, provisioning, and compliance of aggregated Vblock Infrastructure Platforms. UIM simplifies deployment and integration into IT service catalogs and workflow engines, and simplifies Vblock platform deployment by abstracting the overall provisioning while offering granular access to individual components for troubleshooting and fault management.

- Security by RSA enVision (optional)

- Additional hardware required for racking, cabling, uninterruptible power supplies, etc.

VCE also provide advisory, implementation, and integration services for cloud.

- Advisory services include VCE Cloud Strategic Impact Advisory Service, bringing executive stakeholders together for a half-day session and highlighting the anticipated cloud computing benefits to the organization; and VCE Cloud Computing Strategy Service, assessing the organization's existing infrastructure and applications and developing a high-level architecture and roadmap for governance, operations, and facilities.

- Implementation services include VCE Deployment And Implementation Service and Complementary And Additive Implementation Services (including VCE Vframework Service and VCE Data Center Integration Service).

- Integration services include Virtualization and Migration Services, Virtual Desktop Infrastructure Services, Security Risk Assessments, Architecture and Design Services, Operating System Refresh (re-platforming) Services, and Information Technology Service Management Services.

More information on the VCE cloud offerings is available at http://www.vce.com.

Oracle

Oracle's strategy is to offer a broad portfolio of software and hardware products and services to enable public, private, and hybrid clouds, enabling customers to choose the right approach for them.

For private clouds, Oracle offers a portfolio of horizontal and industry applications that run on a standards-based, shared services platform. For private Platform-as-a-Service (PaaS), Oracle supplies middleware and database products, including Oracle Exadata Database Machine and Oracle Exalogic Elastic Cloud. For private Infrastructure-as-a-Service (IaaS), Oracle supplies server, storage, and networking hardware combined with virtualization and operating system software.

For public clouds, Oracle On Demand is a cloud service provider delivering application and platform services to customers. Customers can also choose to run Oracle products in third party public clouds. Many third party SaaS ISVs and other public clouds are powered by Oracle technology. Oracle also offers enables integration across public and private clouds with a set of products for identity and access management, SOA and process integration, and data integration.

Let us take a closer look at the Oracle solutions.

Oracle Cloud Applications

Oracle offers a wide portfolio of horizontal and industry-specific applications, and all modules can be hosted through Oracle On Demand or through service provider partners. Oracle also offers a set of subscription-based services, such as Customer Relationship Management (CRM), Human Capital Management (HCM), and Procurement. Oracle offers a choice of deployment models from subscription-based services and customer-owned applications hosted at Oracle, to managed, on-premise, private cloud deployments.

Oracle supplies a modular set of cloud-ready applications known as Oracle Fusion Applications, and these coexist seamlessly with other Oracle applications. Built on the standards-based Oracle Fusion Middleware, Oracle Fusion Applications include Oracle Fusion Customer Relationship Management, Oracle Fusion Financials, Oracle Fusion Governance, Risk, and Compliance, Oracle Fusion Human Capital Management, Oracle Fusion Procurement, Oracle Fusion Project Portfolio Management, and Oracle Fusion Distributed Order Orchestration.

Oracle's Platform as a Service (PaaS)

Oracle's PaaS is based on Oracle's database and middleware products and is delivered as a private or public cloud service. It offers rapid application development with standards-based shared services and elastic scalability on-demand.

Oracle's PaaS includes Database-as-a-Service, which is based on Oracle Database and Oracle Exadata Database Machine, and Middleware-as-a-Service, which is based on Oracle WebLogic and Oracle Exalogic Elastic Cloud.

Oracle Exadata Database Machine is a pre-integrated, optimized combination of Oracle Exadata Storage Server Software, Oracle Database software, and industry standard hardware components from Sun. Oracle Exalogic is a machine optimized for Java execution in the middleware/application tier.

As well as providing a platform for running applications, Oracle PaaS also includes capabilities for developing and configuring cloud applications, cloud management, cloud security, cloud integration, and collaborating using clouds.

- **Cloud development**: Oracle PaaS includes also capabilities for cloud application development, and supports environments such as JDeveloper, NetBeans, and Eclipse.

- **Cloud management**: For cloud management, Oracle Enterprise Manager can be used to manage all layers, from infrastructure to applications, and across the full cloud lifecycle (setting up the cloud, deploying applications, policy-based scaling, and metering cloud usage for public cloud billing or private cloud chargeback).

- **Cloud security**: Oracle provides products such as Oracle Identity Management to manage users' identities and Oracle Database security options for protection of information.

- **Cloud integration**: To provide integration across public clouds, private clouds, and traditional architectures, Oracle offers Oracle SOA Suite and Oracle BPM Suite for process integration,

Oracle Data Integration and GoldenGate for data integration, and Oracle Identity and Access Management for federated user provisioning and single-sign-on.

- **Cloud collaboration**: Oracle WebCenter is a user engagement platform for social business, delivering connectivity between people and information. It includes tools for building portals, composite applications, and mashups along with full content lifecycle management.

Oracle's Infrastructure as a Service (IaaS)

Oracle offers a range of servers, storage, networking, virtualization software, operating systems, and management software required for IaaS. Oracle's offerings for IaaS include a range of SPARC and x86 servers mounted in cabinets, racks, and blades; storage including flash, disk, and tape; converged network fabric; virtualization options including Oracle VM for x86, Oracle VM for SPARC, and Oracle Solaris Containers; operating systems Oracle Solaris and Oracle Linux, and Oracle Enterprise Manager.

More information on the Oracle cloud offerings is available at http://www.oracle.com/cloud.

NetApp

NetApp provides a number of core technologies and capabilities that can form the foundation for a private cloud solution. These technologies include:

- **NetApp Unified Storage Architecture**: This architecture uses one set of software and processes across all tiers of storage. All NetApp storage systems are configured with NetApp's proprietary Data ONTAP operating system, which delivers massive scalability (NetApp FAS and V-Series storage solutions can scale from a few terabytes to several petabytes), improved management for large-scale deployments, nonstop operations, and support for FC, iSCSI, FCoE, NFS, and CIFS.

- **Scalable and efficient shared IT infrastructure**: Built-in storage features such as deduplication and thin provisioning, integrated data protection, and the ability to address dynamic resource needs by scaling up, scaling down, and scaling out.

- **Automation and analytics**: NetApp offers a suite of management products that enable the efficient management of storage capacity in a shared infrastructure—from policy-based automation to end-to-end cloud management tools from NetApp and partners.

- **Secure multi-tenancy**: NetApp software enables storage to be shared with maximum privacy and data security; this is a feature that is especially important in a multi-tenant environment.

- **NetApp Integrated Data Protection**: Backup, disaster recovery, and compliance capabilities are built in and can be activated as needed without having to deploy additional software and hardware.

In addition to these core technologies, NetApp provide the FlexPod Data Center Solution. This solution is built on Cisco Unified Computing System servers, Cisco Nexus switches, and NetApp unified storage systems running Data ONTAP. FlexPod has been optimized for a variety of mixed application workloads. Validated Designs and Workloads on FlexPod include VMware vSphere built on FlexPod, Microsoft SharePoint 2010 Validated on FlexPod, SAP Applications built on FlexPod, Citrix XenDesktop built on FlexPod, and Red Hat Enterprise Linux built on FlexPod.

NetApp has partnered with a global network of service providers and system integrators to provide a range of cloud services built on NetApp. NetApp service providers offer cloud solutions for many enterprise workloads and applications, including storage as a service, infrastructure as a service, desktop as a service, backup as a service, disaster recovery as a service, messaging and collaboration as a service, and SAP as a service.

More information on the NetApp cloud offerings is available at http://www.netapp.com/cloud.

CA Technologies

CA Technologies provide a range of cloud management and security solutions including service assurance, security, service and portfolio management, virtualization and automation, data management, energy and sustainability, service simulation, and IT management as a service.

Solution categories include:

- **Model Agile Cloud Services**: These solutions can help to simulate the behavior of a required composite service, review policies, security, capacity requirements, and cost structure. Solutions include:

    - CA Cloud 360 enables businesses to validate and select which applications and business services are best suited for private, public and hybrid clouds, or traditional models.

    - CA Business Service Insight enables businesses to manage traditional and cloud-based services by helping to understand which services are currently running in the environment, tracking service performance and SLA performance, and comparing with other internal and external alternatives.

    - CA Capacity Manager enables businesses to plan, optimize, and manage computing resources.

- **Turn-key Cloud**: CA AppLogic is a turn-key cloud computing platform that enables businesses to define and compose a complete service definition in a visual model, and then transform applications by wrapping them with everything they need to become on-demand business services. The CA AppLogic platform is used for composing, running, and scaling distributed applications. It uses advanced virtualization technologies enabling the deployment of solutions based on existing operating systems, middleware, and web applications. CA AppLogic replaces traditional IT infrastructure such as firewalls, load balancers, servers, and SANs with pre-integrated and pre-tested virtual appliances; each is able to run almost any existing multi-tier Linux application. Each appliance runs in its own virtual environment that boots its own Linux OS and appears as a separate physical server to the software that runs inside the appliance.

- **Assure Cloud Services**: These services deliver real-time visibility into how critical cloud services—residing either on- or off-premise—are performing. Services include:

  - **CA Application Performance Management**: Ensures the performance and availability of business-critical applications, transactions, and services as well as the end-user experience and business value of customers that access online services.

  - **CA Service Desk Manager**: Optimizes business users' support experience and automates incident, problem, knowledge management, interactive support, self-service, and advanced root cause analysis.

  - **Nimsoft Service Desk**: This all-in-one management solution, available either on-demand (SaaS) or on-premise, provides action-based workflows built on ITIL standards to coordinate all aspects of service delivery. Functions include Service Catalog and Request Management (the end user interface), incident management, problem management, service level management, change management, configuration management, and knowledge management.

- **Automate Cloud Services**: These services provide unified automation across virtual and physical infrastructure, applications, and services. In addition to the previously discussed CA AppLogic, services include:

  - **CA Automation Suite for Clouds**: This solution provides out-of-the-box, pre-integrated workflows for standard IaaS use cases such as automated self-service provisioning of cloud infrastructure. CA Automation Suite for Clouds enables rapid provisioning of new services, dynamic management of workloads to meet fluctuating business demands, and the control of public and private cloud resources through a single, unified system.

  - **CA Service Catalog**: This solution communicates service offerings in descriptive business language, enabling the automation of service delivery and the provisioning of physical, virtual, and cloud environments.

  - **CA Virtual Placement Manager**: This solution uses advanced analytics for automating the sizing, placement, and balancing of virtual machines. It allows users to run scenarios using both existing and hypothetical infrastructures to allow for infrastructure planning prior to deployment.

- **Cloud Security**: These services are a combination of on-premise and cloud-based security services that deliver key security capabilities such as advanced authentication, identity management, and federated single sign-on. Services include:

  - **CA CloudMinder Advanced Authentication**: This solution protects against inappropriate access by providing multiple forms of authentication to validate user identity. It also provides real-time, risk-based evaluation services that can help secure access and transactions.

  - **CA CloudMinder Single Sign-On**: This solution combines the power of a reliable identity federation solution with the benefits of a hosted, cloud-based deployment model into a single federated single sign-on solution.

- **CA CloudMinder Identity Management**: This is an identity management as-a-service solution that provides capabilities for user provisioning and de-provisioning to on-premise applications and cloud services as well as comprehensive user management capabilities.

- **CA RiskMinder as-a-Service**: This solution provides a secure, cloud, risk-based authentication service. It protects against inappropriate access and transaction fraud by evaluating a variety of contextual factors such as device, location, and user behavior to derive a risk score which is then used to determine an authentication recommendation.

More information on the CA cloud offerings is available at http://www.ca.com/cloud.

BMC Software

BMC provide services and solutions for planning, building, and managing cloud environments. The solutions fall into four main categories: *design, deliver, operate and optimize,* and *compliance and cost-effectiveness.*

- **Design**: The services in this category help customers understand and define the requirements for an optimal cloud environment. Services include:

  - **BMC Cloud Computing Services**: BMC's prescriptive approach for implementing cloud computing ensures each service is designed and configured to meet the needs of the business.

  - **BMC Rapid Cloud Deployment**: Using a prescriptive approach, BMC Consulting Services ensure a successful, on-time hybrid cloud *appliance* or BMC Install Planner that leverages a Linux and Oracle pre-production environment or hybrid cloud using the BMC Install Planner and a Windows and SQL Server pre-production environment.

  - **Cloud Solution Planning Workshop Service**: The BMC Cloud Solution Planning Workshop is a one-to-three week activity that helps with the definition and design of a best-in-class cloud architecture and roadmap.

  - **BMC Capacity Optimization**: This product provides capacity management for all data center resources; including physical and virtual servers, databases, storage, applications, middleware, networks, and facilities.

  - **BMC Atrium Discovery and Dependency Mapping**: This product automatically discovers physical and virtual IT assets and applications and identifies the relationships between them.

  - **BMC Service Cost Management**: Part of the BMC Remedy IT Service Management Suite, this solution enables chargeback and/or showback of costs to the line of business, and helps businesses estimate the ongoing cost of providing an IT service by capturing key cost drivers.

- **Deliver**: The services in this category use sophisticated automation, tight operational controls, and the ability to support a broad range of heterogeneous resources to deliver single and multi-tier, physical and virtual, and private and public cloud services. Services include:

- **BMC Cloud Lifecycle Management Implementation Services**: The aim of these services is to implement a cloud computing pilot in as little as 180 days. Deliverables include detailed architecture design, cloud service blueprints and catalog, documentation of solution implementation requirements, and a fully-functioning BMC Cloud Lifecycle Management solution in a new cloud computing pilot environment.

- **Business Service Catalog Transformation Service**: BMC follows a prescriptive approach to building a service catalog as part of a larger IT Business Management initiative. An initial engagement, usually between eight and ten weeks, focuses on reviewing best practices for the IT Business Management initiative, identifying four business services and up to 20 underlying technical services, identifying the key characteristics of each service in a consistent manner as a model for expansion, and providing a roadmap of additional activities to drive incremental benefit.

- **BMC Cloud Lifecycle Management**: This solution enables IT organizations to deliver complete business services in a flexible, controlled cloud environment that meets business needs and provides intelligent, policy-based, ongoing operations. It features an easy-to-use cloud administration portal and user self-service portal, flexible service design and provisioning with Service Blueprints, secure multi-tenancy, and support for heterogeneity; from physical to virtual, multi-hypervisor, public cloud integrations.

- **BMC Atrium Orchestrator Adaptors**: This product features thousands of pre-built run books based on ITIL good practices, a Graphical Development Studio for assembling workflows, an Integration Mapping Wizard to simplify configuration of application interfaces, an Operator Control Panel for control and monitoring of workflow execution, and a scalable grid architecture with load balancing and high-availability.

- **BMC Network Automation**: Part of the BMC BladeLogic Automation Suite, BMC Network Automation features include automatic generation of change scripts used to implement mass configuration updates, enforce policies, and perform non-disruptive rollbacks; simplification of complex configuration changes using pre-defined jobs and configuration templates; and maintenance of a trusted baseline configuration for one-click comparison and remediation and policy-based compliance.

- **Operate and optimize**: These solutions are designed to help businesses monitor and manage their cloud environments. In addition to BMC Cloud Lifecycle Management, BMC Capacity Optimization, and BMC Atrium Discovery and Dependency Mapping (already discussed), solutions include:

  - **BMC End User Experience Management**: Part of the BMC Application Management Suite, this solution provides end-to-end application performance monitoring and proactive detection and isolation of end-user performance issues.

  - **BMC ProactiveNet Performance Management**: This solution includes performance management, event and impact management, capacity optimization, end-user experience management, orchestration, discovery, dashboards and analytics, service level management, and a configuration management database.

- **Compliance and cost-effectiveness**: These solutions offer configuration and regulatory compliance and IT business management solutions—including chargeback and financial management—across physical, virtual, private, and public cloud environments. In addition to BMC Cloud Lifecycle Management and BMC Service Cost Management (already discussed), solutions include:

  - **BMC Remedy IT Service Management Suite**: This management suite includes a service desk solution, a self-service request catalog, tracking of incident response times and service desk SLA performance, asset and software license lifecycle and compliance management, and real-time performance reporting.

More information on the BMC cloud offerings is available at http://www.bmc.com/cloud.

Strengths of HP Cloud Solutions

HP believes that in order to be successful in cloud computing, vendors need to deliver integrated systems that offer several key characteristics:

- Support for private, public, and hybrid cloud environments

- The ability to include a broad range of business applications, all leading hypervisors, and multiple operating systems

- Unified delivery and control of services across both cloud and traditional IT environments

- Automated lifecycle management of applications and infrastructure

- End-to-end security

- Scalability to meet unpredictable business demands

HP enables the selection of the best method for service delivery, whether that is using traditional, private cloud, or public cloud architectures. HP can also manage, outsource, and finance cloud implementations. HP helps customers *build* their own clouds, and for those customers who do not want to build, HP provides ways for customers to *consume* cloud services provided by HP.

With hybrid delivery (see Figure A-1), HP helps businesses deliver the right services at the right time and at the right cost across all customer segments. Several service delivery models are available, and customers can select one or more of the models depending on their needs and requirements.

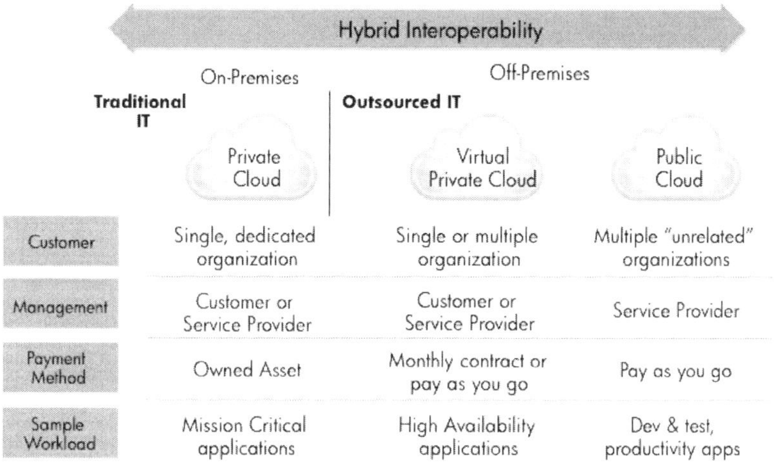

Figure A-1. HP Hybrid Delivery

Customers wishing to *transform* their traditional IT environment to cloud can take advantage of a set of services that support them on the journey. *Management and security* are a key part of the journey to cloud, and HP provides software and services for heterogeneous management, security, and governance across traditional, private, and public cloud.

Build

HP CloudSystem is a fully integrated and open solution from infrastructure to the cloud automation/heterogeneous data center management and services for hybrid cloud solutions. HP CloudSystem is based on a single, unified architecture that combines hardware, software, and services. HP CloudSystem solutions are complete, integrated systems for building, managing, and consuming services across all deployment models (private, public, and hybrid) and cloud service models (IaaS, PaaS, and SaaS) as shown in Figure A-2. Built on HP Converged Infrastructure and HP Cloud Service Automation software, HP CloudSystem delivers unified security, governance, and compliance across physical and virtual infrastructure and associated applications. HP CloudSystem provides a single services view across private, public, and hybrid cloud, supports a multi-hypervisor, multi-OS, heterogeneous infrastructure, includes intelligent automation, and lifecycle management, and is scalable and elastic.

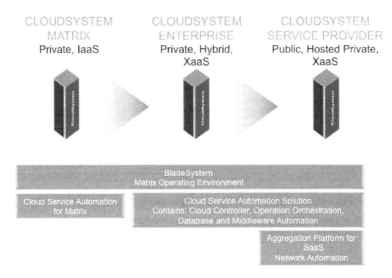

Figure A-2. HP CloudSystem Solutions

HP CloudSystem supports virtualization from VMware, Microsoft, and HP (Integrity Virtual Machines)—all on a common modular architecture. HP CloudSystem supports a wide range of HP server blades, all advanced G7 or greater x86 blades, as well as Itanium-based blades.

Features of the HP CloudSystem solutions include:

- End-to-end automated application delivery and management

- A self-service portal with a built-in service catalog to unify all applications under the control of IT

- Complete lifecycle management of all operations

- Fast-tracking the development of a cloud service catalog with HP Cloud Maps, pre-defined templates for popular business applications

- Support for multiple departments and clients from a single environment

- Converged Infrastructure that maximizes the use of resources and reduces operating costs

- Instant scalability and one-click, just-in-time provisioning

- Open standards that support multiple types of applications, hypervisors, operating systems, and heterogeneous infrastructure

- Burst and flex capacity to meet unpredictable demand across internal and external sources

- A leading automation software suite (HP Cloud Service Automation)

- A cloud service portal that provides a unified view of services and monitors service quality across all sources

- Comprehensive security and intrusion prevention across virtual and physical infrastructures and applications

- Multi-tenant protection and common management of applications and infrastructure operations

HP Cloud Maps are freely available from the HP website and can be used to automatically provision and optimize application and infrastructure resources. Cloud Maps provide preconfigured templates for infrastructure services that can be imported directly into HP CloudSystem to enable new cloud services to be up and running in minutes.

Consume

HP provides enterprise-class cloud computing services in an efficient and flexible consumption model. The services are flexible, scalable, and automated, and no capital investment is needed. HP Enterprise Cloud Services–Compute delivers cloud computing services for core business applications and processes in a globally consistent IT environment with high levels of performance and availability. Hosted in HP data centers, it makes bundles of server, storage, network, and security available to be consumed as a service, and customers pay only for the resources that they reserve. IT capacity can adjust rapidly to meet changing business needs

HP Enterprise Cloud Services–Compute runs on the HP Converged Infrastructure architectural model. It brings servers, storage, network, software, and security together into an optimized and efficient resource pool so applications can share the infrastructure more effectively. Application workloads are securely hosted on physical or virtual servers in HP next-generation data centers.

The HP Cloud Services Program (in private beta at time of writing) delivers public cloud infrastructure, platform services, and cloud solutions for developers, ISVs, and businesses of all sizes. The initial offerings include HP Cloud Compute and HP Cloud Object Storage. HP Cloud Compute allows users to deploy compute instances on demand, customize instances to handle unique workloads, and add new instances through an intuitive web user interface, or programmatically through an API. Customers can configure instances of various sizes for a variety of use cases, such as test and development, basic web applications, complex multi-tier deployments, or large-scale data processing with intermittent peak periods. HP Cloud Object Storage provides scalable, online storage capacity on-demand. Object storage is ideal for archiving and backing up data, serving static content for web applications, and storing large public or private datasets, such as online files and media. When combined with HP Cloud Compute, more sophisticated solutions can be implemented, including logfile storage and analysis, audio and video transcoding, and MapReduce analytics clusters.

HP provides access to the capabilities of the HP IT Performance Suite using a SaaS model. No capital expenditure is required, and the business benefits can be realized quickly. Components include HP Application Lifecycle Management, Application Portfolio management, Asset Manager, Elastic Test, Project and Portfolio Management, and Quality Center.

Transform

HP delivers a broad selection of professional services designed to help with planning, implementing, operating, and securing private and public clouds (see Figure A-3). From initial assessment to design and implementation, HP services experts work with customers to find the right solutions for their unique needs.

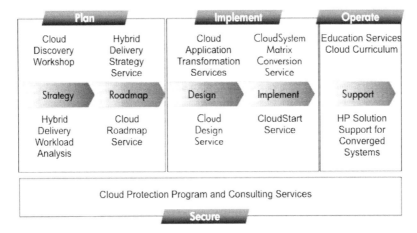

Figure A-3. HP Cloud Services

Manage and Secure

HP delivers management and security solutions for traditional IT, private, and public cloud environments, bringing them together into one security policy framework, and making all of those services available in one centralized portal. This is built on the HP Cloud Service Automation software and integrates with the HP Secure Virtualization Framework, providing a fully automated and highly secure cloud environment that mitigates the risk of downtime caused by human error, misconfiguration of resources, and attack from inside or outside of the organization.

HP Cloud Service Automation orchestrates the deployment of infrastructure compute resources and complex multi-tier application architectures. HP CSA integrates and leverages the strengths of several HP data center management and automation products, adding resource allocation management, service offering design, and a customer portal to create a comprehensive, service automation solution.

Services are designed using a graphical interface, are published to a service catalog, and can then be referenced in offerings presented to subscribers through a customer catalog. Subscriptions are instantiated and processed using a structured lifecycle, with pre-defined integration mechanisms that can be used to invoke external processes.

The HP Secure Virtualization Framework has been designed to implement threat-protection in virtualized environments. The three key areas addressed are compliance, convergence, and consolidation. Compliance deals with the regulations that aim to mitigate the risk of application unavailability and data loss. Convergence deals with the integration of various tools such as firewalls, intrusion prevention systems, content security gateways, policy management systems, Security Information and Event Management (SIEM) tools, and Network Behavior Anomaly Detection (NBAD) tools into a single integrated tool. Consolidations deals with providing a flexible solution for extending the threat protection of the HP TippingPoint IPS Series into the virtualized data center. Components include the HP TippingPoint N-series IPS appliance, Virtual IPS (vIPS) and Virtual Firewall (vFW), and the Virtual Management Center (vMC).

The HP Cloud Protection Program includes HP Cloud Protection Consulting Services such as HP Cloud Protection Workshop, HP Cloud Protection Design, and HP Cloud Protection Implementation. The HP Cloud Protection Reference Architecture covers cloud security from several perspectives, including business, functional, technical, and implementation, and ensures that proper security controls are defined across all dimensions.

HP Cloud Assure is delivered via HP Software-as-a-Service and offers an end-to-end solution for performing security risk assessments to detect and correct vulnerabilities. It provides common security policy definitions, automated security tests, centralized permissions control, and web access to security information. HP Cloud Assure can scan networks, operating systems, middleware layers, and web applications, and perform automated penetration testing to identify potential vulnerabilities.

Index